CIRCLE OF HARMONY

A Case Study in Popular Japanese Buddhism with Implications for Christian Mission

KENNETH J. DALE

with a chapter by

SUSUMU AKAHOSHI

PUBLISHED BY

William Carey Library

SOUTH PASADENA, CALIF.

Library of Congress Number 75-4214
ISBN 0-87808-424-X

Grateful acknowledgement is made to the following publishers and authors for permission to reprint brief quotations from copyrighted material: Macmillan Publishing Co., for *The Rush Hour of the Gods* by H. Neill McFarland (copyright 1967 by H. Neill McFarland) and *Religion, Society and the Individual* by J. Milton Yinger (copyright 1957 by the Macmillan Co.); Princeton University Press for *Aspects of Social Change in Modern Japan* edited by R.P. Dore (copyright 1967 by Princeton University Press), reprinted by permission of Princeton University Press; SCM Press Ltd. for *Japan's Religious Ferment* by Raymond Hammer (copyright 1961 by SCM Press Ltd.); Charles Tuttle Co. for *The History of Japanese Religion* by Masahiru Anesaki and *The New Religions of Japan* by Harry Thomsen (copyright 1963 by Charles Tuttle Co.); Kosei Publishing Co. for *Rissho Kosei-kai* (copyright 1966 by Rissho Kosei-kai); McGraw-Hill Book Co. for *Twelve Doors to Japan* by R.W. Hall and R.K. Beardsley (copyright 1965 by McGraw-Hill), used with permission of McGraw-Hill Book Co.; Kodansha International for *Anatomy of Dependence* by Takeo Doi (copyright 1973 by Kodansha International).

Published by the William Carey Library
533 Hermosa Street, South Pasadena, Calif. 91030

Co-published in Japan by Seibunsha
3-16, Shin-ogawa-cho, Shinjuku-ku, Tokyo

PRINTED IN JAPAN
THE KAWATA PRESS, TOKYO

PRONUNCIATION OF JAPANESE WORDS

All syllables are given equal stresss. Vowels are pronounced similarly to the vowels in Latin, as indicated below, and are always pronounced the same.

a – ah
i – ee
u – oo
e – eh
o – oh

All consonants are sounded approximately as in English. The "g" is hard, as in "get." "Y" is treated as a consonant.

Thus "*hōza*" is pronounced "hoh-zah" (rhymes with "Rosa"). "*Risshō Kōseikai*" is pronounced "ree" (rhymes with "see")—shoh (same as "show")—koh (rhymes with "show")—sei (same as "say")—kai (rhymes with "sigh").

A long mark gives the vowel double the time alotted an ordinary vowel. It is the practice in this book to use long marks only when the word is the Romanized writing out of Japanese, and therefore written in italics, and not to use them in the case of proper nouns or certain other words (such as hoza) considered as Anglicized Japanese words.

CONTENTS

This Book Is Gratefully Dedicated To

My Family

my parents, Sextus and Victoria

my wife, Eloise

my sons, Greg and Ted

for the part they have played

in preparing me for and

supporting me in this task

of living

and loving

and learning

in Japan

PHOTOGRAPHS

(1)
Daiseidō, the Great Sacred Hall of Rissho Koseikai located in Suginami Ward, Tokyo.

(2)
Interior of the Great Sacred Hall, showing the three balconies where hoza takes place.

(3)
A session of hoza.

FOREWORD

MANY alert critics agree that the striking development of new religions is one of the most astonishing phenomena in post-war Japan. In the process of enormous social change from rural, vertically-structured life to urban, horizontal society; from traditional, authoritarian community to modern democratic organization; from an agricultural society to a highly complex technological society, the life style of the people in the great metropolitan centers of Japan has been greatly affected. Some advocate a religionless society or the "death of God" for the contemporary age, but although this might apply to the Western world, it would certainly not apply to the Japanese situation today.

Unexpectedly, in the post-war period we have seen fantastic growth among various new religions which meet the new demands and needs that have arisen among the new urban dwellers. Some scholars characterize this phenomenon in terms of the "rush hour of the gods." Certainly many new images are created and advocated in order to respond to the needs of the new urban community. Some of them are new religions in the strict sense, that is, they have been entirely newly created in the post-war period. But many of them were formed out of an effort to renew old religions traditions. Three of the most striking examples of the so-called "new religions" belong to this category, namely, Soka Gakkai, Rissho Koseikai and Reiyukai. All come from the traditional Nichiren Sect but have made a unique reform and adaptation into today's society.

Dr. Kenneth J. Dale's study of the impact of *hōza* of Rissho Koseikai is a penetrating investigation of the specific method and approach of a particular new religion which has made fantastic growth in the post-war period. There are at least three factors which make this study an outstanding contribution in the examination of the new religions in Japan. First of all, the focal point of the investigation carried out by Dr. Dale is a thorough analysis of *hōza*, which is the key to the growth of Rissho Koseikai. Through this study we can recognize how *hōza* is carried out in actual practice and what are the positive aspects as well as the limitations of *hōza*. *Hōza* is a kind of informal discussion and dialogue circle which takes place daily at the headquarters of this religion. It provides an opportunity for the believers not only to know each other but to share one another's burdens and personal problems. This indicates that in modern society where people have left the homeland of traditional religion, they need a common ground to share their own problems. It clearly indicates that such a small circle of sharing each other's problems is one of the most important functions of religion in modern society.

Secondly, Dr. Dale has not only made an external description of *hōza* but has also made an internal analysis of the group dynamics operative within these groups. He utilizes the case study method in order to give concrete examples of how the groups function. Thus we have here the first account of the operation of *hōza* as seen by a specialist in group counseling and psychology of religion. In this regard his study is unique, that is, it is the first time the Western sciences of group dynamics and group therapy have been applied to a religious group in a non-Christian tradition.

Thirdly, Dr. Dale draws conclusions both in an appreciative way of what *hōza* contributes and in a critical way in showing its limitations. He is not overwhelmed by the impact of *hōza* but makes a realistic estimate of its effectiveness in meeting the emerging needs of urban dwellers. Most of the believers come from the lower strata of the complex metropolises such as Tokyo and have a great need to experience sharing of concrete problems of their daily life. Certainly *hōza* meets such need. But the study also clearly shows that the training of leaders and the methods used to solve problems need continuous attention in order to attain the intended results.

Hōza also provides an enormous challenge to the Christian church, which is so much out of contact with the lower segment of society. If Christianity is a democratic religion for ordinary people and stands for justice for the oppressed and the disinherited, I believe we need a radical change in method of operation in the churches of Japan and elsewhere. This study of *hōza* challenges us to think also about our own way of renewal within the Christian church.

Masao Takenaka
Professor of Sociology of Religion
Doshisha University
Kyoto, Japan

PREFACE

ONE of the significant features of the contemporary scene in the field of religion in Japan is the remarkably effective methods of propagation and mass education found in the fast-growing popular new religious movements. At the same time one of the obvious features of the contemporary status of the Christian church in Japan is its extremely slow growth. Why is church growth so sluggish while the new religious movements are expanding so vigorously? Christians are convinced that the fault does not lie in the content of the Christian message. Does the fault lie in the manner in which Christianity is being propagated through present church structures, theologies and strategies of evangelism?

Out of this concern for Christian propagation and education in Japan we came to have an interest in one of the most popular of these modern indigenous movements, namely, Rissho Koseikai. (For the sake of brevity and ease of pronunciation, this name will be abbreviated to RK throughout the remainder of this book.) Being further prompted by an interest in counseling and in the function of the small group in both religion and therapy, we confined the research to a study of the small group activity of RK known as *hōza*. (Hereafter, this word will be treated as an Anglicized word.) Hoza, which is translated by RK as "group counseling," is said to be the secret of RK's phenomenal growth and the clue to RK's impact on the lives of several millions of people.

In this book we shall examine hoza as thoroughly as possible in an attempt to find out what factors are responsible for the remarkable impact which this activity has had as an agent of religious propagation and education. Section I presents a brief background which shows the religious context in which RK and its hoza exist. Special attention is paid to the "new religions."

The heart of the research is in Section II, which is a case study approach to hoza in which the findings based on attendance at forty hoza sessions are systematized and analyzed. These findings are classified into the following categories: physical environment, organization, leadership, socioemotional dynamics and conceptual content. This section is organized according to "Findings," which endeavor to record objectively what was observed in hoza, and "Interpretations," which seek to interpret the Findings in the light of various related fields of study.

In Section III, the research material of the preceding section is evaluated and discussed particularly from two points of view, namely, from the point of view of comparing RK's hoza with the practices and attitudes of the Christian church in Japan, and from the point of view of the essential difference between Japanese and Western religiosity. It is the writer's sincere hope and purpose that through these interpretations and comparisons those engaged in the outreach work of the Christian church will be enabled to re-examine present attitudes and methods and gain fresh perspectives for the future.

Our approach in this study has been to examine hoza from several different points of view in order to understand its impact. Specifically, we have looked at this activity from the standpoint of its cultural-anthropological and psycho-sociological context, from its setting within the indigenous religious traditions, especially within the framework of the new religions, and from the vantage point of therapeutic counseling and group dynamics. The contribution of this study lies in its findings from a first-hand investigation of hoza, and in interpretations of these findings based on material from a broad variety of sources. It is our hope that such an approach, while it will not fully satisfy either the academician or the popular reader, may, through its broadly synthetic approach, bear some new insights into the dynamics of effective religious propagation.

*

By its very nature, this study is a piece of research in group behavior, and as such is related to that field of social science research known as group dynamics. Methodology in the study of group dynamics has become an exceedingly technical field. Although our approach to hoza was not primarily from the standpoint of group dynamics as such, certain aspects of the methodology of that field were utilized. Our basic orientation was a factor analysis approach by which we attempted to observe empirically and record the various factors which we came to conclude do constitute the effective appeal of hoza.

Our method might be classified as the field study method, that is, we attempted not to disrupt or control the groups in any way. A disadvantage of the field study method is that question must be raised concerning the typicality of the groups studied. There are a variety of hoza groups: those meeting during the day in the Great Sacred Hall, those meeting in homes at night, those mainly for youth, those representing the working class areas, those representing the suburbs, etc. Distinctions could be drawn regarding the group process and subject matter among these different types of groups, but in this study attention is centered on the common elements rather than on elements which might distinguish certain groups from others. Although the writer attended various kinds of hoza groups, the most frequent were the day-time sessions at the Great Sacred Hall.

The writer attended the hoza sessions as an ordinary participant, taking the stance of "participant observer." There was a tendency for other members to make the writer the center of attention, asking about America and Christianity or about his reactions to RK and hoza. At such times, answer was made as briefly as possible in order to avoid having the discussion center on himself. To have participated actively at that point would have made it impossible to hear normal topics of discussion or to experience the normal dynamics of the group.

A practical problem for the observer is to determine what to observe and in what manner to record it. A complete transcript of group interaction was not deemed necessary. Inasmuch as each session was two hours long, such a record would have become too bulky and repetitious. Rather, each significant segment of conversation was noted and jotted down, and these notes were later transcribed into verbatim report form. Observation was made of both the "task-oriented" content of the conversation, that is, the verbal exchanges of information, opinions, instruction, etc., and the "process" factors and socio-emotional behavior, that is, the non-verbal gestures and clues which indicate attitudes and feelings. The chapter titled "Conceptual Content" makes use of the task-oriented conversations, while the chapters entitled "Socio-emotional Dynamics" and "Leadership" utilize especially the observations of non-verbal process factors.

It was the writer's original intention to have the complete observation records included as an appendix to this book, but considerations of length have made it advisable to delete the original record. Instead, only pertinent excerpts have been put into the body of the text, and a list of the hoza groups attended is included as an appendix. The excerpts quoted in the text are written in a highly abbreviated form which expresses only the essential gist of the conversation. To have included the details of the conversations would have added emotional nuance and colorful narrative, but would have resulted in material so lengthy as to be extremely difficult to work with. In the citations, speakers are identified either as leader ("L") or as "Mrs. A," "Mr. B," etc. Names of hoza participants are not generally known to other members of the group, so it is impossible to identify speakers except by a symbol. The "A," "B," "C," etc. designate the order of the speakers during the session. The number at the end of the excerpt refers to the session number according to the descriptive list found in the appendix.

*

The preceding paragraphs might give the impression that we have, out of various ulterior motives, merely "used" the hoza of RK as a case study. This is not the case. We respect hoza for what it is, and we found it to be so fascinating that we wanted to investigate its dynamics more thoroughly, and also to share what we discovered with a wider audience. Both positive and negative aspects of hoza have come to light. An honest attempt has been made to be objective, both in observation and interpretation. It is to be expected that the filtered impressions of a Western "outsider" will not coincide with those of a Japanese Buddhist "insider." Different observations and interpretations from those found here no doubt could and should be made. Each of us can work only from within the scope of his own limited vision and understanding. We hope this writing will not be taken as either a final commendation or condemnation of RK's hoza but as a small contribution to an ongoing dialog between people of different faiths, and an ongoing search for more effective means of propagating religious faith in Japan today.

As this book goes to press and I reflect on the stages of its preparation, I am keenly aware of the debt that I owe to the many people who have assisted directly in making this research and publication possible. Aware that I am omitting the names of some who should be included in this expression of appreciation, I nevertheless want to acknowledge here certain individuals and institutions without whose support and guidance this work could never have been accomplished.

This book is based on the material of my dissertation presented as a requirement for the PhD degree at Union Theological Seminary, New York, and I am indebted especially to Professors Ellis Nelson and Robert Lynn of that Seminary for their academic guidance. Prof. Masao Takenaka of Doshisha University, Kyoto, also gave valuable direction during the writing of the dissertation, and I appreciate his introductory words written as a Foreword to this publication.

A special kind of appreciation is due to the many friends at RK who gave of their time in interviews and discussions to deepen my understanding of Buddhism and of RK's purposes and procedures. Officials of the Public Relations Division, the Evangelism Division, the Publishing Division, and of the Academic Research Institute and Seminary have all given valuable help. In addition to these, I feel deep gratitude to the many nameless hoza participants and leaders whose expressions have found their way into the manuscript. How often my heart was warmed by the open and accepting friendliness of these devout people towards me, an outsider and foreigner!

This book and the experiences and insights which it evidences must be seen in the larger context of our life and work in Japan over a span of more than two decades. Undergirding our career in this country have been the support of the Division of World Mission and Ecumenism of the Lutheran Church in America and the cooperation of the Japan

Lutheran Theological College and Seminary, both of which have graciously provided the opportunity for me to pursue this study.

I should like to say a special "Thank-you" to the Martin Goers family, who have given constant encouragement to us and to this particular project in a variety of ways through the years.

To H. Neill McFarland, whom I have never had the pleasure of meeting, but whose excellent study of the new religious movements of Japan entitled *The Rush Hour of the Gods* has obviously been my companion throughout various parts of this study, I express sincere appreciation. I am also grateful to Fr. Joseph Spae for the helpfulness of both his writings and his personal conversations, and to Kazuko Matsuzawa for several suggestions.

Last but not least, I wish to acknowledge the contribution of my esteemed colleague and collaborator, Dr. Susumu Akahoshi, for enhancing the value of this publication with the addition of a chapter written from his distinctive point of view as a Japanese Christian psychiatrist. His original writing of the chapter in Japanese was a more detailed study of developmental psychology and its bearing upon national mentality and religiosity, but in the process of translating and editing his work to fit into the scope of this small book, portions of his psychological theory and insights regretfully had to be deleted.

Kenneth J. Dale
Japan Lutheran Theological
College and Seminary
Tokyo, Japan
March, 1975

SECTION I

THE CONTEXT OF HOZA

It is necessary first of all to make a few sketches of the general religious background which constitutes the context for understanding hoza. Three aspects of this background will be considered in Section I, the first being the historical religious traditions. Since there is an abundance of literature on the classical religions of Japan, that particular area will be virtually omitted here except for a few paragraphs of introduction included for the sake of the uninitiated reader. The area of folk religious belief will receive somewhat more attention. In the next chapter, the subject of the new religions as a modern movement will be given a summary survey treatment. This material on the new religious movements is extremely important for an understanding of RK and hoza, but has been dealt with by a number of researchers in recent years, most notably by H. Neill McFarland in his *Rush Hour of the Gods*. Finally the subject of RK itself, in which and for which hoza exists, will be introduced in some detail, inasmuch as there is no adequate description of this new religion in English, apart from a translation of Rissho Koseikai's own publication of its self-portrait.

CHAPTER ONE

HISTORICAL RELIGIOUS TRADITIONS

The latest statistics of the Ministry of Education state the following number of adherents for the major religions in Japan.[1]

Shinto	84,717,081
Buddhism	83,646,509
Christianity	884,512
Other	9,325,850
Total	178,573,952

The total of nearly 180 million adherents contrasted with a total Japanese population of some 110 million—a population which is supposedly one of the most secularized in the world!—is intelligible only in the light of the remarkably tolerant Japanese approach to religion in general, and to the intuitive and emotional rather than rational comprehension of religion. Thus it is difficult to describe Japanese religious affiliation in any specific manner. However, for the sake of analysis, a few of the main strands of Japanese religious tradition will be sketched here.

CLASSICAL RELIGIONS

Shinto

Shinto—literally, "way of the gods"—lives in modern Japan as a focus of rites and festivals which recall the past, add celebration to the present, and give a certain sense of identity for the future of the people of Japan. The Shinto concept of *kami* (god) is intimately related to the way of thinking, feeling and acting of the Japanese people as a whole. D. C. Holtom calls it the "national faith of Japan." It is based on a mythology of the origin and destiny of Japan found in two ancient writings, the *Kojiki* and the *Nihon Shoki*. The religion itself claims to be coexistent with Japan from its beginnings. It is still today characterised by primitive, animistic elements. It manifests itself in four different areas: (1) in the ceremonies of the Imperial Household; (2) in domestic Shinto centered in the *kami-dana* (god-shelf) of private homes; (3) in shrine Shinto centered in ceremonies and festivals of the public shrines, and (4) in sect (or religious) Shinto expressed in activities of the various sects.[2]

There was a revival of Shinto in the 19th century, through which it became officially established as the "national faith" of Japan. In 1900 Shinto shrines were officially declared to be non-religious institutions; thus there existed nominal freedom of religion but practical coercion of the citizenry to pledge allegiance to the myths of national superiority. Because of this peculiar position, Shinto was diabolically used in the 1930's by the military clique to demand the allegiance of all Japanese citizens, and imbue them with the assurance that their military advances in the Pacific were divinely inspired designs.[3] With the defeat in 1945 and the establishment of a new constitution which guarantees freedom of religion and separation of church and state, Shinto has had to maintain itself as an independent religion, but even at the present moment there are efforts being made to give at least certain segments of this religion national support.[4]

However, the majority of Japanese know Shinto as a seasonal festival centered in the local shrine, or as a rite of purification and dedication of infants and children and of new buildings or public facilities. Small Shinto shrines are frequently found on the roofs of office buildings and department stores in the major cities. H. Neill McFarland comments that such varied roles of this religion point to its most distinctive characteristic, namely, "the intention to be identified through ritual with the whole range of Japanese history, tradition and aspiration." He continues, "Doctrinally and ethically amorphous, jealous of no absolutes, Shinto acknowledges no necessary contradiction between primitive animism and modern scientism."[5] Salvation in Shinto lies in the happy, healthy life. There is no distinction between man as he is and man as he should be. "When one is healthy, it means he is already in the state of salvation."[6]

Buddhism

Since the middle of the 6th century A. D., Buddhism has been an integral part of Japanese culture. Japanese Buddhism is Mahayana Buddhism, which is characteristically flexible and capable of adaptation. Accordingly, Buddhism in Japan has been adapted to Japanese cultural patterns, but at the same time it has in turn influenced those patterns. The Tendai and Shingon sects were established in the early 9th century, but it was not until the new movements of the 12th and 13th centuries that Buddhism became a truly popular religion. At this time, the *Jōdo* (Pure Land) sects were established under Honen and Shinran, Zen Buddhism was brought in from China by Eisai and Dogen, and Nichiren Buddhism flourished under the dynamic leadership of its prophet and founder, Nichiren (1222—1282).

All of these sects are still influential today. The Pure Land sects emphasize salvation by faith in the Amida Buddha. The mere repetition of the phrase, *Namu Amida Butsu* ("Honor to the Buddha of Boundless Light"), along with a confidence in the mercy of the Amida Buddha, is sufficient for salvation. Zen claims to be the original Buddhism. It finds the essence of religion in the intuitive experience of truth, such as Sakyamuni Buddha is said to have had in his experience of enlightenment while sitting under the linden tree. Zen is not dependent on any sutras as the other sects are, nor even upon rationality, but only upon the direct apprehension of reality in a moment of mystic, intuitive insight. With Zen—which is more a discipline of meditation than a religious faith—came the art of the tea ceremony, flower arranging, archery and other cultural features which became an integral part of the way of life of the samurai, referred to as *bushidō*. It is through these cultural features, still today determinative in defining the Japanese way of life, that the influence of Zen is most widely felt. Nichiren Buddhism, based on absolute devotion to the Lotus Sutra, is unique in its exclusivism, fiery zeal and messianic message. This spirit has been revived in the present time in the form of two of the most powerful new religions, Soka Gakkai and RK, both of which are rooted in the Nichiren stream.[7]

Regarding the ideology of Buddhism, Beardsley gives the following succinct statement:

> Primitive Buddhism taught that "enlightenment," a mystic experience, was the only escape from the sufferings of earthly existence. Without enlightenment one must undergo endless reincarnation and suffer earthly evils. One must strive to achieve release by becoming a Buddha (an enlightened one); the only route is the Eight-fold path...One's progress along this path is determined by one's karma, or "chain of causation," forged in earlier incarnations by one's steps in the right direction or away from it.[8]

The majority of Japanese still today feel at home in the traditions of Buddhist ritual, at least on the occasion of death and funeral services and memorial services for deceased ancestors. Although efforts at revival within the traditional sects are being made, the fact remains that most people see Buddhism as being "almost entirely irrelevant to the preparation of a modern man to the task of decision making in the modern world."[9]

Confucianism

It might well be argued that Confucianism does not belong in a list of religions of Japan. Whether Confucianism itself is a religion or an ethic is a matter of perennial debate among scholars of comparative religion. Although Confucianism as a religious institution *per se* has been all but non-existent in Japan throughout history, its impact as a social ethic has been undeniably powerful. During World War II the Confucian ethic of loyalty of subject to sovereign was officially promoted by the government to undergird the cause of nationalism. For centuries Confucian principles have made deep impact on Japan through the code of *bushidō*, the roots of which lie principally in Zen Buddhism and Confucian ethics. These principles are based on five social relationships and the rights and responsibilities derived from them. These are the relationship between sovereign and subject, parent and child, older brother and younger brother, husband and wife, and friend and friend. These relations are marked especially by the virtues of loyalty and "filial piety."[10]

Christianity

As in the case of Confucianism, it might be argued that neither does Christianity belong in this list of traditional religions of Japan, for Christianity, unlike the other three, has been a relative late-comer on the Japanese scene, and furthermore, unlike the other three, has always been a "non-mixer." Although the number of adherents has never been impressive, Christian impact on Japanese life has become increasingly significant over its four hundred year history in this land.

The history of Christianity in Japan dates from 1549 when the great Jesuit missionary, Francis Xavier, first brought Roman Catholic Christianity to southwestern Japan. This early chapter of Christian history is marked by rapid growth for half a century—the number of Christians is said to have been about one-half million, or two per cent of the population, which is a greater proportion than at any time since—only to be followed by some three decades of intense persecution. In the famous Shimabara massacre of 1638 thousands of Christians were killed at one time. That episode ended the existence of Christianity as an institution for the next 250 years, when an official policy of seclusion from the outside world was strictly maintained by the Tokugawa government. But as was discovered at the end of this period, even during these years of strict prohibition of foreign religion, families had preserved Christian teaching and rites underground through the centuries. These were called the *kakure kirishitan* (hidden Christians).

The first Protestant missionaries came to Japan in 1859 when the new government policy again permitted cultural and commercial exchange with the outside world. Since then both Roman Catholic and Protestant churches and Christian educational and social welfare institutions have grown slowly but surely up to the present. The Christian appeal has been mainly to intellectuals and the urban population. The lower economic and cultural classes, the large rural population and scores of fishing villages remain all but untouched. Even the most generous statistics have not put Christian membership above one per cent of the total population. However, there is a general recognition of the Christian claim that the influence of Christianity is far out of proportion to the small number of church members. Especially through education of the leaders of society and through ethical emphasis and social welfare work, the Christian Gospel has made an unquestionable impact on Japanese culture and institutions.

A boom of interest in Christianity and expansion of the churches, largely through a sudden proliferation of missionary activity, followed World War II. This wave has definitely receded to ebb-tide at the present time. Today's material affluence and nationalistic ideals tend to make Christianity, which is still identified as a foreign religion, unattractive to most people. The sluggish growth of the Christian churches stands in stark contrast to the fast-growing new religions.

FOLK RELIGION

Much of the Japanese religious heritage is of a non-institutional character and remains separated from the official religious systems. "In Japan, there seems always to be an element of residual autonomy in folk-life—a jealous defense of something that the masses know to be real in the face of all sophisticated formulations."[11]

Elements of Folk Religion

Ichiro Hori, a leading authority of folk religion in Japan, claims that folk religion is important for understanding the spiritual life of the Japanese and also their social psychology, for "folk religion always preserves the strong enduring power which perseveres in the lower structure of society and religious institutions." He sees it as something which has "strong digestive power" that enables it to hold together both homogeneous and heterogeneous elements which "form all possible phenomena of syncretism." This kind of religion functions among the common people to satisfy their emotional and religious needs.[12]

Two different systems of belief are discernible within Japanese folk religion: the *uji-gami* type (tutelary or guardian shrine system), which is based on the social unit of the family or clan, and the *hitogami* type (man-god system), which is based on the connection between a certain *kami* (deity) and a particular "holy man" such as a shaman. The *uji-gami* type is inseparable from ancestor worship, which is its symbolic rite. Thus, the social structure of traditional Japanese communities is closely bound up with folk religion and ancestor worship. The *hito-gami* type is expressed through charismatic personalities and their magical practices. Both types interact with each other in various religious phenomena even today.[13]

Shamanism is an important element of Japanese folk religion. It has existed throughout a long period of religious history without being institutionalized in a strict sense. It came into Japan from central and northeast Asia where shamanism has long been prevalent. Most shamanic persons are women. This phenomenon is not confined to the primitive past, for shamans, shamanesses and shamanic mass hysteria "appeared actively among the people at each socio-political crisis or change throughout Japanese history—not only at the transition from Heian to Kamakura...but also following World War II."[14] Hori devotes a special chapter in his book on folk religion to the survival of shamanic tendencies in the contemporary new religions.[15]

Yuji Sasaki made a study of fifty-six shamans in four different localities of Japan from the point of view of his psychiatric profession. He found that they were of two types, those who spontaneously became shamans through a sudden experience and were thus self-authenticated, and those who chose shamanism as a profession and were educated for it. Both types performed the following three activities: (1) prophesying in regard to illness, marital arrangements, business, etc., (2) performance of magic ritual in support of or to ward off the prophecy, and (3) serving as a medium between the client and the soul of a dead person. Some became possessed and talked in tongues while others had revelations or inspirations. Both socio-cultural factors and individual personality factors play a role in the making of a shaman.[16]

Elements of folk religion have visibly permeated the everyday life of the Japanese to no small degree, as any more than casual observation reveals: the presence of the *kami-dana* (god-shelf) in most homes and shops; the celebration of *obon*, a summer festival which commemorates the spirits of the dead; the near-universal practice of *hatsumōde*, the visit to a shrine during the first days of the new year, and many other such phenomena.[17] These practices also reflect Shinto and Buddhist tradition.

In addition to the above phenomena are other folk beliefs which the Westerner is apt to classify as "sheer superstition," but which, to multitudes of Japanese of lower economic and cultural strata, constitute a certain kind of religious orientation. Research reveals an extremely widespread use and acceptance of divination, sorcery, magic, taboo, etc., throughout society. It is prevalent not least in religion.[18] Special mention can be made of *hōigaku*, the art of facing houses and other things the right direction; lucky days, which are widely observed especially for setting the date for weddings; fortune-telling, which is practiced on the streets of any town; *seimei handan* or onomancy (the reading of character and fate from one's name), and similar practices. Turning to such beliefs in time of distress in order to find relief or some sign of hope is a natural response for many Japanese. This response is referred to by the special phrase *kurushii toki no kami-danomi* (turning to a god in time of trouble). Takagi claims that this is the very ground on which the new religions are built.[19]

Ancestor Veneration

The veneration of deceased ancestors is doubtlessly the most significant aspect of folk beliefs in Japan, and plays a major role in the religious activities being investigated in the present study. It is not confined to the so-called religious realm, but for great numbers of people ancestor worship also plays a determinative role in both the social and ethical spheres as well. R. P. Dore's investigation of Shitayama-cho produced the conclusion that although there is considerable apathy toward the ancestral rites, positive rejection of the duty to pay respect to the ancestors' *ihai* or *kaimyō* (tablet which records the posthumous name of the deceased) is rarely found.[20]

"Ancestor worship in its cognitive aspect is an answer to a fundamental human problem: death. But whereas cultures of the West have tended to give the dead a sacred burial rite and then erase them from fellowship with the living, Oriental cultures "have built stronger defenses against the erosive work of time and cherish the memory of the dead through the ages."[21] "Life is not possessed solely by one individual and is not limited to the present. It continues from the past to the future and is related to others. One's life is not isolated but inter-related." The veneration of ancestors should be understood in this sense, says a contemporary Buddhist leader.[22]

The most obvious manifest function of ancestor worship is the integration of the members of the household. Through the worship ceremonies before the *butsudan* or *shōrōdana* (Buddhist altar where memorial tablets and pictures of the dead are kept), the members of the household are united among themselves laterally, and at the same time vertically, i.e., with those who have gone before. Ancestor worship is a religion of the household (*ie*). The necessity for continuity of the household is deeply imbedded in Oriental consciousness. The primary importance of the *ie* as a cultural characteristic and the religious rite of ancestor worship have a mutual affinity for each other and reinforce each other. "The *ie* is a spiritual community and ancestor worship is its religion."[23] Dore's conclusion about the value of the rites is that they serve to strengthen the attitudes of respect and gratitude and also demonstrate such attitudes to society.[24]

From the above, the social significance of venerating ancestors is obvious. So far as religious belief involved in the rites is concerned, this is another matter. It can be said that belief in the actual existence of the departed is all but ignored. The "theological content" of the rites is not taken seriously. The feeling (*kimochi*) prompting them is a matter of considerable importance. If an individual did not take part in the ceremonies, he would be alienating himself from the spiritual community, the household, and this would be the worst reproach.[25]

Some other facets of the meaning of ancestor veneration are noteworthy. One is the vague assumption that a soul, if not made the object of frequent rites from the beginning, might be potentially malicious. Neglect of the rites may issue in evil consequences for both that soul and the neglectful family. The role of such a soul seems to be either that of threatening the household with misfortune, or of wandering about causing insecurity to the living. Such threats can be countered by more faithful performance of the veneration rites.[26]

Many different aspects of the meaning of ancestral veneration were revealed in Dore's interviews with eighty-three people of Shitayama-cho who performed the rites: (1) Worship is primarily for the sake of comforting the *hotoke* (spirit of the dead; the same word as used for the Buddha). (2) If the worship is not performed the *hotoke* might be malignant and vindictive. (3) Worship expresses gratitude for favors received from the ancestors. This was the most frequently expressed opinion. (4) Worship involves a pledge to conform to certain moral standards. The reverse side of this is the fear that if one does wrong, the *hotoke* will punish him. (5) Performing the ancestral rites provides a mystical experience or spiritual training. It is a token of reverence and respect. (6) Some venerate only the close relatives whom they recollect in their memory and this becomes a recollection rather than an abstract experience. (7) Sometimes the rite takes the form of reporting recent family events to the ancestors.[27]

As we turn now to look at the new religions and at RK in particular, the role which both the classical religions and the various elements of folk beliefs play in giving shape to these contemporary popular movements will be obvious. For these movements are deeply imbedded in Japanese religious tradition. In a sense they are the fruit of seeds which have been planted in the soil of Japan from the time of its earliest origins.

CHAPTER TWO

CONTEMPORARY POPULAR RELIGIOUS MOVEMENTS

SURVEY

RK is classified as one of the so-called "new religions" of Japan. As such it must be viewed as part of this larger movement in contemporary Japanese society and religion. In the next section a brief sketch of RK itself will be drawn, but it should be understood that many if not most of its characteristics and activities are shared in common with other new religions. Therefore it is necessary in this section to gain an overview of RK and its central activity, hoza, in its proper context, namely, the context of the new religious movements. Inasmuch as there are several helpful works in both English and Japanese on the new religions, only summary statements are deemed necessary here.[1]

To what do we refer when we speak of the "new religions" of Japan? The term is inadequate and misleading in many respects. The Japanese term, *shinkō shūkyō*, literally means "newly arisen religion" or "newly flourishing religion." However, the word "new" is misleading. Neither in terms of time nor of content are the "new religions" really new. One of them, Tenrikyo, dates back to 1838. Konko-kyo and Omoto-kyo are also 19th century movements. Many of those which developed after World War II had their beginnings in the earlier decades of this century. Of course, in comparison to the established religions of Shinto, Buddhism, and Christianity they are relatively "newly arisen." In terms of content they are not really new either, for most of them are versions of Shinto, Buddhism, Confucianism or Christianity, or syncretistic combinations thereof. These religions are sufficiently rooted in the ancient value system of Japanese culture and religion to allow any Japanese to feel at home in their teaching and practice.[2] However, in application and interpretation, and also in form and practice, there is something new in these movements. They appeal to the modern mind through new rites, new methods of propagation, new systems of organization, etc. The term "religion" is also subject to question inasmuch as many new religions do not meet the definition of that word, which ordinarily includes a regular doctrinal system, established liturgy, and a certain measure of organizational stability.

The term "popular" is more apropos than "new" because it avoids time reference, and places the emphasis on the appeal to the masses, which is in fact a chief characteristic of all the new religions. Sakae Kobayashi says they are qualified to be called "religions of the masses, by the masses, and for the masses".[3] McFarland uses the term "contemporary popular religious movements" to designate his field of study.[4] This phrase accurately describes what we are talking about in this book. Although we will continue to use the term "new religions" for convenience sake, what we are talking about is the phenomenon of the multitude of religious movements, most of which have sprung up in recent decades, and which appeal mainly to the lower middle class of Japanese people.

How large a movement is represented by the new religions of Japan? Accurate statistics are impossible to obtain, for several reasons. In the first place, in response to surveys and censuses, the new religions tend to inflate greatly their statistics, for their primary concern with statistics is to demonstrate their remarkable growth. In the second place, statistics on religious affiliation in Japan are often measured in terms of families rather than individuals. This makes for an extremely unwieldy base for figuring. In the third place, the new religions are constantly in a process of change. Groups emerge and dissolve; membership booms in one place and suddenly declines in another, etc.

With these precautions about the difficulty of obtaining an accurate cross-section of the status of these movements, we will point out the following information. Harry Thomsen, writing in 1963, presented the picture as follows: In 1963, 171 new religions were officially registered with the federal Ministry of Education. A little more than one-third of them were registered as Shinto sects, about one-third as Buddhist sects, a few as being related to Christianity, and the rest were listed as "miscellaneous." Those listed as miscellaneous reported membership of about three and a half million as of January 1, 1958, while the adherents of the remaining 121 groups totaled a little less than 15 million, making a total of over 18 million.[5]

McFarland, writing in 1967, says that the groups which he reports on—Konko-kyo, P. L. Kyodan, Seicho no Ie, RK, and Soka Gakkai—these five alone report memberships totaling more than 15 million.

Soka Gakkai itself claims to have enrolled more than 5 million families, or over 10 million persons.[6]

The latest statistics on ten major groups, as reported by the national Ministry of Education, show the following figures:[7]

Tenri-kyo	1,993,217
Kurozumi-kyo	407,590
Konko-kyo	514,997
Omoto-kyo	143,891
Sekai Kyusei-kyo	662,072
Seicho no Ie	2,414,950
P. L. Kyodan	1,473,187
Reiyukai	4,259,587
Rissho Koseikai	4,849,476
Nichiren Shoshu (Soka Gakkai)	16,201,488
Total	32,920,455

CAUSATIVE FACTORS

Psycho-Sociological Factors

Religion is a multi-dimensional phenomenon. As Richard Niebuhr said of the Christian denominations, "An exclusively religious interpretation, especially a doctrinal one, is likely to miss the point of the whole development."[8] Observers agree that the new religions constitute a significant socio-religious movement in Japan today. What is transpiring here is what Milton Yinger observed in his sociological approach to religion when he says that religion is a part of an interacting system in which religious developments are best understood as reponses to certain social developments.[9] Takagi's thesis is that religious bodies come into being and grow during an age of anxiety, a time when people feel insecure about the future.[10] When for social or political reasons an entire nation tends to feel anxious about its future, there is a good chance that religious movements which can meet the demands of the day will flourish. Unstable government, unjust policies, and impotence or corrupt practices in the existing religions all contribute to anxiety. Hori also attributes the rise of the new religions to social anomie.[11]

The new religions attract mainly an "in-between" group in society, neither the laboring class nor the management class, but the self-employed class of small shop-keepers and workers in small businesses and industries.

Whereas the laboring class is organized in labor unions and have their sense of belonging there, and the management class enjoys the advantages of the strength and prestige of the big corporation, the "in-between" group is excluded from both of these bases. These are the ones who find acceptance, a spirit of belonging, and a feeling of power and unity in the fold of the new religions.

Historical Perspective

The new religions have flourished and become the object of popular attention during the post-World War II period. However, in order to get a true perspective of the whole movement of new religions, it is necessary to take a longer range historical view. We shall look very briefly at some of the social-religious crises of the past before going into a description of the post-World War II crisis in more detail.

Two popular religious movements appeared during the Tokugawa Period which can be called predecessors of the new religions: the Shingaku Movement originated by Ishida in the early 17th century and the the Hotoku Movement originated by Ninomiya in the 19th century. Both of these movements were eclectic, and built around a fusion of religious salvation and economic recovery—a fundamental concept in the popular religious movements.[12]

Masaharu Anesaki says that the social atmosphere of the first half of the 19th century "was redolent with something verging on the Messianic conception of the Jews in the first century before Christ." Faced with severe social and economic distress, the common people were powerless to better their lot through political action. Their only alternative was to flee to religion. Two great religious movements sprang up to fill this need, Tenri-kyo and Konko-kyo, both of which are still vital today.[13]

The last two decades of the 19th century were another period of social anxiety. Social reform seemed impossible in the face of rapid modernization and political absolutism. During this period Omoto-kyo had its beginning. The early 20th century presented a situation of a widened gulf between those growing rich through the new industrial and commercial success of Japan, and the disprivileged classes. There was also a revival of interest in religion as such, centered around renewed interest in Nichiren, the great Buddhist prophet of the 13th century. In 1912, Tokumitsu-kyo, and in 1925, Reiyukai were founded. The latter is the parent of a number of influential sects which broke away from it later, among which RK is numbered.[14]

Two factors combined to cause a spectacular growth of popular religious movements in the immediate post-World War II period. One was the simultaneous collapse of the old authoritarianism and removal of religious restrictions which came with the fall of the imperial system. Takagi interprets the new religions as popular thought movements among the masses (*taishū shisō undō*) and sees their proper context to be among other mass thought movements occurring since the beginning of the Meiji Era, the principal movement being the one which successfully developed the emperor system (*tennō-sei*) by giving it a religious (Shinto) base. When the emperor system collapsed, and simultaneously the restrictive Religious Bodies Law of 1939 was removed, there were both the motivation and freedom to start new mass religious movements.

The other factor was the desperate economic, social, moral and spiritual situation which prevailed throughout the nation, which lay in ashes and rubble, physical exhaustion and spiritual bankruptcy. The crushing defeat in the War left the nation in chaos. Material destruction along with the destruction of what had been a glorious vision of Japanese imperial conquest shattered self-confidence and created a need for a faith among the masses. McFarland asks, "Given the traumatic experiences of the Japanese nation, to what alternatives might the masses have turned if the new religions had not been available?"[15] to which Takagi replies that, actually, the complete destruction of traditional Japanese social, cultural and political structures was averted by the rise of the new religious movements.[16]

Ethico-Religious Factors

What about the factors which could be called more specifically religious? These movements are religions, not merely social movements. We have seen how religious movements have arisen in response to sociological needs, rather than to what would be ordinarily described as a specifically religious need, but we can also point to some factors in the ethical and spiritual life of the masses, particularly in the post-World War II period, which are significant in tracing the rise of the new religions. The established religions proved incapable of showing a way of salvation to the millions of desperate people in Japan at the end of World War II. Arnold Toynbee wrote shortly after the War:

> In our time all traditional ideologies, philosophies, and faiths have been shaken off their pedestal by the explosive intellectual force of modern science, and Japan's traditional ideology, like all others,

> would have been undermined by the progress of science if it had not been shattered by the shock of military disaster...The cataclysm (of the War) seems to have produced a sort of moral and spiritual vacuum which will surely have to be filled.[17]

In 1945 there were reportedly long waiting lines outside the Iwanami Book Store in Tokyo, where people were waiting to buy a copy of a popular book presenting the Nishida school of philosophy. This dramatically evidenced the desperate search for guidance by people who had suddenly lost the philosophical foundations of their nationhood and personhood.[18]

So there was a natural searching after the hope and faith which religion offer. But the established religions at the end of the War were in a state of impotency. A textbook of one of the new religions comments on the state of the old religions in these bitter words:

> From the standpoint of actual practice and practical application, the religious world today has degenerated and forgotten the truths discovered by former great sages. The leaders of today have become nothing but clown-like priests or monkey-like religionists, pretending to know the truth and rattling it off in a pompous manner. One cannot help but be shocked; one cannot help but be dumbfounded.[19]

The old Buddhist denominations had not been vital or aggressive since long before the War. Shinto was identified with the ultranationalism and emperor deification, and therefore automatically collapsed with the surrender in 1945. Christianity provided an answer to the crisis of the times for many, but it suffered both from its connection with the West and from its whole atmosphere, which was alien to Japanese mentality and tradition. It was out of such a context of socio-psychological and ethico-religious turmoil that the scores of post-World War II religious movements arose and flourished. Theodore Jaeckel aptly summarizes their role with these words: "They are a socio-religious movement of a Japan in transition...They depict the struggle of a nation which is fighting for spiritual survival."[20]

CHARACTERISTICS

In order to give a more adequate description of these popular religious movements, a number of their salient characteristics will be sketched below. Although each new religion does claim uniqueness, there is much more that unites them into the common stream of a recognizable phenomenon than there is to set them apart from each other. Nearly every student of the new religions produces his own list of characteristics, all of which agree in essentials. Our description will be made in the form of ten summary characteristics, all of which apply not only to the new religions in general, but to RK and its hoza in particular.

Concrete Benefits

This is mentioned first because here is one of the most significant clues to the mass appeal of the new religions. *Goriyaku Shūkyō* (literally, honorable profit-making religion) is a pejorative phrase commonly applied to them. They are accused of exploiting the universal human desire to be "healthy, wealthy and wise" by making extravagant promises of material benefits on one condition—joining the religion. On the positive side, it must be recognized that they, unlike the established religions, bring religion out of the realm of theological abstraction and interpret it as that which brings practical blessings into the believer's everday life. Religion must be integrated into life, and the purpose of religion is to improve the quality of life in a tangible way.

Charismatic Leadership

The new religions have their source in a charismatic leader. *Ikigami* (living god) is the term often applied to the founder or foundress, who exerts a near-divine authority over the followers. The founder often claims shamanistic powers, and claims to have received special divine revelation commanding him or her to start this new movement. "In almost every instance, some kind of mystical manifestation of power is offered as primary evidence of the validity of the religious mission."[21]

Social Solidarity and Individuality

One of the benefits of participation in a new religion is the restoration of social solidarity to those who suffer alienation and its consequent insecurity. There are two dimensions to this boon of social solidarity, one being the opportunity to participate in mass activities where sheer numbers and spectacular size buoy up the otherwise isolated individual. Rallies in rented stadia, pilgrimages to the national headquarters, gala processions, and spectacular public festivals are all part of the "cultus" of the new religions. The other dimension is the opportunity to participate in group discussions, variously called *zadankai* or hoza (cell groups, discussion groups) where the individual finds an outlet for loneliness and frustration within the atmosphere of a small intimate cell group. These cell groups, among which RK's hoza stands as a prime example, function as informal social gatherings, as confessionals, and as a place to plan and evaluate the activities of the organization. In this cell group system, participants are given a new sense of individuality, dignity and personal worth which has been notably lacking in the past. Thomsen suggests that "we are perhaps witnessing the first beginnings of a change from national religion into personal religion."[22]

Hierarchical Structure

Authoriatarianism, vertical stratification and feudalistic patterns of relationship characterize most Japanese organizational structure, and these characteristics are obvious in the organization of the new religions. This hierarchical pattern, with the charismatic figure at the top spreading his authority through successive sub-authorities down to the last individual, makes for efficient administration and communication, but also tends to produce a blind obedience which works counter to the incipient spirit of democracy being fostered in present-day Japan.

A Religious Mecca

Most of the new religions have constructed a spectacular "mecca," an imposing national headquarters and central worship hall, which serves as a focus of interest and pride for all the adherents. These buildings are often magnificent or luxurious or bizarre to the point of defying common sense. They have been built at tremendous cost, both in terms of the sacrificial service rendered by the adherents, and in terms of money, the source of which remains an enigma to most observers. They serve as a kind of paradise on earth for the followers, whose lives are characteristically monotonous and drab.

Emotional and Physical Participation

In the worship rites there is a powerful appeal to the emotions. Corporate chanting is the most basic element of the service. Thousands of voices chanting holy phrases in unison rouses a sense of unity, strength and enthusiasm. Frequently there are rituals involving dancing, gestures, or banner-waving. Another aspect of physical participation is even more significant. That is the "total life" participation of giving time and energy to service projects of the organization, usually known as *o-yaku*. Members are expected to contribute a certain number of days to serving their institution. This might be in the form of maintaining the grounds and property through such tasks as cleaning, serving food, etc., or in the form of helping in the actual construction of new buildings and facilities.

Effective Propagation Methods

The new religions are zealous in the promotion of their faith. They use new and effective methods which the established religions have never attempted. They capture the interest of the masses by appealing to them at the level of their need. The effective use of the small discussion group is one of the most appealing strategies. It can be observed that many of their methods were learned from the Christian Church: the idea of personal counseling, evangelism through mass media, home visitation, use of hymns in worship, and the "Sunday School" for educating children.

Optimistic Simplicity

The final points which will be brought out in this list of characteristics relate principally to the nature of the teaching. First, simplicity should be noted. The new religions have streamlined the old institutions and their dogmas. The religious organization itself is easy to enter, the teaching is easy to understand, few demands are made, and the ritual is simple. Most of the founders of the religions had no higher education themselves, so naturally their teachings are simple, direct, and earthy. Although usually based on one or more of the traditional religious teachings, the old complicated systems have been skillfully reduced to a lucid scheme which can be understood by even the most unlearned day laborer.

One aspect of this simplicity is a kind of simplistic optimism which characterizes the theology of the new religions. Human nature is seen as fundamentally good; all that is necessary is to brush off the dust which mars man's beautiful soul. There is a strong belief in the possibilities of success in life. Kobayashi concludes tht "an optimistic viewpoint is a predominant attitude which we find in all these new religious movements"—an attitude which has its origin in the Shinto outlook on human nature.[23]

Syncretism

Ryōbu Shintō (dual Shinto)—a joining of Shinto and Buddhism which resulted in a folk faith in the *shinbutsu* (god-buddha)—has been a phenomenon in Japanese religion for centuries and finds a natural expression in the new religions. Although most sects are primarily identified with Buddhist, Shinto or some other stream of tradition, most of them see religious belief as a relative matter, and unashamedly incorporate elements of various religions, including Christianity, into their teaching and practice.

Superstition, Magic and Folk Beliefs

Mention must also be made of the incorporation of magical, shamanistic and superstitious elements, and other elements common to folk religion. Divination and astrology, to say nothing of emphasis on ancestor veneration, side by side with sophisticated concepts of classical Buddhism or humanistic philosophy, are characteristic of the "theology" of the new religions. Shamanism is deeply rooted in the spiritual life of the Japanese, from the period of the Ainu and the *Kojiki* down to the time of the founders of the new religions, says Taika Sugai. Therefore these religions must be dealt with both on a sociological and existential basis, and also on the basis of folk beliefs, including the traditions of shamanism, animism and fetishism.[24]

SIGNIFICANCE AND ROLE

In conclusion to this brief survey of the contemporary popular religious movements, a few comments can be made about their general significance and their possible role in Japan's future. It is possible that the new religions, rather than dealing a death blow to Buddhism and Shinto, may force them into a new phase of rejuvenation and accommodation. Can these movements be seen as the much needed spiritual renewal in the life of Japan? Is the religious quality of these movements such that they actually have the power to move Japan's millions toward renewed spiritual life? Doubtlessly that is an unrealistic expectation, inasmuch as they themselves are deeply rooted in traditional religious concepts, such as ancestor veneration, shamanism and other aspects of folk religion. Therefore they have offered "mainly a sanctuary and a palliative, largely revisionary in character which imparted a measure of hope to many among the frustrated masses, but offered nothing to the nation as a whole."[25] Tillich concluded that "no transformation of society as a whole, no aspiration for the radically new in history, can be observed in these movements."[26] The salvation they offered has not touched the depths of either the human predicament or the social malaise.

Public reaction against them is, by and large, severe. "*Shinkō shūkyō*" (new religions), as a Japanese expression is almost synonymous with the idea of a bogus religion. Many people find their eccentric teachings and fantastic claims of divine revelation, etc., to be curious and amusing. Many find their irrational statements and their big business methods repulsive and alarming. The faith healing of some is seen as a regression from modernization to the primitive, and the political alliance of the most powerful of them, Soka Gakkai, is seen as a threat to democracy. Many Buddhist leaders are alarmed at and critical of the inroads made by the new movements, judging them to be impure in doctrine, opportunistic in their methods, and misleading in their promises of benefits received.

At the same time it can also be said that many people feel more positive toward the new religions than toward the old established religious institutions, for they are at least aware of individual persons and their problems, and are dynamically involved in helping them on the level of their conscious needs. The established leaders recognize the ineffectiveness of the old teachings and methods. It must be admitted that the old religions have given room for the activities of the new religions, for most of the sects of Buddhism have long since lost their power.

So there are certain positive remarks that can be made about the religious adequacy of the new movements. For one thing, the very efficiency and authority of their organizational structure has produced a disciplined religious practice which contrasts favorably with the amorphous character of the old religious traditions. Teachings, practices, and rituals have been made lucid and meaningful to the common man. For another thing, the success of these movements leads the way for a new relevance of religious faith to modern life. Emphasis falls on individual and social ethics. Religion is real only if "it works" in everyday life. At the same time it is also hopeful to observe that the trend at the present time is for the new religions to become more theologically oriented, more "spiritual," and less magic and material oriented.[27]

McFarland states that these religions answer the quest for a "vocational symbol" for contemporary Japan, to use Tillich's term.

> It now appears that the loss of their sense of national identity and purpose remains almost the sole instance of major wartime devastation that the Japanese have found to be irreparable. But it is a vast hiatus, the closing of which is unquestionably Japan's greatest current need.[28]

Doubtlessly, nationalism is the most durable source of mass enthusiasm, and nationalistic fervor in one form or another often provides the "vocational symbol" for a nation. However, the intense nationalism that began with the Emperor Meiji in 1868 and drove the nation on its desperate road to conquest, only to end in self-destruction, is now repulsive to post-war Japanese. Within this milieu the new religions have been in certain respects substitutes for nationalism. Their leaders in many cases function as emperor substitutes. For the masses, the belief in centralized authority and the need for authoritarian leadership have been as strong after World War II as they were before. The new religions have been sensitive to this need and capitalized on it as an opportunity for uniting the masses into powerful social units.[29] The Japanese way of life is a way built on communal patterns in which social solidarity is a supreme value. The new religions offer just what is needed: a close-knit social group which at the same time emphasizes respect for human personality.

It is likely that the new religions will not decline, but will play a significant role in national life for some time to come. Some observers think that this role will be an increasingly reactionary one. Others believe that, focusing on world peace as some do, they will not follow a reactionary path of imperialism, but will be a link to the future in building a more responsible life for both individuals and nation. Some Christian observers see them as preparing the way for Christian development in Japan in that they are making the conscience of the current materially minded generation more sensitive to moral and spiritual concerns. We agree with McFarland's conclusion that "it does not yet appear what they will become, but at least for the forseeable future it seems certain that they will continue, and it seems likely that they will contribute importantly, both for good and ill, to the emergent life of Japan. Let them not be judged with haste, but let them be observed with care."[30]

CHAPTER THREE

RISSHO KOSEIKAI

HISTORICAL BACKGROUND

RK was founded by Mr. Nikkyo Niwano and Mrs. Myoko Naganuma in 1938 in Tokyo. The best approach to understanding the origins and development of RK is to become acquainted with the life activities and "spiritual journey" of these two people.

Mr. Niwano was born in 1906 of a pious Buddhist farm family in Niigata Prefecture. At the age of eighteen he decided to make a career for himself in Tokyo, where he went and worked for small shopkeepers for several years. He served in the Japanese navy with distinction, and after discharge opened his own small pickle shop in Tokyo.

During this period, Mr. Niwano gave himself to what he calls his "pilgrimage for seeking after truth." For some years this pilgrimage consisted of the study of various popular folk beliefs, including *rokuyō* (belief in lucky and unlucky days), *kyūsei* (a kind of astrology), *hōi* (choice of certain directions for facing a house when building and directions for other actions), *shichishin* (divination in which everything is determined by seven gods), *tengū-fudō* (a faith cure), and, in particular *seimei-handan* (onomancy, or the interpretation of one's fate through analysis of his name). He thought that through such means he could help eliminate misery and suffering in the world.

In a further attempt to eliminate suffering brought on by the crisis of a serious illness of one of his children, he joined Reiyukai, one of the new religions which was flourishing at that time. His daughter was healed. Then, largely through his contact with an influential Buddhist teacher in that religion named Sukenobu Arai, Mr. Niwano became strongly attracted to the teaching of the Lotus Sutra, which was the Buddhist scriptural foundation of Reiyukai.

In Reiyukai Mr. Niwano had his first experience in the small discussion groups called "hoza." He became a faithful hoza member and eagerly learned from others about the Lotus Sutra and everyday problems during these informal sessions. He even changed his job from shopkeeping to delivering milk so that he could contact more people and convert them to his faith. One of his converted customers was Mrs. Myoko Naganuma, a woman seventeen years older than himself.

Mrs. Naganuma was born in 1889 into a poor family of Saitama Prefecture. She went to work in a factory in Tokyo at an early age. She was married for eleven years to a barber, whom she divorced because of his disolute life, and married again. Bad health was a constant plague to her, but after joining Reiyukai she was said to be cured. Mrs. Naganuma was a shamanic type of person, a charismatic spiritual leader by nature.

From 1935 to 1938 Mr. Niwano and Mrs. Naganuma were zealous Reiyukai members working as a team for the promotion of that religion, but in 1938 a clash occurred between them and Mrs. Kimi Kotani, the leader of Reiyukai. RK claims the reason for the schism between this team and Reiyukai was the indifference of the latter to the Lotus Scripture, as taught by Mr. Arai. Meetings began to be held in Mr. Niwano's home in 1938, with some thirty adherents. Mrs. Naganuma was the spiritual leader and Mr. Niwano was the organizer and promoter. The content of their teaching was essentially the same as that of Reiyukai, with emphasis on the Lotus Sutra. The name chosen for their new organization was *Dai Nippon Risshō Kōsei-kai*, which literally means "The Great Japan Society for Establishment of Righteousness and Achievement of Fellowship."[1] The "*Dai Nippon*" (Great Japan) was dropped from the name after the war.[2]

Membership grew rapidly during the desperate pre-war and war years reaching about 1,000 in 1941, and about 3,000 by the end of the war, in 1945. After that, with the granting of religious freedom and the search for security and moral guidance after the war, RK became the fastest growing new religion, doubling its membership every year until 1950.

A notable event in RK's development in the 1950's was the so-called Yomiuri Affair. In 1956 the Yomiuri Newspaper published a series of reports that RK was guilty of malpractice in purchasing land, was working against democratic principles, was deceiving its members, etc. Even the national Diet took up the affair and leaders were summoned for questioning. This incident was cause for considerable reflection by RK leaders, but within a few years the public image had been restored.[3]

Mrs. Naganuma died in 1957. With her death there came a change in RK's basic approach. From 1958, which Niwano called "the year of the manifestation of truth," shamanistic practices, charismatic powers and divination which had characterized her leadership were soft-pedaled. In place of this, although basic teaching remained unchanged, institutional efficiency, systematic instruction in doctrine, and everyday ethics came to the fore under President Niwano's leadership.

Two of the principle thrusts of the 1960's were religious cooperation, and, along with that, world peace. President Niwano takes an active leadership role in several nation-wide religious federations and leagues. He went to Europe in 1963 as a representative to the Peace Delegation of Religious Leaders for Banning Atomic Weapons. In September, 1965, he had a private audience with Pope Paul VI, during which these two gave their blessings to each other and exchanged views on the contribution of their respective religions to world peace. This interview was of momentous import for President Niwano, who wrote thus about it:

> I clearly felt that there is little difference between God's love as taught by Christ or the love for humanity and the idea of compassion as advocated by Buddha...The great ideal of religious cooperation for which I have spent 27 years of activity centering around RK...is now steadily going to be established.[4]

DOCTRINE

RK is Buddhism without monks or priests, the tone and direction of which have been set mainly by two laymen. President Niwano is not at home in Buddhist scholasticism. All leaders—national officials, worship leaders, preachers, hoza leaders and theologians—are laymen in the sense of not having been "ordained" as priests. That does not imply that none of these are professional full-time workers in the organization. Doctrine based on the Lotus Sutra, is interpreted in modern, simple terms by laymen for laymen.

A statement of the RK Creed, recited by all members at every worship service, provides a focus readily understood by the masses for the many points of the doctrinal system:

> We the members of RK, under the leadership of our revered teacher, President Niwano, recognize the essential way of salvation in Buddhism and pledge our best efforts, in the spirit of Buddhist laymen, to perfect our character and realize in our lives the Bodhisattva Way. To this end, by improving in knowledge and practice

of the faith, in personal discipline and in leading others, we will endeavor to realize a state of peace for the family, the community, the country, and the world.[5]

RK leaders admit that the early period (up through 1957) was, in a certain sense, a period of accommodation to popular folk beliefs.[6] However, there is no question but that, ever since the "year of the manifestation of truth" in 1958, RK has been moving toward "a more recognizably Buddhistic definition of its life character."[7] In this section we shall present an outline of the doctrinal system according to the presentation of RK itself through her official publications.[8]

RK doctrine is based on the Lotus Sutra (*Myōhō Renge-kyō* or *Hokekyō*), the most influential of all the Buddhist scriptures in Mahayana Buddhism. It is thought to have originated in India around the beginning of the Christian era. It is in the form of an apocalypse, in which the Buddha speaks not as an extraordinary man, but as the Eternal Buddha. It claims to be his final and authoritative discourse in which he promises that through faith and the practice of righteousness all mankind will be saved. This sutra presents the bodhisattva ideal, that is, a compassion for others and a zeal to bring others into the fold of salvation. The bodhisattvas are the great spiritual beings or saints who could enter the final bliss of Buddhahood, but deliberately postpone this for the sake of helping others. It also presents the idea of messianism as a controlling motif in the interpretation of history; i.e., various bodhisattvas have appeared from time to time throughout history, each time as a savior during a period of decay. Another feature is the promise to confer happiness and every blessing upon believers. The Lotus Sutra makes the most extravagant promises of health, prosperity, etc., upon all who believe and propagate the faith.[9]

The elements of "Fundamental Buddhism," however, are not confined to the Lotus Sutra, but come rather from the earlier Hinayana stream of Buddhism. What is original about RK teaching is that it combines both the emphasis on saving one's self according to the way of the "Four Noble Truths," which is characteristic of Hinayana Buddhism, and the emphasis on saving others, which characterizes the Lotus Sutra and Mahayana Buddhism. Both of these streams are combined and applied in a "redemptive" way toward the practical solution of the problems of contemporary people.

Many doctrines and doctrinal formulae will appear in the study of the content of hoza conversations. Without an overview of the structure of RK's systematic theology, these teachings will be confusing. The doctrinal structure can be most easily grasped if seen from the perspective of the Four Noble truths (*shitai*) of classical Buddhism. The major teachings can be organized around these four central concepts.

1) The truth of suffering (*kutai*). "How to solve sufferings found in our environment or among ourselves is the great task of religions..."[10] First of all, one must grasp the real condition of suffering or misfortune which he is now experiencing. The important thing is that a person must take the responsibility for his suffering upon himself, blaming neither environment nor other people for it. There are principally three kinds of suffering: spiritual suffering, physical suffering and economic suffering.

2) The truth of cause (*jittai*). "It is not right to be resigned to one's sufferings...The Buddha Sakyamuni taught the Four Noble Truths to overcome suffering in this life.[11] Acknowledging his suffering, one must investigate its cause, if he would be rid of it. Every suffering has a definite cause. The law of cause and effect covers all phenomena of the universe and is basic to the understanding of Buddhist concepts. An analysis of the causes of suffering is arrived at through the use of two corollary doctrines:

(a) The doctrine of the reality of all existence (*jū-nyoze*). This doctrine refers to the interaction of all things in the physical and moral realm. When actions (primary cause) come into contact with certain conditions in the environment (secondary cause), the result is an effect which in turn produces an appropriate reward or retribution, from where the cycle starts over again.

(b) The twelve-linked chain of causality (*jūni innen*). This doctrine, similar to the preceding one, explicates the interrelations of life, but mainly from a chronological point of view. The important concept of karma comes to the fore here. "In the consciousness possessed at our birth, the karma accumulated in our previous life—all our deeds done in the past world—is working as the latent conciousness."[12] Transmigration from one existence to another is assumed.

3) The truth of extinction (*mettai*). This is the quiet stage where all sufferings have been extinguished, where all spiritual, physical and economic distresses have been removed by discovering and eliminating their causes. This is the ultimate aim of Buddhism. To understand the truth of extinction one must be aware of the three truths called the "three cardinal signs," which are as follows:

(a) All things are transitory (*shogyō mujo*). All things in the universe are in a constant process of change. Man changes every moment from birth to death. Changes may be either for better or for worse.

(b) All things are non-substantial (*shohō muga*). The meaning of this term for RK is that nothing in the universe stands alone or in isolation from other things. All things, including people, exist in inter-dependence upon all other things and people. This realization issues in gratitude towards all things and in a life lived in harmony with all that exists.

(c) Nirvana is bliss (*nehan jakujō*). Bliss, or quiescence, means the quiet stage where one is in harmony with all and free from selfish attachments to anything. After the realization of the transitoriness and inter-dependence of all things comes this stage of perfect freedom from adherence to temporary and superficial problems.

4) The truth of the path (*dōtai*). This is the truth which shows how to move from the state of our present sufferings to the bliss of nirvana. Two formulas give the clue:

(a) The eight-fold path (*hasshōdō*). When one has analysed his suffering and its cause properly, he must act the right way in order to break the former chain of interaction and begin a new chain of cause and effect. This right way is broken down into eight specific ethical imperatives: see rightly, think rightly, speak rightly, act rightly, live rightly, endeavor rightly, remember rightly and meditate rightly.

(b) The six perfections (*rokuharamitsu*). In contrast to the eight imperatives, the following six injunctions are not for those who simply want to be saved themselves, but for those who have advanced beyond that stage to the stage of giving one's life to save others. This is the way of the saints, or the bodhisattvas (*bosatsu*). It is the way of charity, observance of the precepts, patience, assiduity, meditation and wisdom.[13]

ORGANIZATION

Inasmuch as the focus of this work does not lie in the area of organization and facilities, only the briefest sketch of these aspects of RK will be introduced here. This introduction is deemed necessary so that the reader will have some idea of the impressive scope of the movement with which we are dealing. The entire organization is centered in the Great Sacred Hall (*Daiseidō*) in Suginami Ward of Tokyo. This is not only the center for worship and teaching, but the central organ of administration as well. Here, under the leadership of President Niwano and the Board of Directors, doctrinal emphasis and missionary strategy are determined and business management is carried out.

The nation is divided into 30 dioceses (*kyōku*), each of which has several churches (*kyōkai*, 222 in all), and the churches in turn have sub-units called branch churches (*shibu*), where the actual work of propagation of the faith is carried on. Each church has a full-time head plus volunteer staff workers. Each church has a training hall which is the center for local evangelism. Each church has an average of 7,000 households, while each branch church consists of approximately 1,200 households.

The branch churches are divided into regional groups called *chiku*, which consist of an average of 200 households each. These are again subdivided into smaller units (*kumi*, about 40 households each), and these in turn are broken down into neighborhood groups (*han*, about 10 households each). Each of these units has a responsible head. The whole organization, therefore, is a tightly knit pyramid structure with direct vertical lines of authority. It should be noted that all these units are established on the basis of geographical division. Leaders of the units are responsible not for a group of isolated individuals who live here and there, but for a certain geopolitical unit which generally coincides with the administrative units of the city government.

RK has a Men's Division and a Women's Division, but puts special emphasis on the Youth Division. Retreats for youth at the elaborate facilities at Ome Retreat Center, where 120 boys and 120 girls at a time go for three days of intensive inspiration and education, are one of the most promising areas of actvity for the future.

FACILITIES

First must be mentioned the Great Sacred Hall (*Daiseidō*) which towers as a mammoth landmark along one of the main arteries of traffic in Suginami Ward, Tokyo. This building, finished in 1964 at a cost of four billion yen (about eleven million dollars), can accommodate thirty thousand worshippers at one time. Built of pink tile and lavishly paneled with black and red marble on the inside, the Hall is seven stories high, topped by a huge dome. The cavernous central worship hall is circled by three broad, flat balconies where hoza groups meet in circles on the carpeted floor. The building is equipped with a large cafeteria, reception hall, elevators, and closed-circuit television, and with a magnificent German-built pipe organ. The commanding statue of the "Eternal Original Buddha" at the focal point of the sanctuary is some twenty-five feet high, painted predominantly in gold.

A second building of even greater proportions than the Great Sacred Hall, located directly across the street from the former, was completed in April, 1970. Called Fumon Hall, it is a gorgeously appointed five thousand seat public auditorium where the public can enjoy the arts, hear lectures, attend concerts, etc, and where RK members can be addressed by their leaders. The word *fumon* implies a gateway through which all men can enter and know the truth. It was built at a cost of ten billion yen (about twenty-eight million dollars) and is the largest theater-auditorium in the Orient. Its acoustical engineering and stage facilities are second to none in the world.

For twenty years President Niwano has lived by his motto, "One Thing a Year" and built one great institution after another, never rushing into a blind business venture, but never stopping. In 1948 the original Hall and headquarters was built. In 1949 the Kosei Nursery School, in 1953 the Kosei Library, in 1955 the Kosei High School for Girls, in 1956 the Kosei High School for Boys, and in 1958 the Kosei Home for the Aged were established. In 1959 the small Kosei Hospital founded earlier became a general hospital having 338 beds. The new Kosei Publishing House was completed in 1969, and the Kosei Office Building was finished in the spring of 1970. Mention should also be made of the vast Kosei Cemetery and elaborate Retreat Center, both in the suburbs, the Kosei band and chorus, martial arts society, and not least, the "Kosei Group" which sponsors television broadcasts.

Besides the publication of many books by President Niwano on Buddhism, the Kosei Publishing Company produces the *Dharma World* (an English monthly), the *Kōsei Shinbun* (a weekly newspaper), the *Kōsei* (a general monthly), *Mamille* (a monthly for women), and the *Yakushin* (a monthly for youth). A journal of academic and theological research, *Shinri to Sōzō* (Truth and Creation) and a journal for school teachers called *Shin no Kyōikusha wo Mezashite* (Becoming True Educators) have appeared in recent years.

ACTIVITIES

A glance at some of the activities in which all members are expected to participate will suggest what RK faith means to individual members. Personal evangelism (*michibiki*) is extremely important. Every member, even though he is still new and immature in the faith, is expected to share the blessing he has received with someone else, urging him to join RK. Thus he will supposedly increase his own happiness as well as lead others to salvation. All members in the Tokyo area contribute about one day out of fifty to actual service (*oyaku*) for the organization, assisting in cleaning, ushering, serving of food, etc. at the Hall. Faithful members attend public worship from 9:00 to 9:45 a.m. any day of the week at the Hall or at local meetings at set times. Worship consists of chanting portions of the Lotus Sutra and the singing of a hymn. Members who wish to achieve merit and advancement in the organization attend training sessions where they receive intensive instruction in doctrine and teaching methods. Periodic examinations are given, and if the individual successfully passes the examinations he is promoted to a higher level of leadership.

The festivals, in which tens of thousands participate at one time, must also be mentioned. The ceremonies are considered to be of great importance both for the individual and the community. Sixteen festivals constitute the large, public annual events, among them being such varied occasions as New Year's Day, the birthdays of Lord Sakyamuni and President Niwano, and the *Oeshiki*, the most spectacular of all, which commemorates the death of St. Nichiren.

Finally, mention must be made of hoza, the focal point of this study. It has already been noted that many of the new religions have small group discussions, which are called by various names. RK uses the term "hoza," which literally means Law (*hō*) and sitting (*za*), in order to express the major purpose of these groups, namely, to sit together and learn the meaning of the Buddha's Law. Hoza is one of the practices inherited from Reiyukai, the parent body of RK. However, RK has given this particular activity a theological foundation and needs it to fulfill its basic function of saving people. That is, the spirit of the *sanga*—"the congregation of people closely united, who have recourse to Sakyamuni Buddha and his teachings"—is vital for RK, and the spirit of the *sanga* is realized in no better way than through hoza.[14] RK believers pledge allegiance to the "Three Treasures", that is, the Buddha, the Law and the community of believers in what is called *Sanbokie*. It is recognized that man is weak by himself and needs the support of a community. Hoza offers this moral and social support.

These hoza groups meet at the Great Sacred Hall every day of the week from 10:00 to 12:00 in the morning and 1:00 to 3:00 in the afternoon. They consist of groups of about a dozen people each who sit in the traditional Japanese squatting position in circles on the three broad, flat balconies of the worship hall. They are arranged on the balconies according to the local geographical units to which they belong. The leaders, volunteer laymen, come regularly, but the group participants change from day to day. On weekdays, when most men are at work, the participants are mainly housewives. Groups also meet in homes and at local halls and branch churches, but this study is largely confined to the groups which meet in the Great Sacred Hall.

SECTION II

AN ANALYSIS OF HOZA

SECTION II constitutes the original research of this book. It is an analysis of hoza carried out through an investigation of the factors which account for the effective impact of this activity as a means of religious propagation and education. Five factors are delineated: factors pertaining to physical environment, organization, leadership, socio-emotional dynamics and conceptual content. These factors are analyzed by using two types of material: Findings based on personal observation of hoza sessions, and Interpretation of the Findings based on studies in Japanese mentality, social structure and religion, and also in psychotherapy and group dynamics.

CHAPTER FOUR

PHYSICAL ENVIRONMENT

The physical and esthetic aspects of the environment in which hoza takes place, the first factor to be considered, makes a large contribution to the total impact of what goes on within the sessions themselves.

(*Findings*)

PHYSICAL FACILITIES

The Great Sacred Hall is an edifice of auspicious proportions. Its sheer size is overwhelming. The pink tile exterior, the deep red marble walls and columns of the grand staircases, the multi-colored mosaics of Indian design, the brilliant colors of the floor, the high-vaulted aluminum ceiling, and the pure gold pinnacles of the domes—these and many other features invariably impress the visitor with the magnificence and opulence of this mecca for all RK believers. The architectural pattern and artistic form of both the exterior and interior are patterned after an Indian temple, and tend toward gaudy brilliance.

The Great Sacred Hall is kept immaculately clean at all times. This is accomplished by the corps of volunteer workers who take turns serving in various capacities as monitors for the Headquarters. Stairways and hallways are being dusted or scrubbed continuously during the day. The Hall is adequately heated by a central heating system in the winter, and comfortably air-conditioned in the summer. Another practical environmental advantage is the fact of access to an excellent cafeteria where the hoza participants can enjoy an inexpensive lunch during the noon hour between morning and afternoon sessions. If members prefer to bring their own lunch and buy only a beverage or dessert, such facilities are also conveniently available. Cookies, candy and drinks are sold at discount cost for children at all times. Even clothing, jewelry and cosmetics are sold in the cafeteria at discount prices.

ATMOSPHERE

A more significant observation in regard to the environmental factors which contribute to the impact of hoza is one that concerns the specific conditions of the group itself during the meeting. However, this subject will be only sketchily treated here, since it will be further developed in the section on socio-emotional factors.

The first and most obvious of these conditions is the fact that no chairs are used on the balconies. Instead, all participants, except the secretaries who sit at small desks located at strategic places, sit on the floor in the traditional Japanese squatting position. During the moments of worship at the beginning and end of the sessions all sit in the formal squatting position on their knees with hands placed on forelegs, or, at certain moments, in the prostrate position of reverence. But during the discussion men relax in the cross-legged squat position and women also take a more relaxed posture.

Mothers are free to bring their children with them to hoza. This poses no problems, for the broad carpeted floors on the balconies make an excellent playground for pre-school age children, and there is no hesitation about holding babies in arms while participating in hoza. Babies are welcome guests who provide amusement for the other women. Neither are mothers embarrassed to breast-feed babies in the circle whenever the need to do so arises. Children not only run about the balconies freely, but squeal and yell at their playmates uninhibitedly. Mothers as well as other participants seem oblivious to the commotion caused by children.

Children are not the only source of noise during hoza. In the Great Sacred Hall there is always a background of noisy bustling during hoza sessions. This is inevitable with so many people talking at one time throughout the building, all the parts of which are comprehended in one enclosure. On festival days or other special days the floors are so crowded with people that the setting could better be described as a din than a hum of noise. It is all but impossible for hoza participants to hear one another. The most blatant noise is the loudspeaker system which frequently pages individuals or announces activities of the day, or inquires about a lost child, a car parked in the wrong place, etc. Moreover, people are constantly moving about, coming late, leaving early, dropping over to another circle to see a friend, running to the secretary's desk to make some report, etc. Monitors make the rounds passing out and collecting attendence lists, distributing literature, and transacting various business.

WORSHIP AND HOZA

The architecture of the Great Sacred Hall is skillfully planned and executed from the point of view of effective religious impact. The central area of the Hall is high-domed, spacious and majestic in atmosphere. The brilliant altar area which focuses on the great statue of the Buddha gives an aura of awe and splendor to this central worship area.

The atmosphere on the balconies, where hoza is conducted, is in striking contrast. Here the floor is richly carpeted; the ceilings are very low. Plants and flowers add beauty and warmth. Everyone removes his shoes before walking on the carpet, the same as he would do when entering his own living room. In short, here on the balconies the participant feels perfectly at home, relaxed and "cozy."

The significant thing is that these two areas are skillfully juxtaposed. That is, when one is worshipping in the holy awesomeness of the great Hall, the balconies with their intimate fellowship are always in sight beckoning him. Likewise, while one is participating in the informal fellowship of hoza on the balconies, he cannot help but be aware of the sanctuary and its holy symbolism, for the balconies face and open into the central worship area.

Acts of worship and hoza discussions are also integrated through skillful timing of the various activities, which is made possible by the architectural design of the building. The day begins with an hour of formal worship in the central sanctuary, from where members quickly take elevators or stairways to their respective locations on the balconies. There they immediately squat on the floor in the company of their friends and the conversation begins. There is no loss of time nor breaking of mood such as would occur if it were necessary to move from one building to another, or if worship and hoza were conducted at different times of the week.

At noon a sonorous gong from the chancel area sounds, and everyone immediately orients himself toward the altar and image (*gohonzon*), whereupon the entire membership chants the sacred formula, "*Namu Myōhō Renge-kyō*," in unison with hundreds of other voices, for three or four minutes. Then there is a brief silence while all prostrate themselves facing the altar. The ritual ends with expression of gratitude to Mr. Niwano, the founder and leader. Finally all sing together the theme hymn, to the accompaniment of the great pipe organ. Following that, participants again face each other, bow to one another and express gratitude for the session. Leisurely they disperse for lunch in the cafeteria below.

(*Interpretation*)

ESTHETICS

The gaudy auspiciousness of the architectural style of the Great Sacred Hall is puzzling to the observer of Japanese art and culture. Its brilliance, opulence, and lack of the "quiet taste" which supposedly characterizes the Japanese artistic sense is baffling, especially in view of the fact that this is not an esoteric movement, and one which, moreover, is characterized by conservatism. Where is the sensitivity to and harmony with nature, the restrained beauty, the simplicity and plainness which are accepted as the predominant characteristics of Japanese esthetics? The following considerations are an effort at interpretation.

An ostentatious style of architecture is a peculiarity of nearly all the new religions. The grandiose headquarters building is a mecca and source of pride for adherents of these religions who make pilgrimages from all over the nation to spend a day in the glorious main temple.[1] McFarland points to the religious escapism which this emphasis on a magnificent religious edifice produces (the "edifice complex"), but notes that through it "grandeur becomes accessible, at least occasionally, to people who are debarred from it in almost every other avenue of their existence."[2]

The acceptance of this style of art and architecture can be viewed as a manifestation of the Japanese tendency to embrace simultaneously a multiplicity of heterogeneous elements, and the tendency to assimilate foreign elements without critical evaluation of them. Japanese culture does not attempt to be logically consistent, either in the realm of the conceptual or the material. Foreign cultural elements are readily absorbed, but this absorption is often uncritical and not thorough-going. Foreign elements which serve a practical purpose are readily assimilated, but since this borrowing is done intuitively and directly rather than rationally, the result is likely to be a divorce between external patterns and fundamental principles.[3] RK leaders admit that the facilities contain a variety of styles, and that this very thing makes them characteristically "contemporary Japanese."

But it is impossible to define narrowly what actually constitutes the

Japanese esthetic style. A distinctive quality of Japanese esthetic sense is expressed in the concept of "quiet taste." "In the past Japan maintained a consistent general trend throughout its civilization, retaining always the love of restraint...as characteristic." The sensibilities of the Japanese were characterized by a rejection of the ornamental and the gaudy, and love for reserve. The terms which express this specific type of restrained, modest beauty, this "cultural restraint imposed on the vital impulses," are *wabi* and *sabi* (a wistful, meloncholy mood) and *mono no aware* ("the sadness of things").[4]

However, a parallel but sub-dominant movement toward the lavish and spectacular has also been an important stream in Japanese cultural history. This is exemplified in the ornate and colorful shrines of Nikko. These are typical of the opulence of the Tokugawa Period. The earlier Momoyama Period culture was noted for its glitter, but even then there existed at the same time a trend toward restraint, the spirit of *wabi* and *sabi*. "It is a tradition of Japanese civilization that the glittering and the majestic should always be accompanied by its opposite."[5]

It should be noted, accordingly, that Japanese architecture is, generally speaking, compounded of two different traditions: the native Japanese and the Chinese. The former tends toward modesty, the latter towards grandeur and brilliance. "Architecture intended to be publicly imposing...has tended to take the continental style, while the native style has been preferred more often in domestic dwellings."[6]

ATMOSPHERE

The atmosphere of hoza is alive with bustle, commotion, interferences and noise. How can this be conducive to counseling and religious instruction? Yet all the commotion appears not to have an adverse effect on the members, who not only manage to communicate well despite the bustle and noise, but seem quite oblivious to it. Some reasons for this may be found.

The group orientation of the Japanese is a primary cultural characteristic. Japanese tend to live their entire lives in the context of a human collectivity. This point will receive further elaboration in subsequent sections. Suffice it to say here that the Japanese are basically a group-oriented people. This way of life possibly has its roots in the geography, climate and population density of the country.[7] Privacy in the sense of Western individualistic privacy is virtually unknown. In the traditional house, for example, there are few solid walls; instead, sliding paper doors (*fusuma* or *shoji*) are used to divide rooms. Thus children live with their family all hours of the day. They cannot help but be aware of the presence of other people, even when "doors" are closed. This collaterality of Japanese life finds natural expression in the collaterality of the hoza balconies in the Great Sacred Hall.

Moreover, urbanized Japanese, especially those of the shop-keeper, small business class, are accustomed by necessity to living in close and crowded quarters facing the narrow, bustling, shop-lined streets where vendors, fish-market men, etc., shout out their bargain prices from morning until night and coax passers-by to stop and buy. In Dore's study of *Shitamachi* (the relatively low-class section of Tokyo), he notes among the cultural differences between these people and the *Yamanote* (higher class residential area) people that "the wide-open, no-secrets communal life of the *Shitamachi* family contrasts with the greater individualism and privacy of the *Yamanote* family." He also notes that "whereas the *Shitamachi* family typically lives in a crowded street in a densely populated area, the *Yamanote* family divides itself from its neighbors with a garden and hedge."[8] The townspeople of Japan are no strangers to bustle and noise! Therefore, the noisy, bustling environment of hoza actually contributes to the "at-home" atmosphere of the Great Sacred Hall, at least for the shop-keeper class of people.

The squatting position in which the hoza participants sit is the most characteristic traditional Japanese posture. Although Japanese men are accustomed to sitting on chairs in their offices, as are students, most women feel more at home sitting on the floor in the squatting position than they do on chairs, inasmuch as this is the accustomed way of living in a Japanese house. Most of the rooms of a traditional Japanese home have *tatami* (grass mat) floors, on which chairs are not used. Sitting on the carpeted floor rather than on chairs is a significant positive feature of the environment of hoza.

The comfort and convenience of the Great Sacred Hall, with its central heating and air-conditioning, its cafeteria and discount shops, its cleanliness and richness, and its broad places for children to play are in themselves no small reason for the popularity of hoza. Most of the participants are housewives of an economic class where the family lives in crowded, unattractive quarters, and where the housewife enjoys little if any recreation. The average housewife rarely has an opportunity to eat at a restaurant. For these individuals, the experience of spending part or all of a day in the inviting atmosphere of the Great Sacred Hall is sufficient reward in itself, apart from the content of the hoza discussions.

Furthermore the care of children is a primary concern for young mothers, who could not attend hoza if there were restrictions on bringing children, or if there were no place for them to play. But on the balconies the children enjoy the extremely permissive handling which is characteristic of Japanese child-raising—distracting to the Westerner, but taken for granted by the participants in hoza.

INTEGRATION OF HOZA AND WORSHIP

Thanks to the arrangement of the balconies for hoza as part of the grand sanctuary of the Great Sacred Hall, intimate social experience is never far removed from sacred things, and the idea of the holy is never far removed from the discussion of everyday problems which constitute hoza. Here is an integration of the atmosphere of holiness with the atmosphere of intimacy, and the integration of the act of worship with the act of socializing, both of which effect a mutual reinforcement. Both are skillfully related in subconscious feeling, through the atmosphere, as well as in conscious acts. The stated purpose of hoza is to apply Buddhist teaching to everyday life problems, and this kind of environmental arrangement effectively helps to further this purpose.

Moreover, this physical arrangement has added significance in the Japanese context. Part of that significance is related to what was mentioned earlier about collaterality. The single enclosure which comprehends both common public worship and all the discussion groups meeting at the same time, is a strong expression of group solidarity, of close fellowship, and corporate thinking and acting. "Behind the message and the promise, perhaps the single most important boon that the new religions have had to offer is the opportunity to belong to a community."[9]

Is there not something profane about letting worship, religious instruction, recreation, child-care and small talk become intertwined in this way? Does not the diversion interfere with devotion? Not in the Japanese naturalistic approach to religion and life which sees *kami* (god) as one with man, and men and nature as one with *kami*.[10] For religion to be accepted by the Japanese it must be "involved in the warp and woof of life." There are no absolute distinctions between sacred and secular, or religion and recreation, in this culture colored by centuries of Shinto history.[11]

CHAPTER FIVE

ORGANIZATION

The remarkable growth and power of RK are due in no small measure to its efficient structural organization. Here we are not concerned about the over-all structure of RK as such, but only about the organization of the hoza system. Three related topics dealing with different aspects of organization, namely, principles of organization, the constituency of the hoza groups, and the use of pressures in maintaining the groups, will be dealt with in this chapter.

Organizational Principles

Under this topic will be included several items pertaining to the structure, composition and procedure of hoza groups. Matters pertaining directly to group dynamics as such will be discussed later.

(*Findings*)

NETWORK OF PERSONAL CONTACT

The hoza circle is not an artificially created social group. Rather, it is a group which has roots in person-to-person contact and in geographical community, both of which features are extremely important in maintaining social groupings in Japanese culture. RK itself is propagated largely through personal contact of each member persuading his acquaintances to join the religion. This activity is known as *michibiki* (leading). Every RK member is expected to tell others about the benefits of the religion and urge them to join. First he is expected to persuade others in his own family. Anyone who has people working under him is expected to urge his employees to join. Members are urged to visit the sick and those in trouble, using the opportunity of their distress to tell them that joining RK will surely produce a concrete benefit for them. Sometimes there is a veiled threat that evil will befall the member if he fails to be diligent in propagating the faith.[1]

Almost everyone who attends hoza has come through the invitation of a member, and is physically brought to the circle by that member. The member introduces the newcomer and often speaks on his behalf, as is evidenced in the following typical observation:

> Mrs. B: (Accompanied by Miss C) My friend, Miss C here, just found out this morning that she has acute appendicitis and must have an operation this very afternoon. She's not going to the RK hospital, which is unfortunate, but to a small neighborhood hospital. Do you think things will turn out all right? (25)

The older woman was playing the role of spiritual parent, or the role of "go-between." Miss C said nothing during the session.

The writer himself was frequently asked during hoza, "Who is your *michibiki-te* (the one leading you)?" and the reaction to his status as one who came on his own was one of mild surprise and, "In spite of that, we're glad you're here."

In the following case in Session 30 the important role of the *michibiki-te* is obvious.

Mrs. A, a housewife in her late twenties, was attending for the first time and presented a problem of marital difficulties. The discussion of her case went on for about half an hour on the level of husband-wife difficulties, without getting far. Then Mrs. B, the friend (*michibiki-te*) who had brought Mrs. A, revealed the deeper dimensions of the problem, which involved a triangle love affair between the husband, his wife, and his brother's wife. Significantly, it was the "go-between" who took the responsibility of exposing the deeper problem and getting to the core of her trouble.

GEOGRAPHICAL BASIS

Hoza groups are organized according to geographical areas. As one walks around the balconies of the Great Sacred Hall, plates indicating the ward of the city are posted conspicuously so that even the newcomer has no difficulty finding his own ward. He will go to his ward section and there give his address to the receptionist at the desk. He will be told what circle he should attend, for the whole structural plan of RK is based on geographical units.

This system of organizing is not only efficient, but has the advantage of automatically providing common experience and common problems for discussion. In many cases it also means that people of a common economic and cultural level will be meeting together. There is a commonality among the members by virtue of this geographical division, and this tends to offset the disadvantage of the constantly varying membership of the groups, which will be noted later.

Because of the personal network among members and the commonality resulting from geographical structuring of the groups, leaders know how to get conversation under way and how to bring common concerns to the fore. The following are typical examples:

L: Mrs. E, how is your son who went to Hokkaido to live? (36)

L: Mrs. A, how did things work out in regard to the boundary dispute on your property? (24)

L: Mr. A, you recently went to a retreat at the Training Hall. Please tell us about your experience. (31)

Inasmuch as each of these individuals comes only occasionally to the Great Sacred Hall, the leader would not know about these personal matters were it not for geographical proximity, which allows him to call on that person or to know about him through neighborhood gossip. But since the leader knows these items of personal concern, the hoza session can run on the momentum of neighborhood contacts and personal acquaintance.

CONVENIENT SCHEDULING

The time schedule for hoza meetings is highly advantageous. Groups meet every day of the week, except on festival days, when there are other activities, and on certain other rare occasions. Thus, a member can attend on whatever day is convenient for him. Almost any worker can find one or two days out of the month which are free, and he knows that whatever day of the week this might fall on, hoza will be in session.

The hours of hoza are from 10:00 a.m. until 12:00 noon, and from 1:00 p.m. until 3:00 p.m. Inasmuch as the majority of participants on weekdays are housewives, these hours are conveniently accommodated to the housewife's schedule. It is essential that the Japanese housewife be on her way home by 3:00 p.m. in order to do the daily shopping and preparations for the evening meal. Therefore, the entire public activity of the Great Sacred Hall ends promptly at 3:00 p.m.

Participants may attend only in the forenoon or only in the afternoon, or stay for both, having lunch in the cafeteria between sessions.

Furthermore, the time of going and coming is completely flexible. Although the sessions start at 10:00 in the morning, members continue to arrive until almost noon. The same is true in the afternoon. Or if one needs to leave early, there is no pressure whatsoever to stay until the closing hour.

Hoza sessions are also held in RK members' homes in the afternoon for housewives and in the evening for youth and men. In this case both time and place are conveniently adapted to the needs of the members, since the home meeting is for the people of the immediate neighborhood.

(*Interpretation*)

THE IDEA OF HOZA

The Group in Japanese Society

The Japanese are a collectivity-oriented people. Their traditional value system is one which finds the locus of value in the limited nexus of a defined human group, rather than in either the individual or in a universal concept. Individuals are defined as group members and have no identity independent of the group, says Bellah.[2]

"Whatever has happened in the realm of explicit ideology, it remains true that the 'human nexus' continues to be more powerful and salient in Japan than either ideas or individuals."[3]

In short, Japan's traditional value system is a system of values realized through groups and collectivities. These groups are integrated with the structure of reality and endowed with sacred religious characteristics, exemplified by the veneration of ancestors.[4] The unconditional belief in a limited human nexus is one of the chief characteristics of the Japanese way of thinking. Man the individual is subordinated to man in a group. Man is conceived primarily in terms of human relations. Thus a human event is not a personal event, but is primarily a social event. Whereas religion usually advocates transcending specific human relations, this facet of religion is scarcely seen in Japanese religions. Even classical Buddhism was adjusted to fit into this pattern.[5]

> The commitment of an individual to his own group is much stronger than any commitment to a transcendent value system or to a professional or union organization tying him to others occupying the same position in other groups. The basic cleavages in Japanese society have not been between different social classes but between one

> corporate group (composed of people of different social positions) and other corporate groups. The strong commitment of an individual to his group...has been conducive to a very high degree of solidarity and conformity within any single group.[6]

In the context of this way of thinking, the idea of hoza—a small group organized in a religious setting—is not only adapted to Japanese interests, but partakes of the very essence of the Japanese social spirit and personal need. Hoza is one means of restoring the solidarity of the group and offering the opportunity to belong to a community to those who have experienced the break-up of the old solidarities and the break-up of the family system.

Throughout Japanese history various organized groups have appeared on the local level as a response to this need. Notable among these are the many kinds of *kumi* (associations),[7] from the *goningumi* (five-man group) of the Tokugawa Period to the *tonarigumi* (neighborhood association) and the *buraku* (local community) and *chōnaikai* (local neighborhood organizations) of the present day.[8] The *tonarigumi* were strong and influential throughout the nation during World War II. They were organized with the deliberate intention of unifying all the the people on the basis of geographical units. This aspect of the *tonarigumi* disappeared after the war, and in its place came the *chōnakai* (local neighborhood association) and other informal groupings, the nature of which varies from community to community.

Parhaps the most significant organized group to serve as an analogy of and predecessor to hoza is the *kō*.[9] Especially in past centuries, this flexible, local organization functioned to integrate the community in the religious, economic, and social dimensions. The dictionary definition of *kō* is "club" or "association." Today it usually has the more specific meaning of a mutual aid society. It is a kind of religious and/or economic organization. When centered at a certain temple, or when composed of a definite membership, it is called *kōju*. At first *kō* was a kind of religious institution, like a "home prayer meeting", or Buddhist worship rite. The neighborhood gathered together for prayers at a certain household, but the religious service was followed by a discussion of matters of collective community interest. In such meetings the *buraku* residents reaffirmed their collective unity. This kind of *kō* meeting is still commonly practiced in certain rural areas. In a study of the community of Niiike it was found that the *kōju* functioned not only as a religious ceremonial, but as the "cooperative work unit, the mutual assistance unit, the unit of management, protection and solidarity of the *buraku*."[10] Embree, studying Suye Mura in the mid-1930's, found the financially oriented *kō*, sometimes called *tanomoshi-kō*, which can be translated as "cooperative credit club", to be a wide-spread and important form of community cooperation.[11] It is obvious that in *kō* there is a significant historical precedent for RK's hoza. RK has selected this extremely indigenous, traditional mode of social organization and has skillfully adapted it for efficient functioning in the contemporary urban setting.

Theological and Sociological Interpretations

This leads to a further comment on the relation between the theological and sociological meanings of hoza. There can be little doubt that the idea of hoza was inherited from RK's parent body, Reiyukai, from accustomed participation in various *kumi* and from the *kō* organizations. But RK speaks only of the theological dimension of hoza by linking it with the doctrine of *sanga* (the congregation of believers) and the practice of Sakyamuni Buddha's gathering a small circle of believers around him when he taught. Hoza, RK states, is an expression of the third component of the trinitarian formula, called *sanbōkie*, which exalts the Buddha, the Law, and the Congregation (*sanga*). Hoza, seen as an expression of the *sanga*, is the embodiment of the spiritual fellowship of Buddhist believers.

If this theological interpretation is placed alongside the observations of Japanese social structure and group consciousness noted earlier, a revealing illustration of Max Weber's concept of "elective affinity" is found. Weber says that "in time, ideas are discredited in the face of history unless they point in the direction of conduct that various interests promote. Ideas, selected and re-interpreted from the original doctrine, do gain an affinity with the interests of certain members of special strata; if they do not gain such an affinity they are abandoned."[12] The theological "ideas" of the Buddhist *sanga* found affinity with and so have been promoted by the sociological "interests" of the Japanese, i.e., their propensity for thinking and acting in group context.

CHARACTERISTICS OF HOZA ORGANIZATION

Network of Personal Relations

The peculiar Japanese code of personal ethics called *bushidō* is based on concepts of honor, obligation and loyalty (*giri*, *gimu*) which produce what has been called the "web" of Japanese society. This web establishes a network of social relations which makes it imperative for every individual to take his proper place in a vertically oriented pattern of interpersonal relatedness.[13] Hoza capitalizes on this pattern by setting up its own structure of personal contacts. People are brought to hoza through *michibiki* ("personal evangelism"), which is the invitation of a member to a non-member to join the organization. The one who thus leads another becomes the *michibiki no oya* (parent) of the one who is led, who is the *michibiki no ko* (child).[14] This familial relationship—the strongest bond possible in Oriental culture—is maintained from that time on. Chie Nakane, in discussing the various characteristics of group formation, concludes that "Japanese group affiliations and human relations are exclusively one-to-one: a single loyalty stands uppermost and firm."[15] In further delineating the structure of the group she states that "an organizational principle in terms of parent-child relationships constitutes the basic scheme of Japanese organization."[16]

This network of relations is evident in Japanese society in the practice of having a "go-between" (*nakōdo*) play a mediating role for important transactions, such as marriage or making a contract or joining an organization, rather than taking direct action oneself. The *michibiki no oya* serves as this go-between in leading people into hoza and into RK membership. Or, again, the network of close-knit social relations is evident in the traditional *iizutae*, or passing on of news throughout the community via a set route of person-to-person communication.[17] RK, using this same pattern, keeps every member informed of high-level decisions, and keeps track of every member by using this same pattern of *iizutae*. The *shunin* communicates regularly with the *kumi-chō*, the *kumi-chō* with the *han-chō*, and the *han-chō* in turn communicates with every individual in his *han*[18].

Tightly Knit Organization

RK maintains a tightly knit hierarchical administrative organization, beginning at the top with the leadership of President Niwano and going down to the last small local sub-unit called the *han*. The new religions are typically organized in pyramid fashion with the founder or head, maintaining an office at the national headquarters, at the top. Under the national office will be regional offices and officers, under these the district, which in turn will be subdivided into various local groupings, each with its respective head. Organizational policy is in the traditional pattern of personal relationships, loyalties and obligations, principally the *oya-ko* (parent-child) relationship, rather than in the pattern of constitutional rules and regulations. This makes for a remarkable operational efficiency, one in which the Japanese feel quite at home, and indeed one for which many have genuine need—the need to find status within a group, and the need to submit to authority. "The astonishing success of these new religious groups," writes Nakane in speaking of one of the contemporary Japanese religions, "seems to be attributable mainly to their system of vertical organization."[19] Thus authority and discipline are woven into the religious body. It is this kind of discipline that accounts for the vast numbers who attend hoza daily. Leaving attendance merely to individual whim and feeling of need would undoubtedly not produce the same results.

Geographical Division

The minutely developed organization referred to above is laid out on the basis of division into successively smaller units according to geographical area. This division on the basis of geographical locality is of no small significance in view of the fact that "residence factors" are extremely important in constituting Japanese groupings. Residence factors, whether it be one's home prefecture, or one's local neighborhood in a city, are, in many cases, more significant than common interests in determining groups. Silberman points out that "the outstanding characteristic of the important associations of the *buraku* is spatial contiguity."[20]

Hierarchical Structure

This characteristic of the hoza groups will be examined in more detail in the subsequent chapter on leadership, but it should be mentioned here that, apart from the nature of the leadership as such, hoza is unquestionably organized in the pattern of a hierarchical or authoritarian group. According to the definition offered by group dynamics, an authoritarian group has its source of origin outside the group, and has a person designated by the outside source to control it from within. The group is managed by this leader, who is assumed to have superior knowledge to the members of the group. Communication is mainly in the form of statements from the leader with responses to him from the group.[21] Significantly, this is an accurate description of the organizational principles of hoza. This kind of group organization is well adapted to the traditional Japanese social organization, which is largely defined by Confucian patterns of vertical relationships, and by the spirit of *bushidō* with its pattern of obligations and loyalties. This kind of authoritarian structure is a natural manner of socialization for Japanese, in everything from the family system to the emperor system.[22]

Norbeck says with regard even to the voluntary associations in a Japanese community, that there is nothing inherently democratic about them, and they can be used for either democratic or totalitarian purposes.[23] Nakane points to the hierarchical organization of Japanese Buddhist sects, particularly with reference to the controlling power of the main temple over its subordinate branches.[24]

Constituency

(Findings)

SOCIAL CLASS

The determination of the social class of members of the new religions is a matter which has been investigated by various sociologists of religion, and so has not been a matter of primary concern in this study. However, during attendance at hoza sessions, note was made of any reference to occupation which came out in the conversations. On the basis of this, the following observations can be made. The specific references to occupation, either that of the one speaking or of her husband in the case of a wife, showed a preponderance of the following kinds of work: small shopkeeper, office worker and tradesman. Observation of dress and manners also indicated a preponderance of middle to lower middle class styles.

These observations can be corroborated by the findings of an investigation of occupational distribution of hoza members made by Watanabe in 1968, which showed the following distribution:

Self-employed	20.4 per cent
Salaried workers	20.4 per cent
No occupation (virtually all of which were housewives)	59.1 per cent

The enterprises of the self-employed were small businesses which employed from two to five workers. Among the husbands of the housewives, 48 per cent were self-employed and 52 per cent were salaried workers, most of whom did clerical work. The self-employed usually referred to shop keepers.[25]

Regarding educational level, observation of manner of speaking indicated secondary level education. As will be discussed elsewhere, the type of religious message or conversation which appealed to them definitely indicated a manner of thinking not above secondary level education. These observations can be compared with the findings of Wada, whose survey of forty RK members chosen at random showed that twenty-two had graduated from only elementary school, fifteen from high school and three from college.[26] Watanabe found in her sampling of ordinary members that 34.9 per cent had only elementary education, 44.2 per cent had secondary education and 20.9 per cent had some higher education.[27]

Although there is considerable variation in the percentages recorded by these different surveys, taken together they give a picture of hoza members as a group whose occupational status tends toward the small shopkeeper or clerical office worker class, whose educational status tends to be limited to elementary or secondary education, and whose social class therefore tends to be in the area between middle middle (sic) and lower middle class.

THE ROLE OF WOMEN

The great majority of those who attend hoza in the daily session at the Great Sacred Hall are middle-aged women. Notation was made in the Observation Record of the sex differentiation of twenty-four typical groups attended. There was an overall average of 77 per cent female and 23 per cent male attendance in these sessions. This observation may be compared with Watanabe's survey which showed that out of a sample of 75 members, 49 were female and 26 were male. According to her survey, age distribution of the females was as follows:[28]

20—29	22.5 per cent
30—39	18.4 per cent
40—49	36.8 per cent
50—59	16.3 per cent
60—69	6.0 per cent

Age distribution among males was parallel. These statistics give a general picture of hoza groups being constituted predominantly by middle-aged women.

Hoza sessions are conducted in homes in the evening so that men may more conveniently attend. However, these are scheduled only once or twice a month in most areas, and the number of participants at these sessions is relatively small. (At Session 31, eight men attended the home meeting.) It is also true that on Sundays and holidays many men attend the Great Sacred Hall hoza sessions, but even then they are definitely a minority.

It is significant to hear how this dominant role of women in religion is interpreted by the women themselves in the following two cases:

> *Mrs. B*: Men should be more zealous in their religious practice. That would make it easier for us women. Our husbands are often irritated when we come home a little late from hoza and don't have supper ready for them.
>
> *L*: Men should take the lead in religion and we women would gladly follow, but unfortunately we women usually have to be leaders. (12)

> *L*: Our religious discipline as wives is to learn to acquiesce to our husbands. When our husbands see that we are really more obedient and humble wives, they let us go to RK willingly. But until they do willingly consent to our coming here, what a trial it is for us! That trial is our religious discipline. The men themselves usually don't feel the need to come to hoza. They are so busy at work that they really can't be expected to attend here. The important thing, anyway, is that they willingly allow us wives to come. That is evidence of their good heart, and that is their service to the Buddha. (23)

In these two cases are two approaches to the fact of the predominance of women. In Session 12 there is the attitude of resignation toward the fact that men, unfortunately, do not take the lead, so therefore women must do so. In Session 23 there is a more positive interpretation of the feminine role, the conclusion being that women represent their families in the religious area, and as long as a husband gives voluntary assent to the wife's activity, his religious obligations to the household are being taken care of. Regardless of the interpretation which might be made, the fact remains that hoza's main appeal is to women.

(*Interpretation*)

REGARDING SOCIAL CLASS

Although there is a wide range of occupational roles and educational status among the participants of hoza, there is obviously a preponderance of people in the lower middle class range, having little or no higher education. Sociologists of religion appear to be unanimous in their analysis of the new religions as being a movement which has special appeal to the lower social and economic class, the principal reason being that these people are relatively unorganized, rootless and lacking in the sense of belonging and social solidarity which is so important for Japanese. The sociologist Mita finds a very dark situation facing workers in small enterprises. Such workers suffer chronic deprivation, lack of sufficient social welfare, and lack of security so that they are forced to depend on the paternalistic care of their employer. "Unfortunately, such dependence constantly reproduces the attitudes necessary to pre-modern morality and the continuity of 'feudal' human relations."[29] The new religions are perhaps the sole institutions of society to be relevantly concerned to alleviate the plight of the lower middle class.

The lives of this class of people are troubled with many anxieties and concrete problems because of their economic and social insecurity, and hoza promises to hear these problems and give a concrete answer to them. The new religions are often disparagingly referred to as *goriyaku shūkyō* (literally, honorable profit-making religions). They promise the establishment of the Kingdom of God on earth here and now. Saki calls the new religions eschatological and utopian, for they set up for the dissatisfied sectors of society the ideal of recreating a new world of peace and prosperity (*yo-naoshi no yume*).[30] Hoza also serves as a medium of expression for the common man who would otherwise have no platform for making his voice heard. Affiliation with hoza affords to the nameless and powerless a chance to affiliate with some persons who are socially and culturally above them, and to educate themselves so they, too, can rise on the social scale.[31]

The significance of the social class which is found to predominate among the members of RK, as among members of most of the new religions, has been discussed in the section on causative factors in the rise of the new religions (Chapter II), and has been given exhaustive treatment by Hori, Saki, Takagi and others. Because of this, and also because the thrust of this study lies in a different area, no further interpretation of the findings on the social class of hoza participants will be made here.

REGARDING THE ROLE OF WOMEN

The majority of the participants in hoza are middle-aged women. The appeal of hoza would be much less successful if its goal were to get men involved in religion. The experience of coming together regularly for several hours for informal conversation is more adapted to the needs of women than of men, and particularly adapted to the needs of the contemporary Japanese housewife.

Generally speaking, the Japanese housewife has a hard lot. The traditional position of women in Japan has been one of inferiority and virtual bondage. The daughter was subordinated to her father and the wife to her husband. Under the old Civil Code, the husband's authority over his wife represented a master-servant relationship. He could, for example, divorce his wife without her approval and was under no obligation to contribute to her livelihood after divorce. The wife when widowed had no inheritance rights. The primary concern of a woman was to be an obedient wife and to bear children, especially a male child, who would maintain continuity for the *ie* (household).[32] Under the post-war constitution men and women are accorded equal rights. On the whole both men and women now "do express attitudes of approval regarding the new legal principles of sex equality and emancipation of women, but in practice both men and women to a great extent still accept the subordinate positions and the inequalities which continue to exist."[33]

The city wife, who usually sees her husband only in the early morning and late evening, has special needs for socialization. Vogel, describing sociological effects of urbanization and migration to the cities in modern Japan, comments on the effect of this movement upon women's life.

> The wife who moved to the city was completely dependent on her husband for support, typically did not have a job of her own, and would be disgraced if she had to return to the country because she had not completely satisfied her husband. As a result the basis for husband authority in the city was maintained.[34]

Furthermore, "the wife in the city was usually extremely lonely for lack of any social contacts." Her life is bound to her children inasmuch as she does not have in-laws to take care of them, nor does the father's long working hours away from home permit him to give time to the children.[35]

But there is ferment for change toward emancipation of Japanese women today, "The greatest democratic change that has come to postwar Japan...is the liberation of women."[36] New freedoms have been awarded to Japanese women today, and they will never allow themselves to go back to their old servitude. They need a place where they can express frustrations and their heretofore inhibited aggressive tendencies. No activity could be more ideally adapted to providing exactly what the frustrated Japanese housewife needs at this point in history than hoza. The new religions have sometimes been called a movement of women's liberation, and hoza fits perfectly into this pattern. It is commented by some that at first hoza was little more than an *idobata kaigi* (a humorous expression meaning "well-side conference," coming from the activity of women gathering at the neighborhood well to do their washing and gossiping there), and that the religious feature was added as a later stage of development. Be that as it may, later chapters will make it clear that hoza is indeed a popular program for middle-aged women.

Use of Pressures

Attending hoza we also observe that means of promotion and persuasion which smack of coercion are sometimes used to maintain interest and participation in the groups.

(*Findings*)

There is frequent talk in hoza about how wonderful RK and its activities are. There is frequent overt praise of the leaders, praise of the teaching, praise for what RK is doing for society and for individuals. There is loud acclaim given to the bigness and power of the organization itself. Often praise is accorded to speakers for their impressive speeches given at public rallies.

Of course, this might be taken as spontaneous gratitude and praise for the teaching and the organization which has been helpful to them. But the impression received is that this elaborate, ostentatious praise is a kind of barrage of propaganda to induce other people to join the organization, or a verbal pressure on the participants to be more enthusiastic and supportive of the organization. In Session 17, Mr. A, whose father is an official of RK, and who himself is on the borderline between participation and antagonism, stated that RK's boastful self-promotion was his chief complaint against the religion.

> *Mr. A*: One thing which stands between us and the community is that we are too cock-sure of ourselves and use too much pressure and propaganda. We're always saying, "Look at us; see how happy we are because we belong to RK." We're always waving the RK flag in front of us. Wouldn't it be better if we simply led a good life and let people judge for themselves whether or not they want to join our organization? (17)

Another category of pressures observed in hoza is the pressure applied in telling people that they will have or continue to have problems if they do not participate in RK, or in telling people that they will meet with some adversity unless they cooperate with RK. The following case illustrates this point.

> *Mr. B*: I have trouble getting along with my wife and children. It seems like we're always quarreling. What's the matter?
>
> *L*: Does your wife believe in the Buddha? (No.) Then you must pray for her and for your children. If you see that the fault for your trouble lies with you, as President Niwano teaches us, your life will straighten out. If you should get discouraged and quit RK now, something terrible is sure to happen in your life. (29)

The atmosphere and arrangement of programs both at public meetings and at hoza sessions must in some cases be characterized as manipulative. The use of mass psychology and intense emotional appeal in the speeches given at certain public rallies is an attempt to manipulate the will and feelings of the audience. In hoza certain people who have had emotional religious experiences are brought to the sessions to tell their story and move people to respond. The case of Mr. A in Sessions 26 and 29 is a good illustration. This attractive-appearing young man who spoke with emotional force as well as with personal charm was brought into several groups to tell his story. He always left the listeners deeply moved.

The writer himself has frequently been the object of coercive persuasion during hoza. In Session 40 about half an hour was given to trying to persuade him to believe RK teaching. First Mr. A tried to persuade him to show gratitude to his ancestors by venerating them. Then Mrs. A took over:

> *Mrs. A*: Please read our literature and you will gradually come

to understand our teaching. Become a member first of all, and then go on from there. I used to be a Christian myself, but I have gradually come to see the light. (40)

Then Mrs. B tried to convince him that Christ and his teachings are included in the way of the Buddha. One after another the members of the group all tried to teach him the Buddhist way of salvation according to Mr. Niwano's interpretation. They gave no opportunity for the writer to express doubt or to ask questions; they were not inclined to let him make a free decision regarding religious loyalties.

There is frequent verbal urging and pressing of members to work more diligently for the organization. Members are urged to be more zealous in winning others to the RK faith, and in bringing others with them to hoza. Frequently the leader goes around the circle asking each one how he is progressing in his efforts to lead others to the faith.

L: Mrs. D, you must try to win Mrs. A to RK. She is in the hospital now, you know. Most people join RK in time of sickness or some similar crisis, so don't pass up this opportunity. (22)

The question of pressures used on members to make them contribute financially to the organization has from time to time become a matter of public concern. A few observations relevant to this can be made. One is the daily practice of members' giving their contributions during hoza. A common procedure in giving an offering is for a member to take a bill or bills out of her purse, wrap it in the special offering paper provided for this purpose, write the amount along with her name, reach out ostentatiously across the middle of the circle and lay the gift in front of the leader, who collects and records the contribution. This act is performed at the members' convenience; there is no set time for the offering. The observer cannot help but feel that this procedure for making the offering is used because of the indirect pressure it places on each member of the circle not to be outdone by his neighbor.

There are also more direct pressures applied to make financial contributions. The leader in Session 38 made the logically persuasive argument that the ultimate goal of RK is to create world peace, but in order to teach society the way of peace a large hall to accommodate mass gatherings is necessary. RK is about to build such a public auditorium, but it can be done only if everyone contributes generously of himself and his money. Therefore, to create world peace, she urged that all must give larger offerings.

(*Interpretation*)

Coercion and manipulation in group process must be negatively evaluated from the point of view of an egalitarian philosophy. Principles of group dynamics as defined in the West are based on the ethical premise of absolute respect for the equal rights and privileges of each and every member of the group. Ethical conduct of the leader in this context means that he does not coerce others to follow his own convictions and preferences, and that he does not manipulate the group toward his own judgments.[37]

However, if the reason why this approach is tolerated to the extent that it is be sought for, it can be at least partially explained by what has been indicated above regarding the authoritarian and hierarchical structure of traditional Japanese group life, in which unquestioning obedience is a virtue. What appears to the Western observer to be acts of coercion and involuntary submission might simply be to the persons in a hierarchically oriented society proper expressions of authority and obedience. A danger is involved, however, in that there is but a short step from authoritarian procedures to coercive procedures, for power resides in authoritarian leadership, and legitimate power (based on the leader's right to prescribe behavior for others) and expert power (based on the leader's special knowledge or expertness) easily slip over into reward power and coercive power (based on the leader's ability to mediate rewards and punishment).[38]

CHAPTER SIX

LEADERSHIP

The examination of leadership in hoza proves to be one of the most significant aspects of this study, from the point of view of both understanding Japanese social patterns and understanding what constitutes effective religious leadership in contemporary Japan. Observations are focused around the following three topics: charismatic qualities, teaching ability, and the authoritarian posture of leaders.

Charismatic Qualities of Leaders

(*Findings*)

Max Weber's concept of charismatic authority as constituting a unique kind of social leadership, to be differentiated from routine, bureaucratic leadership, is helpful in attempting to analyze qualities of leadership in RK in general, and hoza in particular. Weber defines the charismatic leader as the holder of a special gift, who gains authority solely by proving his strength. People obey him because of his extraordinary personal qualities.[1] Mrs. Naganuma, the co-foundress of RK, was unmistakably such a charismatic leader. And this same charismatic quality also characterizes many hoza leaders, if not in the full sense of Weber's technical definition, at least in the sense of the common definition of charisma as "that special spiritual power or personal quality that gives an individual influence or authority over large numbers of people."[2]

There is a consciousness on the part of leaders that they are part of a hierarchy which is a kind of divine institution. The hierarchical structure of RK, with President Niwano at the top and the ordinary believers at the bottom, has been pointed out in the preceding chapter. President Niwano is the bearer of the Buddha's power and revelation, and the actual distinction between the Buddha and Mr. Niwano is vague, because the Buddha can be identified with either the "Truth of the Universe," or with the historical Gautama Buddha, or with later historical personages who have received enlightenment and been vessels of enlightenment to others.

In public speeches as well as in hoza, frequent reference is made to the church heads, to President Niwano and to the Buddha as being in a direct line of authority. Group leaders claim that authority for their answers to people's problems comes by direct insight into the will of the Buddha. In Session 21 the leader was asked whether he could always be sure of having the correct answer for the problems brought up in hoza. The leader affirmed with conviction that he always had exactly the right answer to every problem. In answer to the question as to how he could be so sure, he replied:

> *L*: If your heart is clear and pure, then you can understand clearly what the will of the Buddha is. Our answer does not come simply from our own reason, but it comes from beyond us. We are like a TV set. Tune it right and the picture comes from beyond on to the screen. (21)

What are some of the personal characteristics that define the charismatic personality? Weber speaks of "special gifts of the body and spirit," "inner determination and inner restraint," "personal strength," and "personal heroism or personal revelation."[3] Observation indicates that many hoza leaders do radiate these very qualities. The typical leader is a brilliant, confident personality. The following comment describing a leader is representative:

> In the midst of the session the area chief burst into the circle and took over for the time she was there. She interrupted what was going on without apology. She was a commanding and powerful personality, aggressive and self-confident, quite different from the stereotype of Japanese femininity. She had unmistakable intelligence and leadership capacity. She wore fashionable clothes and make-up. (2)

Leaders are generally people of powerful, attractive personality, capable of capturing the interest and allegiance of group members. Fluent speech and persuasive oratory characterize nearly all of them. The following descriptions can be cited:

> This leader was a good public speaker. She talked forcefully without stopping for 45 minutes. She was a very poor group leader but a splendid preacher. (3)

> The leader was a skillful public speaker with magnetic personality. She did almost all the talking in the session, but all listened with keen interest. (38)

The state of emotional rapture is an obvious characteristic of leaders at the large public rallies or retreat meetings and, to a lesser degree, in hoza. At the Ome youth retreat meetings, speakers become almost violent with emotional appeal. Talking with fast, loud, high-pitched intensity, they constantly elicit emotional response from the audience by shouting "Do you understand?" or "Are you with me?" to which the whole audience shouts in unison, "Yes!"

This same phenomenon is observable in hoza to a certain extent. In Session 15 the leader was characterized thus:

> This leader talked fast and boldly and positively, sometimes with such emotion that she was carried away with herself. She was stern and never smiled; she sometimes scolded people. She had forceful gestures of her hands and head; she gave direct commands to do this and that. (15)

(*Interpretation*)

The charismatic qualities of hoza leadership can be viewed from several perspectives, all of which show how natural it is to find this particular kind of leadership in this particular setting. Seen from the perspective of group dynamics, any adequate leader must perform a dual function if his group is to reach its goal successfully. He must operate in an instrumental capacity to perform the tasks and decisions which constitute the task orientation of the group. But this alone is not enough. He must also maintain the internal existence of the group, that is, hold and unite the members' interest and allegiance. The affective tone and emotional aspect of the leader-follower relation is exceedingly important in group process.

Seen from the perspective of the historical background and context of RK, it will be recalled that Mrs. Naganuma, the co-foundress of RK, was herself a shamanic type of person and a charismatic leader in the fullest sense of the word. In this she was typical of the founders and foundresses of many of the new religions. The powerful charismatic personality of the founder or foundress if often the key to the success of the religious movement. These individuals are people "whose very presence bespeaks personal power and authority, and to whom, therefore, popular loyalty is given almost involuntarily."[4] They are often called the *iki-gami* (living god). Although the leader is usually not called a god in the doctrinal statements of the religion, in the mind of the masses he or she functions as such. The function of the founder of a new religion is sometimes compared to the function of Christ in Christianity.

This suggests a religious perspective on charismatic leadership peculiar to Japan which must be understood before the idea of *iki-gami* (living god) can be grasped. The Japanese idea of God is the concept of *kami*, and *kami* is not a transcendental being. *Kami* can pass from the realm of the metaphysical to the realm of the natural and human. The phenomenal world itself is absolute and no transcendent being beyond the phenomenal world is thinkable. The word *kami*, usually translated "God," stands in such contrast to the Western concept of God that religious issues are often confused even by translating *kami* as "God." "Diety" or "the sacred" are better translations.[5] Thus it is not surprising to find the phrase *yaoyorōzu no kami* (eight million deities) used by Japanese. The significance of this term is not in the numbers, but in the religious consciousness which expects *kami* to appear anywhere in the whole range of life's phenomena. "Gods, spirits, men, and any natural objects or phenomena pass easily...from one realm to the other."[6] Thus it is possible for President Niwano, although not claiming to be "a divinity" in any doctrinal sense, to play the role of *iki-gami* in the minds of common people, in that "divine" power resides in him.

In addition to this basically Shinto coloring of the feeling about religious leadership is the idea of Messianism which is a controlling motif in the interpretation of history according to the Lotus Sutra, the Scripture on which RK doctrine is based. Several Buddhas have already appeared in history, and in each corrupt age a new messianic figure, a new Buddha is anticipated as savior.[7]

Because of the hierarchical structure of authority in RK, this semidivine power and authority does not stop with the top man, but is passed on down the line of the pyramid. It has been said that the key to hoza's success lies in this sense of the leaders' fitting firmly into the line of authority of the "divine hierarchy."

Recognizing hoza leaders as charismatic figures gives rise to a further interesting observation from the sociological point of view. A cardinal point of Weber's theory of leadership is that "the genuine charismatic situation quickly gives way to incipient institutions, which emerge from the cooling off of extraordinary states of devotion and fervor." In other words, "a charismatic movement may be routinized into traditionalism or into bureaucratization." This "routinization of charisma" occurs when the original doctrines are "intellectually adjusted to the needs of that stratum which becomes the primary carrier of the leaders' message."[8]

Recent trends in RK are a remarkably apt illustration of this process. The efficient institution-builder Niwano in a certain sense represents the "routinization" of Mrs. Naganuma's charisma. 1958, the year after Mrs. Naganuma's death, became "the year of the manifestation of truth" in RK history. At this time the emphasis on shamanistic practices and divination gave way to an emphasis on institution-building and systematic instruction in doctrine, which still continues today.

The routinization process can also be seen in hoza leadership, where, in recent years, increasing emphasis is being placed on the theological education of the leaders through training classes. As will be indicated below, many of the current leaders can more accurately be described simply as good teachers than as charismatic personalities.

Leaders as Teachers

(*Findings*)

The hoza leader theoretically is a counselor who leads the "group counseling" sessions, but actually his status is much closer to that of teacher than counselor, and the group session is more aptly described as a teaching session than a counseling session.

Hoza leaders are not professional teachers with academic qualifications. They are laymen and laywomen who have been appointed to this position on the basis of their actual ability to lead and teach people. By virtue of this position the leader occupies an authoritative position, regardless of educational qualifications. In RK one becomes a leader not by a routine educational process, nor by a process of election, but by appointment. Appointments are made on the basis of actual ability to win converts and influence people. Most hoza leaders are eminently effective as teachers of the standard RK "theology", i.e., the standard RK approach which offers a solution to the problem of human suffering. The following comment could apply to many if not most of the leaders:

> The leader was a very poor group leader, but a splendid preacher.

> She knew RK doctrine thoroughly, and taught it in a way that made it easily understood by all. (3)

Participants do not take notes during hoza sessions. The kind of learning process presupposed in hoza is a process of half rational, half intuitive absorption of certain doctrines and ways of thinking by hearing the same thing repeated over and over again, and hearing these principles applied again and again to various problem situations.

In regard to teaching method, it has just been indicated that the principal approach is a kind of rote method of repetition and absorption. Teaching is often done through an indirect method in which cases are used to illustrate a point, rather than through logical reasoning as a conveyor of ideas. Hoza sessions are geared toward the solving of members' actual problems, and toward relating personal testimonies of how faith has affected one's life. Such "case studies" constitute a teaching method which the group leaders use very effectively, and which is peculiarly well adapted to the listeners' "readiness."

The following cases are representative of this method. In Session 3 Mrs. A presented the problem of her friend's second son who failed his entrance examinations into three leading universities and who has thus brought disgrace on the family. This case was used by the leader to teach lessons in several areas. First of all it gave her an opportunity to teach the group how to raise children, noting especially the differences between handling a first and second child. It also gave the opportunity to teach a lesson in humility, for the conclusion was that it was to the ultimate advantage of the whole family that he failed, for to have entered the university would doubtlessly have made the son and his parents conceited. The leader went on to elaborate further her teaching on the virtue of learning humility through failure by telling the following story:

> About ten years ago I wanted to have a maid in the house, but my family didn't want me to have one. Finally, however, I got my own selfish way and got a maid. But this maid never did things the way I wanted her to do them. She was actually a grief to me. In the end this turned out to be the will of the Buddha for me, because through this maid he taught me to be more humble and tolerent. Failure was turned into blessing, just as I know the failure of your friend's son will turn out for good, because he will be humbled by it. (3)

In another session, the leader impressed the group with the virtue of respect for parents and the vice of holding resentment toward anyone by relating this episode:

> My neighbor had bad stomach trouble, which shows he was disrespectful toward his parents. He was asked to have hoza in his home, but didn't want to have it, even though he is a member of RK. But the day he refused to have the hoza, he collapsed while he was at the public bath. So he decided to have the hoza meet at his home after all. After that he and also his brother both changed. Now they respect their parents and understand that you shouldn't feel resentful toward anyone, but should see both good and bad as the will of the Buddha and give thanks for both. Let's all learn the same lesson they learned. (26)

(*Interpretation*)

These few examples of teaching through case presentation rather than through logical reasoning or theoretical teaching are typical of the procedure in hoza.

The authoritarian position of hoza leaders is natural in view of the fact that the status of teacher (*sensei*) is a prestigious position in Japanese culture. The *sensei* commands respect, loyalty, and obedience, especially from his own pupils. The Japanese instinctively attribute to the *sensei* "expert power"—the perception that a leader has special knowledge or expertness which can be transmitted through association with him.[9]

The almost mechanical repetition of stereotyped doctrinal formulae is characteristic of hoza teaching technique. There is a lack of note-taking and lack of questioning and "give-and-take" between leader and member. This method, although negatively evaluated in the West, is traditional in Japan. Rote learning is the method of education to which Japanese are accustomed from kindergarten through university. In the rote learning method it is important that the subject matter be reduced to standardized formulae which can be passed on in precise form from teacher to pupil and from generation to generation. This is also the way in which the traditional arts of Japan—flower arranging, tea ceremony, *koto* (harp), etc.—are taught. RK theology has been conveniently reduced to a relatively few standard formulae which are expounded in the standard textbook, *Konpon Bukkyō no Hongi* (Principles of Fundamental Buddhism). There are also a few standard charts which graphically show how all the teaching can be integrated around the Four Noble Truths, which in turn is summarized in the simple formula of *in-en-ka-ho* (cause-condition-result-reward). This doctrine is taught systematically to the leaders in special training sessions, and is repeated in that precise form over and over in hoza.[10]

It is significant that no source other than the teacher himself is deemed necessary as authority for what is taught. The Scriptures and books are alluded to but are not used directly. Authority lies in persons rather than in Scriptures. This fact speaks significantly about the absolute character of the "limited human nexus" in Japanese culture. Bellah, in describing the ultimate value of the human collectivity in Japanese culture, in contrast to the metaphysical Absolute which is found in Western culture, says that there is no need for an abstract, universal code of ethics, because all that is required is to fulfill one's obligations to the group. Loyalty and filial piety are the fundamentals, and these are not abstractions; they have no universal meaning. They apply only to a particular group context.[11]

The most effective teaching in hoza is done through the telling of narratives. Japanese have a special affinity for the case study method. Subjectivity and the primacy of intuition and experience are characteristics of the thought processes of Japanese. In Japanese thinking there is an identity between subject and environment, between actuality and reality. In the learning process, mutual understanding and trust among subjects is more important than abstract reasoning. A corollary of this for teaching is that a real life story is more effective than a rational statement. The Japanese assign priority to living experience rather than to logical reasoning. Intuitive understanding and direct perception are the unproved foundation of proofs. The Japanese attitude is phenomenological, that is, phenomena are accepted as wholes, without analysis or definition.[12] In the light of this philosophical milieu, it comes as a natural corollary that a narrative of personal happenings and living experience which has direct, emotional impact is far more effective in teaching than is the logical statement or doctrinal analysis.

Despite what was said about the primary importance of experience and natural endowments as qualifications for leadership, leaders do also receive formal training. Training courses lasting from one to several weeks are held seasonally, at which times leaders are given intensive indoctrination. Many leaders hold the rank of "official teachers" (*sei-kyōshi*), and these teachers must have passed several examinations and have proven themselves capable not only in the area of doctrinal understanding, but also in the area of practical ability to lead a group and enlighten others.

Authoritarian Posture of Leaders

(*Findings*)

The personal characteristics of leaders and their ability as teachers have been observed. However, perhaps most significant of all is the general attitude assumed by leaders. With hardly any exception this attitude can be described as an authoritarian posture. In attending hoza one becomes immediately aware of the authoritarian stance taken by the leader. The leader commands attention; he speaks with conviction and force; he exhorts and reprimands and teaches members with authority. It is not easy to quote specific words which reveal this attitude, for the authoritarian position is evidenced more in personal bearing, attitudes, manner of speaking, etc., than in words. Nevertheless, some relevant observations can be made.

Almost every case of problem-solving dealt with in hoza is an opportunity for the leader to give authoritative advice as to the cause and solution of the individual's problem. The "counseling process" itself consists of a minimum of interchange within the group. Rather, it consists of the statement of a problem by a member, after which the member says, "*Onegai itashimasu*" (roughly translated, "Please grant me your help."). Thereupon the leader might investigate the problem by means of a few questions to the member, and then launch into a lengthy soliloquy which consists mainly of advice and indoctrination.

This advice or answer is generally a stereotyped approach, the content of which will be discussed in detail later, but briefly stated consists of the following points: Be thankful for this trouble because it has caused you to reflect upon your life and see your evil heart. This trouble is the result of something evil which you or your ancestors have done in the past. But it is not too late to rectify it if you repent and be more faithful in your ancestral veneration and allegiance to RK. If you do this you will surely be blessed with happiness and many benefits. If you fail to do so, you will surely suffer worse trouble. This "advice" is given boldly and explicitly, with positive force emanating from religious authority and charismatic power.

The above formula for solving problems comes not as the result of counseling dynamics, nor is it merely the advice of the leader. It is more accurately described as an authoritative exhortation or command. The "counselee" is not given a chance to arrive at insight for himself, for the leader tells him directly and sternly what he must do. A typical example indicates this pattern.

> *Mrs. E*: My child lost fifty yen in school. We blamed a certain boy for having taken it, so I told that boy's parents about it, and they returned the fifty yen. Why did this loss of money happen to us?
>
> *L*: What do you make of the situation? What is your attitude toward money?
>
> *Mrs. E*: I tend to be stingy, and rather cunning in handling money. The boy who took the money comes from a pathetic home situation. The father drives a dump truck, and is separated from the mother. They used to have money but wasted it all. They are my close neighbors so I know all about them.
>
> *L*: That boy's parents are a mirror to you so you can see your own midshandling of money. Don't be stingy or greedy with money any more. And you must bring the boy's mother with you here, for she will continue to be miserable until she comes and learns the true law through RK. It is your duty to help her by bringing her to RK. (20)

The leader makes a dogmatic statement of the solution, and gives a comment regarding both the member's attitude (that is, not to be stingy any more) and activities (that is, to bring the other lady with her to RK).

The authoritarian posture of the leader is even more obvious when the leader not only commands and exhorts, but directly chides and reprimands members. In Session 40 the leader became indignant with the members for not understanding her teaching.

> *L*: You must understand that we have all come from a previous life. Without the understanding of the former life, you cannot understand the concept of cause and effect, for causes are rooted in our former life. I have to tell you this time and time again, but you never seem to grasp it! (40)

In session 30 the leader directly reprimanded a member for having had a "romance marriage" arranged by herself rather than a family arranged marriage.

> *Mrs. A*: I find my husband very hateful. He's a good-for-nothing!

I've tried my best to be a good wife; our trouble is all his fault.

L: We all say that at first, but we learn differently after learning the Law.

Mrs. A: I insist that in my case it's not my fault. At least there was nothing wrong in my life before marriage.

L: Was yours a romance marriage? (Yes.) A romance marriage always leads to suffering, because a romance marriage means you wanted to do just as you pleased rather than follow parental guidance. Your romance marriage is the source of your trouble! (30)

To understand the dynamics of this kind of leadership, it is necessary first of all to understand that the people who come to hoza come with the presupposition that in coming to a place of religion they are coming to a place which is expected to provide sure answers to their problems. Almost without exception people come to hoza seeking authoritative advice for their situation. In fact, this is precisely what hoza is advertized to be—a place where people come to receive answers to their problems. The manner of stating one's case in hoza, as referred to earlier, namely, by ending the presentation with the phrase "*onegai itashimasu*" ("Please grant me your help") sets the tone, or is indicative of the frame of mind for the whole procedure of hoza. The stage is not set for dialog, but for supplication and submission on the part of the member, and instruction and command on the part of the leader. The group shows a humble, submissive attitude toward the speaker. No matter what the leader says, it is accepted without question. It seems never to occur to the participants to doubt the validity of the leader's words, or even to ask for further explanation of what is being taught. The characteristic response is one of gratitude for whatever answer is given.

(*Interpretation*)

AUTHORITARIAN LEADERSHIP

The leadership of hoza is highly authoritarian, and the members expect it to be this way. It is instructive for Westerners to compare the results of American group dynamics research on authoritarian leadership and its effects on the group with the results of our observation of authoritarian leadership in hoza and its effects in that setting.

Research in group dynamics makes a considerable issue of authoritarian leadership in contrast to other types of leadership. Leader behavior in hoza corresponds to the marks of authoritarian leadership as described by American researchers, who characterize the authoritarian group in the following way. First of all, the group's origin lies outside the group itself. The group has a status person designated from the outside to control it from within. Often this "status leader" appointed by the outside authority is not the "real leader" who has a relationship of trust and interdependence with the group members. Such a leader who has his internal status from an outside source of authority has the almost impossible task of becoming an emergent leader of the group.

The authorities behind the group assume they have superior knowledge to that of the group members, and assume that the members are inadequate to acquire the necessary knowledge. This kind of control of knowledge from the outside limits the possibilities of the members to develop their own potential capacity to discover knowledge for themselves. Planning and major decisions are in the hands of the external authorities. Members are allowed to use their own judgment only in matters of relatively minor import. The responsibility for the success of the group functioning rests with the leader. If he does not manipulate the group to do what the authorities require, he may lose his status.[13]

White and Lippitt's experiment with leadership in three different "social climates" has become a classic. Their experiment was with groups of boys who were made to experience authoritarian, democratic and laissez-faire leadership. Several significant differences between the authoritarian and the democratic systems were found. Member satisfaction was higher in the democratic group than in the autocratic. Autocratic groups manifested much aggression or overt apathy which hid suppressed aggression. The output of work was the same, but the democratic groups showed more interest and enthusiasm for their work. The researchers concluded, among other things, that (1) autocracy can create much hostility and aggression, including aggression against scapegoats; (2) autocracy can create discontent that does not appear on the surface; (3) there is more submissive and dependent behavior and less individuality in autocracy; (4) there is more group-mindedness and friendliness in democracy.[14]

However, it is extremely significant that the findings of hoza show quite different results of authoritarian leadership. There are no signs of hostility or suppressed discontent, and no impersonal coldness in the atmosphere. How can this incongruity be explained? It is important here to realize that cultural context makes a decisive difference in the determination of what constitutes proper and effective leadership for any given society, or with any given group. Group dynamics research also indicates that it is erroneous to conclude that a certain method of leadership is superior in all situations and for all leaders. It has been found that where members expect the leader to play an autocratic role, "attempts to introduce more democratic procedures usually result in members dissatisfaction and low productivity which is similar to that usually associated with autocratic leadership in a democratic culture." Effective leadership depends on the personality of members and culture in which the group exists, and upon the needs and goals of the group.[15] It also depends on whether the leaders can be comfortable in a certain style of leadership, and whether the members have had experience under this type of leadership, and finally whether the procedure used is in accordance with the accepted procedures of the institution.[16] Especially within a hierarchical organization, leadership shows a peculiar characteristic. In such a case the leader will be accepted and valued to the extent that he helps members reach their goals. Rules for effective leadership are to be determined within the context of the organizational setting in which that leadership is exercised. Thus it behooves the observer of hoza leadership to examine carefully the entire social and cultural milieu which constitutes the setting for hoza before passing judgments on the characteristics of leadership found there.

THE NEED FOR AUTHORITY

Contemporary Japanese have special need for authoritative and authoritarian leadership. The social anomie of the post-war upheaval resulted in the masses losing their sense of national identity and historical continuity, and losing even their ethical foundations. In this situation of instability and lostness, the new religions have appeared as movements which function to unify large masses of people under the leadership of authoritarian charismatic leaders. It was pointed out earlier in the introduction to the new religions that before the war, the Japanese people had been united under the *tennōsei* (emperor system), the essence of which was the absolutism of an ideology and a person. All the nation was unified under the common authority of one man. The collapse of this system was, significantly, not due to any anti-autocratic or anti-*tennōsei* movement. The collapse was forced on the people by their conquerors. The need for centralized authority and authoritarian leadership was as strong after the war as before.[17]

The deeply ingrained Japanese virtue of *chū* (loyalty to emperor) united the nation in strength during the 1930's and early 1940's to fight a war in loyalty and fidelity to their emperor, their *iki-gami* (living deity). The concept of and feeling for authority is still very much alive, although it, along with other social and psychological factors in Japanese culture, is in the process of change today. Although the new post-war Civil Code abolished patriarchal authoritarianism, the Japanese still today carry on the tendency to fear authority and respect power, for they have been nurtured in a social atmosphere where might is right.[18] C. Nakane interprets both Japanese groups and Japanese society as a whole as being characterized by vertical organization and vertical relationships in contrast to horizontal relationships. She goes so far as to say "without either 'frame' (her technical word) or 'vertical links', it seems almost impossible for the Japanese to form a functional group."[19] This authoritarian type of vertical relatedness is very much in evidence in the structure of hoza, where the leader has the "habit of command" and the members "the habit of docile obedience."

Added to this general cultural factor of vertical social organization is the factor of traditional expectations with regard to religious leadership. RK leaders readily admit their authoritarian approach and advocate it as a necessary approach for religious propagation. They say that religion is in essence an authoritative truth, and so it must be presented with authoritative force. People expect this of religion. The common people will not listen nor respond to a non-directive, philosophical, or calmly reasoned approach. In religion one must use imperatives: "Do this!" "This is the truth; believe it!" It is assumed that some people, especially university students, tend to resist this, but the leader simply takes this as a challenge to hold his own and win whatever argument might be propounded. The ideal is to have people see for themselves the meaning of the teaching and how it applies to their life, but if a person is not able to do that for himself, if a person desires guidance from someone, then the leader had better be prepared to give such an authoritative answer. This is his duty as a teacher of religion.

The new religions have appeared today as the heir to all these streams of tradition—the cultural tendencies, the present social milieu and the attitude toward religious authority—and have capitalized on them, won popular support, and achieved success. Critics characterize the new religions as being a revival of authoritarianism, and claim that they are an attempt to revive the old feudal spirit which had found its highest expression in the emperor system, but broke down in the 1940's. Many new religions are greatly concerned about the power structure within their own organization. They allow no criticism of their authority. Their structure can be characterized as the system of *ikkun-banmin,* that is, "All citizens following one lord." While recognizing the naturalness and effectiveness of this pattern of organization within the context of Japanese vertical society, we cannot be blind to the insidious possibilities of trends toward totalitarianism.[20] In the 1956 "Yomiuri Affair" involving a newspaper charge against RK, this organization was accused of working against democratic principles. Critics say that democratic, creative tendencies among the members are squelched in favor of the organizational principle of vertical relations based on religious authority.

We are faced with a far-reaching problem in trying to interpret hoza leadership and determine what does constitute appropriate and effective leadership in Japan today. The masses still today, as in the past, need, expect, and favorably respond to authoritarian leadership. At the same time, the sinister aspects of autocratic control are also inherent in groups which deliberately utilize these proclivities of the Japanese people and which encourage their leadership to take the authoritarian stance.

CHAPTER SEVEN

SOCIO-EMOTIONAL DYNAMICS

We turn now to a different aspect of hoza, namely, the emotional dynamics which are found to be operative there. We will look at hoza as an effort in group counseling, which it claims to be. The broad term "socio-emotional" is used because it is impossible in the case of hoza to talk in narrow, technical terms of the emotional dynamics of counseling. There is very little here to correspond to the dynamics of counseling, technically conceived. There are several reasons for this. In the first place, counseling in the sense in which that word is used in the West is still not widely known or practiced in Japan, nor is its effectiveness as a means of solving problems generally recognized. In the second place, the hoza leaders are laymen, without professional training in either counseling or theology. A certain degree of participation in doctrinal training courses is required, but there is only a minimal, if any, acquaintance with the principles of counseling as such. It should also be borne in mind that hoza is primarily a religiously-oriented meeting, and is not oriented to personality change as such, except as this may be a by-product of a religious "change of heart." At the same time, RK does advertize hoza—the official English translation is "group counseling"—as a place where anyone may come to have his personal problems solved. RK assumes that religious faith will invariably produce concrete changes, both in personal attitudes and in one's life situation.

The chapter will be divided into two parts, the first dealing with factors relevant to group counseling or group therapy. Here the description is focused on five significant factors in determining the therapeutic effects of counseling. The second section deals with factors relevant to general socio-emotional needs of the members.

Group Therapy

(*Findings*)

ENVIRONMENT

The first of the factors relevant to therapeutic experience is group environment, by which is meant the various physical and situational factors which together constitute the atmosphere in which hoza takes place. The assumption is that the nature of the setting for a group is a significant determinant of the therapeutic functioning of the group. In the earlier chapter on Physical Environment we noted the uplifting atmosphere of the main hall and its sanctuary; the intimacy of the low-ceiling, plush-carpeted balconies where the groups meet; the feeling of "at-homeness" created by the comfortable squatting position; the liberty allowed to children, and other features. These are all favorable factors in the creation of good counseling atmosphere.

Two other factors which are directly relevant to the effectiveness of counseling, namely, group size and group seating arrangement, deserve special consideration at this point. The average size of a hoza group is about twelve members. This must be stated in approximate terms, because not only do the groups vary in number from one group to the next, and from one day to the next, but they also vary considerably from one moment to the next within any given session. Some participants arrive late; some leave early; many leave for a while during the session. At times the number drops as low as four or five people. In this case personal business or gossip is likely to replace the usual conversations. Sometimes the persons left in such a small group are asked to join with another group for that day. On the other hand, frequently a group grows to twenty or twenty-five persons. In such a case, again it is difficult to carry on the usual kind of problem-solving, and the speaking tends to become purely teaching or a "solo performance" by someone with a dramatic testimony. If leadership is available, such a large group will be divided in two. However, if a speaker is a fascinating person, the group will probably be allowed to remain as it is.

The way in which group seating is arranged is another significant factor in group dynamics. In this respect there is constancy and positive advantage in the method used in hoza. The general arrangement was described in Chapter IV. Participants are always seated comfortably in the style they are accustomed to, namely, squatting on a soft floor. They are always arranged in a circle, and this circle is always closed, that is, there are no empty spaces or gaps in the ring. Members always sit close to one another. This is not by chance. When an empty space occurs because of someone's leaving the circle, the leader will immediately ask people to move together to close the gap. Or when a person has just arrived and squats down outside the circle, the leader will insist that room be made for him in the circle proper.

If the leader is asked why this is done, he would say that the spirit of hoza is the spirit of harmony (*wa no seishin*). "*Wa*" is the pronunciation for both the ideograph meaning circle and for the one meaning peace, harmony and unity. This double meaning is frequently alluded to as being the motivating spirit of hoza—a circle of people who are helping one another to live in peace and unity. However, beyond this "theological" explanation, the therapeutic value of keeping the group seated in a closed, intimate circle is unquestionable. This intimacy makes discussion easier and enhances the atmosphere of warm mutuality.

One other aspect of the group arrangement deserves mention. That is the custom of the members' piling their purses, shopping bags and other parcels in the middle of the circle, in full view of everyone. Doing so serves several purposes. It frees the individual from having to hold his or her own bag, and it provides a safe place to deposit one's belongings without going through the effort of checking them in and out from a check-stand. But in addition to these obvious conveniences, that massive pile of belongings on the floor in front of the participants seemed to this observer to be an aid in creating a homey, earthy atmosphere. Participants do not stare at a cold empty space in the middle of their circle, but instinctively feel a warm mutuality via the clutter of handbags and parcels in front of them.

But some other elements of group atmosphere must also be observed, elements which would appear to prevent hoza from being therapeutically effective. First of all there is the constant rumble of noise from the other circles which provides an accompaniment for hoza conversations. On days when there is large attendance, there are thousands of people in the temple sanctuary and the balconies, and no walls separate any part of the balconies from any other part of the Great Sacred Hall. This inevitably produces a background of jumbled noises. Often it is difficult even to hear what the speaker is saying.

L: Everybody, please try your best to listen even though it is hard to hear today, for Mrs. A is making a significant confession. (25)

Many mothers bring their small children with them to hoza, and the presence of these children, who are permitted to run about and play freely on the balconies, is another source of commotion. In Session 15 it was observed that there were five three-year-olds playing tag, wrestling and and yelling at one another during the whole session, and no one restricted them. It was also observed that the circle members did not seem concerned or distracted by this noise or this kind of uninhibited behavior. The frequent blast of the loudspeaker system is another distraction. Individuals are frequently paged to come to this office or that. Announcement is made of children lost from their parents. Drivers are asked to move their automobiles parked in the wrong place, etc.

Session 2 provided an example of another kind of interruption—an interruption in the flow of conversation due to the abrupt visit of an official:

> In the midst of the session the area chief burst into the circle and took over for the time she was there. She interrupted what was going on without apology...She asked me to tell about religious life in the U. S., but gave me no chance actually to do so. (2)

Even more disturbing than these elements is the constant flow of business which takes place in and around the circles. The observation at Session 15 is typical:

> There was a constant flow of business during the session: making the offerings, keeping records, distributing materials, delivering messages, etc. All but four people of the group were absent from the circle for part of the time. (15)

RAPPORT

Another element relevant to group therapy is the quality of group rapport, that is, the affective interaction or relationship between counselor and counselee, or among the members of a counseling group. This is an important factor in assessing the therapeutic effectiveness of any counseling situation. What kind of rapport is found among the participants of the hoza group?

Some excerpts will be cited, and later some general conclusions based on the observations will be stated.

Mrs. E: There is a bar next door to my house, and late at night men come out of the bar drunk and urinate on our front gate. They also park their cars in front of our gate so we can't get out.

Mrs. F: Individuals are all good, but in a group they tend to do bad things. So we must watch ourselves so we aren't led astray by the group.

L: True, the world is evil, but if each person would come to RK and learn the right way, society would gradually improve. Don't complain about little things, but put yourself in others' places and try to see things from their point of view.

Mrs. G: My acquaintance also had a problem like that, but things improved after she joined RK.

Mrs. H: I had the same problem as you, Mrs. E. A bar came in next door to my home, and I used to get so irritated by the loud music late at night and by the men urinating on my front gate. But then I joined RK, and after that I found that I just didn't notice those troubles any more. The music doesn't even bother me now. Furthermore, the situation has improved somewhat after we decided to build a wall between the bar and our house.

L: There is surely something you can learn from all this, Mrs. E, if you will only reflect upon your own life and see if you haven't done something wrong to someone else in the past. (26)

At the end of that session, the following observation was made:

The whole group took Mrs. E's problem very seriously. They all joined in giving reproof, advice and encouragement. (26)

Session 30 gave another example of warm mutual feeling:

Mrs. A: I find my husband very hateful. He's a good-for-nothing! I've tried my best to be a good wife; our trouble is all his fault.

L: Yes, I know your situation well. It was just like mine. You're in trouble, but it's not too late.

Mrs. B: Mrs. A's problem is very deep. There's a triangle affair between her and her husband and the husband's brother's wife. She has suffered in silence over this situation up till now, and has somehow tolerated it.

L: Let me tell you about my own misery...

Mrs. C: If you have faith, bad circumstances can be turned into good circumstances.

Mrs. D: You have to start by putting forth some effort yourself. (30)

We are not now concerned about counseling techniques nor about the content of the responses, but only about one factor, namely, the existence of concerned involvement and interaction among the members of the group. This kind of rapport was obviously present in the sessions cited above. The function of problem-solving was not confined to the leader. Many in the group shared in solving the problem, either by relating a similar experience, by giving a word of sympathy and support, or by giving advice. Although all sessions do not by any means achieve this degree of rapport, many similar sessions could be cited. Side by side with these positive elements in rapport there is the problem of constantly fluctuating group membership. The members of any given group vary from day to day. The group meeting place on the balconies is fixed in a general way, inasmuch as each geographical unit is assigned a certain section of a certain balcony for its regular meeting place. Therefore, individuals from a certain neighborhood are likely to meet each other at hoza. But no one knows exactly what persons will constitute a particular group on any particular day. According to observation, in an average circle of a dozen participants, about half of them seem to have a nodding acquaintance with each other; most of the rest would know two or three others in the circle; a few would know no one except the person who brought them there.

ACCEPTANCE

The third category of factors relevant to group therapy is the category of acceptance. This is closely related to rapport, but it touches a deeper level of mutual respect and support as well as the level of interpersonal warmth. There is no overt rejection of anyone who attends hoza. All are warmly welcomed. All are made to feel at home. Everyone is allowed a chance to speak about anything he wishes. The description noted in Session 6 might apply to many if not most of the sessions:

> During the session there was much laughter. There was a wonderful atmosphere of warmth and fellowship. After the prayers at 3:00 p.m., all bowed deeply and thanked each other for mutual help. I was impressed with the atmosphere of mutual concern which was expressed. (6)

The testimony given by a young man during Session 24 expresses the importance of this kind of acceptance for the emotional well-being and sense of belonging of participants:

> *Mr. D*: I am still very young, but I have already experienced many sorrows and troubles. I have no parents, so I was raised in an institution. There I experienced great loneliness and hardship. That's why I come to hoza, for I find comfort and close fellowship here. (24)

Not only is there an atmosphere of emotional acceptance and belonging during the sessions, but there is also the concrete promise of mutual support outside the sessions as well. In Session 2, after a young housewife had come to a new insight about her bad attitudes in the past and about what she ought to do from now on, the leader concluded, with great warmth and encouragement:

> *L*: This is a great day in your life, Mrs. B! This has been a wonderful experience for you and for all of us here in this hoza today! From now on we'll all try to help you every time you come here, or when we meet you on the street. (To the group) You see, we all take responsibility for fellow RK members by following up on them. (2)

However, some negative observations must also be noted. The following observations could apply to many sessions:

> There was not much cohesiveness in the group itself. There was no warmth or affection shown among the members. They simply all listened politely while the leader spoke. (9)
>
> The leader did not have good eye-contact with the people to whom she gave answers. This is characteristic of many leaders. They mouth their "answers"—which often are a stereotyped form—fast and fluently as though they had gone through this a hundred times before.
>
> During Mrs. E's long narrative regarding the double suicide, the leader left the circle to talk with someone else, and three other members also left to do other business with the secretary. An official came around distributing cards for people to use in promotion. Mrs. E was left telling her story to the lady next to her, talking in such a low voice that no one else could hear, even if they wanted to. (36)

EXPRESSION

The factor of free expression is decisive in determining the therapeutic value of any kind of counseling. Does hoza provide an opportunity for free expression? Again there are both positive and negative observations to be made. First, a number of sessions where free expression was encouraged and where members did freely express emotional burdens during hoza can be cited:

Mr. C: I'm frustrated because I have to work until about 10 p.m. every day, yet I'm expected to do my serivce for the RK youth division regularly too.

L: My purpose is to help you discover the real cause of your difficulty. Tell us more about your problem.

(Details and discussion followed.) (14)

L: Mrs. E, how is your son who went to Hokkaido to live?

Mrs. E: Well, I'm quite worried about him.

L: Your worry is like electric waves, which will reach him even in Hokkaido. You will be miserable if you keep your worry to yourself. You had better confess your feelings here in our circle.

(Mrs. talked at length about her situation) (36)

In the above cases, not only did the leader directly encourage uninhibited expression, but in each case the group member responded by pouring out details of the situation that was bothering him. The following examples are deemed to be cases of genuine cathartic expression, that is, relatively uninhibited verbal unburdening of emotional problems, which gave indications of having a psychologically healthy effect on the speaker. Notice the non-verbal signs accompanying the speeches.

L: Mrs. E joined RK just three months ago. She used to be so miserable, but look at her beaming face now!

Mrs. E: I came here once for a festival day celebration, and at the same time attended hoza. But I was determined I would not say anything myself. I had such a deep problem I was embarrassed to speak about it. However, the atmosphere of the hoza group drew out my problem and before I knew it I had told everything. My husband lived with a mistress, and came home only to bathe and get clean laundry. I had become a bath house attendant! He drank heavily, and he gave me no money. When I I told my story here the first time, I cried and cried! (30)

Mr. D (Excitedly): Please help me; I'm having a terrible time with my parents again. They are RK members, but they don't want me to spend so much time doing my service for RK. You see, I visit people several nights a week and go to RK meetings, getting home late, and they criticize me severely for this. They say I should give that time to my work. Tonight when I left the house to come here, they said, "Leave and never come back again if you're going to spend so much time away from home for the sake of RK!" I feel terribly bitter and angry toward them. I just can't make myself step down and listen to them as I know I should. (He was weeping during most of this speech.) (34)

It can be concluded that hoza at its best does offer a therapeutic experience to group members by giving them the opportunity for free verbal expression of emotional burdens.

The preceding examples of free expression must be supplemented with other cases where verbal expression is definitely inhibited by the leader's over-aggressiveness and monopolization of the conversation. After looking first at general instances where expression is hindered, we look further at two characteristic types of leader response which have the effect of cutting off expression: the failure to listen to and attempt to understand what the speaker is trying to express, and the premature giving of advice.

The following comment on the leadership of Session 3 applies to many other sessions as well:

> This leader was a good public speaker. She was a very poor group leader, but a splendid preacher. She talked almost the whole session, even interrupting when others talked. At one point she talked without stopping for about 45 minutes. She occasionally called for others to comment, but before anyone had a chance to speak she was on her way again. (3)

In Session 34 the leader arrived very late. There had been good group interaction up to the time she came on the scene, but the character of the meeting changed completely after the leader came and took over. She did most of the talking herself, which consisted of authoritarian giving of advice.

The following are glaring examples of the failure of the leader to respond to the feelings of the speaker through insensitivity to the real concern of the speaker.

> *Mrs. B*: My friend, Miss C here, just found out this morning that she has acute appendicitis and must have an operation this very afternoon...Do you think things will turn out all right?
>
> *L*: Everything depends on your mental attitude. I used to be resentful because I was mistreated by my mother-in-law. She treated me like a floor mop!...Now I see it was not the people around me who were of fault, but my misery was my own fault because I did not have the spirit of gratitude. Miss C, you had better go talk to your area leader, and then go and pray before the altar. (25)

This case reveals a blatant disregard for Miss B's own feelings at this moment of crisis and anxiety, which went unheeded while the leader told of her own experiences. Likewise, each response of the leader in the following case shows an ineptness in being able to catch the emotional slant of the speaker's problem.

> *Mr. C*: I'm a plasterer by trade, but I quit work recently. My former boss is angry with me now for quitting. But the reason I quit was to work for my brother-in-law, who is a contractor.
>
> *L*: If you do good work, there will be much demand for your services as a plasterer. That's a rule for all tradesmen.
>
> *Mr. C*: I had worked for six years with my former boss, so he says I'm obliged to stay on and continue with him. But there are so many disadvantages working for him. For instance, I get no pay for rainy days, when of course I can't work.
>
> *L*: Well, you've already made the decision to quit, so there's nothing I can do for you at this point.
>
> *Mr. C*: But my boss is after me right now, giving me a hard time. Yet my brother-in-law wants me to work for him. So what shall I do?
>
> *L*: You should be grateful that they both want you. But don't work just for money. And remember you can change all your bad circumstances to good. (33)

We cannot rule out advice-giving as a legitimate part of hoza "counseling," inasmuch as the presupposition is that answers based on the Law of the Buddha will be found or given for every problem brought to hoza by members. However, this advice is often given prematurely, so that further expression of negative feelings or confession is inhibited or blocked. Furthermore, the advice is given at such an early stage in the conversation that it is improbable that it could be truly appropriate for the situation, for the whole situation is not yet known.

Miss B: I have a problem in getting along with my mother. I want to tell you about all the grief I have at home.

(Before she had a chance to tell details of her problem, the leader interrupted with the following:)

Leader: Show by your good life how much RK has done for you, and your family will be convinced of the truth of RK. You're an exceptionally fine young girl to face up to your sufferings so early in life. (4)

Mrs. A: My grandchild is quite sick, but is at home now. Her father says she should be in the hospital, but the doctor says she can stay home if she has no fever. Her father says the mother simply wants to have her home for her own comfort, that is, because she selfishly wants to have the child close to her. What do you think is the right thing to do?

L: Everyone, listen to this problem, for it is one we should all consider. What do you think about this case? Obviously the child is sick because there is no gratitude on the part of the child toward her parents. How do I know this? Because we know the mother is selfish, and this is inevitably passed on to the child. But, Mrs. A, this unhappy situation eventually springs from you, for you are the the grandmother, and the word of the Buddha is that deeds pass on through three generations. The solution here is for grandmother, mother and child all to repent together. This will restore harmony and happiness to your home again. (38)

These typical cases indicate the lack of sensitivity and a listening posture on the part of the leader. One quickly senses the leader to be a person with a pre-determined answer which he is eager to give as a panacea for any problem, whatever it might be. With this approach, it is not essential to listen to the details of each case.

INSIGHT

"Insight" here is taken to mean a new and deeper perception of the the reality of one's self and one's situation, which enables the individual to work toward the solution of his problem. This subject is somewhat different in kind from the preceding topics of this section, for in a sense it is a result of the therapeutic process, rather than an element conducive to the process. To ask the questions, "Does it work? That is, are people really healed and helped, do they actually achieve insight through the counseling of hoza?" leads into evaluative considerations which are not being dealt with here.

Moreover, it is impossible to say whether insight was actually attained or not in most instances. Especially in Japanese culture, so characterized by self-restraint, what lies behind the polite and proper expressions of gratitude for help received is very difficult to assess. According to our observation, during all the sessions there were only two obvious cases of deep-level response which could be called genuine insight. They are noted below:

Mrs. B: I have so many problems at home. My husband and I don't get along well. He doesn't treat me with consideration at all. I also have trouble with the lady who lives below us. She is complaining all the time, and criticizing me. Why are people so hard to get along with anyway? Why can't I have a good husband and good neighbors like other people have?

L: (To the group) How do you folks think Mrs. B looks? Does she look like a happy person or a gloomy person?

Mrs. C: To be quite frank, Mrs. B has a rather sour look on her face.

Mrs. B: That's no help to hear that! My husband always tells me that I look sad, but he wishes I had a smiling face. But how can I look happy when he's so mean to me!

L: But you see, your husband has simply been mirroring your attitude toward him. If you don't treat him smilingly and tenderly, you can't expect him to treat you with consideration either.

Mrs. D: Yes, that's right! The process has to start with you. Don't blame your husband for the trouble; look to yourself first.

Mrs. B: Maybe you're right. I haven't treated my husband very well.

L: Now you're coming to see the truth of the Law, Mrs. B. Change your mind right now, and repent of this critical attitude you've had toward others. Begin to be a brighter person yourself from now on!

Mrs. B: (In tears) I see now that I haven't been a good wife or neighbor. I'll try to do better from now on.

L: This is a great day in your life, Mrs. B! This has been a wonderful experience for you and for all of us here in this hoza today! You've understood for the first time that to change a bad situation to a good one, you have to start with yourself. (2)

Mrs. B: My two children both have aches and pains in their legs. And the other day one of them got a very bad nosebleed. What is wrong with them?

L: The cause of this condition is lustful thinking. Trouble in the legs always points to a problem of sexual lustfulness. You yourself probably have a problem with this, don't you?

Mrs. B: (With embarrassment) Yes, I do. I am a person of very strong passions, but my husband is even more that way. We've had so much trouble between us. (She tells the story of her marriage.) But today my husband is at an RK retreat seeking spiritual help.

L: Oh, how obvious the nature of your trouble is! A wife should be the first one to apologize and repent, but here we have the opposite happening. Your husband has gone to the spiritual retreat before you have. He is the first to repent. But his religious exercises won't do him any good if you don't humble yourself before him right away. Go meet him today when they return from the retreat, and immediately apologize to him and do everything you can for him from now on.

Mrs. B: (Weeping) Oh yes, I will surely do that! I see now where I have been wrong.

(Everyone joined in telling Mrs. B that she must be more meek, and that today offers an especially crucial opportunity for their marital life to take a turn for the better, and that the Buddha has prepared the way for a new life in their family.) (28)

(*Interpretation*)

Five elements of group counseling as observed in hoza have been presented: environment, rapport, acceptance, free expression, and insight. Under each topic it was observed that hoza displayed both positive and negative elements, depending on the leader and his method, and also depending on the cultural context from which we view the various phenomena. It is therefore dangerous to make a general statement about the validity of hoza as group counseling. Furthermore, extreme caution must be exercized in setting up a general standard for what constitutes a positive or negative element inasmuch as any such standard of judgment is highly subject to cultural conditioning.

In the following interpretation some contrasts between Western and Japanese assumptions, processes and goals of therapy will be noted, and following that, comments on the five specific elements which were observed as aspects of therapy will be made.

COUNSELING: WESTERN AND JAPANESE

The assumptions of group counseling or group therapy according to researchers in group dynamics are that the group is a dynamic system of forces in which several people have psychological relations with one another by all contributing actively and responsibly to the group. In the pattern of Western research, some common characteristics of group counseling are the following: 1) All members of the group have a common problem. 2) The counselor functions as a resource person from within the group. 3) A permissive atmosphere which allows for free expression prevails. 4) Interaction and mutual help among members is essential. This is done by letting each member express his own reactions about the problems or his suggestions for handling it.[1] In either individual or group counseling, the counselor struggles empathetically to understand what each client is feeling and thinking. The client gains increased self-acceptance and new understandings of himself. He learns to assume increasing responsibility for his actions and solve his own problems more effectively in the future. A deep confidence in the ability of most people to be responsible for their own lives is the basic requirement. The counselor must not evaluate what is good and right for other people. The counselor has "respect for their integrity as individuals, for their right to the strength-giving act of making and living by their own choices."[2]

Obviously these Western standards for therapeutic group interaction do not fit the pattern of hoza. Does this indicate that participants are disappointed in hoza and find no help there? No, on the contrary the Japanese feel at home in hoza because here is an operating procedure which springs from their own peculiar tradition of "counseling." For instance, it can be noted first of all that the group context for counseling is in keeping with the group orientation of Japanese life in general. The history and culture of Japan having taught people to think in terms of the extended family and the close-knit group; the natural impulse for a person in distress is to turn to one of the clan or group for help. This group orientation, in contrast to individual orientation, is evident in the language of hoza where the characteristic expressions of the leaders are expressions which appeal to the circle as a group, rather than as a collection of individuals. "*Minasan*" (everybody) is the characteristic pronoun used in address. "*—mashō*" (let us...) is the characteristic verb form. The address and appeal is a corporate one. Again the group orientation is evident in the tendency so often observed in hoza to treat the problem presented as a personal problem by a member, not as an individual problem, but as a "symptom" of a universal problem common to everyone. The approach to counseling runs like this: "Why should the individual be left to find what he thinks is a unique solution to what he thinks is his own unique problem, when the truth is that there is no such thing as a unique problem or a unique solution. We all share in a common human misery, and salvation lies in being restored into the the common solidarity of the group through being brought into the realm of the one universal Law."

Alongside of this observation should be placed another observation which at first sight appears to be contradictory. That is the tendency in hoza to individualize problems rather than to understand them in their context as a problem of society. This tendency is found both in counseling in general and in the hoza principle, "The fault lies with yourself." Two significant elements appear here, the tendency to individualize or personalize a problem which actually cannot be solved apart from reform in the larger social unit, and the tendency to be resigned to living with problems. The latter expresses the sense of *mujōkan*, or the ephemeral character of human existence which is a trait of the Japanese way of thinking. This tendency thus appears to individualize every situation, whereas the emphasis on group solidarity tends to generalize every situation. However, two different dimensions of a problem are involved here. The first is the dimension of existential identity, and declares the individual's identity to lie with the corporate group. The second is the dimension of functional activity, and declares that the way to solve any particular problem is either to do your best to "brighten the corner where you are," or otherwise be resigned and patient with your lot if the problem cannot be solved. This solution tends to oversimplify ethical problems by overlooking the individual's responsibility to function at the level of social action, and confines his responsibility to the ethics of personal piety and to the mood of resignation.

Chapter VI pointed out the phenomenon of authoritarian leadership in general. Here we see that the authoritarian attitude also applies to the counseling situation. A study of letters to newspaper counseling column editors revealed a strong inferiority feeling and a submissive desire to receive advice from an expert authority.

> Actually clients await not the consultant's advice, but his order. They cannot judge their own situations for themselves, so they want to find authorities who can judge. The stereotyped concluding sentence in these letters is 'I don't know what I should do! Please help me.' People are looking for a magic helper from outside.[3]

The counseling relationship in Japan, in other words, is built on the same model as social behavior patterns in general, namely, upon a vertical way of thinking. The individual in himself tends to lack self-confidence and has a feeling of powerlessness. "The Japanese want to find something on which they can rely. If they can find such a thing they feel secure."[4]

The counselor-counselee relationship is a superior-inferior relationship, with the counselor taking the role of the authoritarian teacher (*sensei*). A counselee expects his counselor, if he is a worthy counselor, to be able to understand his situation and give proper advice as to how to cope with it. A report by an American family counselor in Singapore gives the following insights into some of the peculiar counseling dynamics which he discovered among Asian people.

> The counselee tends to expect the counselor to be able to see through his situation, advise, manipulate and arrange properly. If one doesn't do this, then the counselor is seen as an uncaring, unable superior. Most relationships are those of 'superior' to 'inferior' rather than to peers. Consequently, most relationships are structured and/or perceived to be on lines of up and down authority. Communication then is basically expected to be authoritarian; for example, lectures, advice, morality, techniques, etc.[5]

The authoritative manner of the hoza counselors is obviously in harmony with these general patterns of counseling relationships among Asian people.

The existence of dependency attitudes in the Japanese personality has frequently been noted. Dependency on the authority figure and on the mode of socially approved behavior is deeply ingrained in Japanese character. Individual self-confidence and self-determination are not the expected nor desired goals of counseling.[6] Psychiatrists point out the passive dependency syndrome, the never fully satisfied desire to be loved, as a peculiarity of Japanese psychological make-up. Japanese psychotherapists see that health for their patients lies not in leading them to self-sufficiency but in letting them depend on the counselor as a maternal figure.

Caudill and Doi, in a special research project where patients responded to pictures, found that welfare of the group and harmony with the consensus of the group were the primary goals of the patients. In other words, their values were oriented to the group rather than to the individual. In sexuality, for example, the desire and need was not primarily self-centered erotic need, but rather an "aim-inhibited" libidinous reaction, or the passive desire to be loved by those around him in contrast to the aggressive desire to satisfy one's own sexual needs.[7] This passive dependency syndrome is described by a special expression, *amae*, a word which derives from the verb *amaeru*, which has no equivalent in English, but which refers to the wish to be loved by others. The sense of *amae* is encouraged from infancy, when the Japanese mother characteristically fondles and feeds her child rather than let it cry. Psychiatrist Takeo Doi claims that the concept of *amae*, or passive dependency, is a key to understanding both Japanese personality and cultural patterns. He says that the Japanese person's feeling of dependence and "the unwillingness to be separated from the warm mother-child circle and cast into the objective world of 'reality'...are somehow prolonged into and diffused throughout his adult life, so that they come to shape, to a far greater extent than in adults in the West, his whole attitude to other people and to 'reality.' "[8]

Identification among Japanese people occurs according to the pattern of parent-child relations, which is one of dependence and complete trust in protective maternalism. The Japanese therapist, therefore, becomes a maternal or paternal figure, and the client finds healing in relating to him as a child, in returning to the protective maternal relationship of the childhood paradise. For in childhood the Japanese child has all the love and trust and freedom possible. Neurosis tends to develop in Japanese when the protected child has to separate himself from parental care and stand alone in society. Healing lies in discovering appropriate dependency relationships, and maintaining a proper group-centeredness, rather than in learning to stand alone.[9] The contrast between these presuppositions and the presuppositions of Western counseling is striking —if not baffling— and provides a significant key for understanding the techniques of hoza leaders and the reaction of hoza participants.

THERAPEUTIC ELEMENTS

We now attempt some interpretation of the five specific factors taken up in the findings as being relevant to the therapeutic effects of group counseling.

Environment

First, regarding group environment, particularly group size, it was observed that the average number of participants in a hoza group is twelve, and that this is considered by the leaders to be an optimum number. Group size is one focus of interest in the field of group dynamics. A "group" can be defined thus:

> We mean by a group a number of persons who communicate with each other often over a period of time, and who are few enough so that each person is able to communicate with all the others, not at second hand, but face-to-face.[10]

Thomas and Fink conclude that the variable of group size should be included in theories of group behavior, distinguishing if possible between the effects that result from the interaction of group size with other independent variables. The study of hoza has produced corroborating evidence for their statement that "group size is an important factor in determining the amount of yielding to conformity pressures".[11] Kishida did a study on group size in relation to conformity, using three groups of Japanese university students, numbering five, ten and thirty persons per group.

> Subjects responded individually to an opinion questionnaire, then received true feedback as to the majority opinion, and finally responded a second time to the questionnaire. Although there was a shift toward conformity in all groups, magnitude of opinion change showed a curvilinear relationship to group size, being greatest in ten-person groups and least in five-person groups.[12]

In contrast to either a smaller or larger group, the ten-person group showed the strongest tendency toward conformity and consensus. As noted in the Findings, the optimum size for hoza groups, both according to leaders and actual practice, is twelve persons. In the light of the above research findings, and in the light of the peculiar importance of conformity and consensus in hoza, this number of twelve is surely significant.

Rapport

The establishing of rapport—the personal trust relationship between two or more people, and the sense of cohesiveness or belonging in the in the case of a group situation—is essential to therapy. In the beginning stages of the life of any group, the group may be not more than a collection of individuals, but if it is a healthy group it soon develops into a system of social interaction. This is what is meant by cohesiveness, or group rapport. It is the sense of "we-ness" among the members. It is characterized by mutual respect, friendliness and loyalty among the members, by interpersonal attraction and wholesome interpersonal relationships.[13] Cohesiveness built on outside pressure is not stable and "it dissolves when the threatening condition or fear of a punitive status authority is no longer present."[14] Group dynamics principles assume that only growth from within based on mutual acceptance and affection produces genuine rapport.

Yet, interestingly enough, hoza groups do not have this kind of internal cohesiveness, indeed, cannot have it because of the constantly fluctuating membership. Membership, it was discovered, changes daily; many members have no personal acquaintance with most other group members. Is it really necessary for a group to have intimate rapport in order to have therapeutic effect? Clearly the counseling of hoza does not depend on deep-level interpersonal relationships. The theological basis for hoza is plain about this, for the assumption is that all people are, in the nature of things, interrelated; there is no independent ego existence; all share the same Buddha nature, regardless of whether they are personally acquainted or not. This indeed constitutes a kind of relationship, an ontological unity of all individuals. But it is not a unity based on a personal knowledge of the other, nor upon an attempt to understand the other as a unique self with a unique spirit of his own—concepts deemed essential in counseling in the Western tradition. In fact, these are the very elements that are denied in the doctrine of *shohō muga* (non-existence of the ego), which will be explained in the following chapter.

Acceptance

The experience of acceptance by the other is an essential element in any psychotherapeutic process. What do the findings at hoza reveal about this point? Although there is no overt rejection of anyone and cordial formal acceptance of all participants into the circle, it was observed that there was frequently a casualness which bordered on the impersonal, and which is close to indifference toward the individual and the feeling he is trying to express. People bring their problems to the group, and they and their problems are accepted in a kind of experience of absorption. That is, the group, without judging or setting him apart, or without really listening to the peculiar circumstances of his problem, all empathize and say they know just what the problem is, and if he will keep coming to their group, he will find the solution through a gradual process of identification. Here again the doctrine of *shohō muga* comes alive: there is no such thing as independent existence; all things exist in inter-dependence. Likewise, the Japanese "collectivity orientation" discussed earlier can be seen in application here.

Expression

Free expression of thoughts and feelings is another essential in any kind of counseling. The assumption is that the counselee's act of expressing his thoughts and feelings freely is a cathartic and health-producing process. The findings showed that there is broad variation in the extent to which free expression is actually practiced and permitted. At their best, hoza leaders provide excellent opportunities for free expression of problems. At their worst, leaders are insensitive to the individual's particular needs and inhibit free expression by their authoritarian manner and their premature advice.

Counselors sensitive to cultural differences are concerned about the Oriental person's not being able to express himself openly, because the values of his culture work against the open expression of emotion. The 1968 Bangkok Conference of Counselors dealt with this problem, asking questions from three angles: 1) Is it possible for people trained under certain assumptions to tell how they feel? 2) Is it proper for people in certain cultural contexts to express themselves on emotional subjects? (3) What kind of feelings would a person in a given situation be allowed to express? These questions are relevant to any discussion of counseling with Japanese, who are known as a peculiarly reserved and restrained people. But in spite of this, one observer found that Japanese couples discuss problems with each other more frequently than American couples do. "Japanese wives win first prize for emotional openness," he says.[15] The factor of social class also plays a role. Dore's observation of class difference in regard to expressiveness also speaks to this point. He draws a contrast between the "wide-open, no-secrets communal life" of the lower class community of Tokyo with "the greater individualism and privacy" of the higher class community.[16] The preponderance of lower middle class participants in hoza should be borne in mind at this point.

Insight

Regarding the element of insight, a distinction can be drawn between insight as used in a technical sense as a goal of counseling, and insight as used in a religious sense of coming to an understanding of the truth. Yuji Sasaki's psychiatric study of comparison of personality change resulting from attendance at hoza and the personality change resulting from psychotherapy concluded that therapy changes personality more radically than does hoza. That is, it makes an individual more relaxed, flexible, adaptable, etc. In contrast, hoza attendance produced little of this kind of change, but did produce religious change, which Sasaki describes as a change in life orientation, a change of values and direction.[17] Whether this is indeed less radical than psychotherapeutic change depends entirely upon what kind of insights are deemed to be of greatest value.

General Socio-Emotional Needs

In this chapter we are describing the socio-emotional factors responsible for the impact of hoza. Inasmuch as RK translates hoza as "group counseling," factors that are directly relevant to counseling as such have been taken up first. Now we turn to socio-emotional factors interpreted in the broader sense of anything which serves to satisfy the individual's needs for emotional well-being, which includes first of all his need for warmth and acceptance from other people. This experience, which might be called the sense of belonging, or simply fellowship, can also be thought of as a therapeutic experience—therapy for the general socio-emotional malaise of alienation, in contrast to the therapy offered by counseling for the healing of specific emotional problems. This more diffuse therapeutic experience is a vital part of the dynamics of hoza—perhaps the determining factor in accounting for its appeal and popularity.

In the following chapter four categories are used to describe the content of hoza conversations: problem-solving, instruction, testimonies and institutional maintenance. The assumption is that the bulk of hoza conversations falls into one or more of these categories. However, a type of conversation which functions in a different manner should not be overlooked. It is one which has special relevance to the socio-emotional dynamics of hoza, namely, gossip. We use the term "gossip" here not in a pejorative sense, but in the sense of "easy, unrestrained talk—especially about persons or social incidents."[18] Hoza provides a perfect opportunity for sharing this kind of conversation. These conversations are included here rather than in the section on content because their function is deemed to be more socio-emotional than conceptual.

(*Findings*)

In view of the intention of hoza to be a place where religion is taught and applied to everyday life, it is noteworthy that there is no small amount of material which actually has no religious reference at all. The following cases are typical.

In Session 5, Mrs. B made a long recital of details regarding an acquaintance who had various kinds of trouble with her pregnancies. Mrs. C chimed in with a detailed account of a friend who had to have an abortion because of ill health. Others joined in with further talk about abortions.

In Session 18 a great deal of the time was taken up with a problem concerning division of the family property.

> *Mr. A*: I'm having a problem in getting my just share of the family inheritance. I live with my aunt and uncle. I'm a second son, and my elder brother won't give me my just share of the inheritance.
>
> *L*: Dividing up the family property is indeed a great problem. Your name is Sato, isn't it, and families with the name Sato have the bad fate of having selfish eldest sons. That's too bad, but inasmuch as you are an RK member, you must be patient and longsuffering, and not cause an ugly situation. Accept your lot; suffering makes you strong.
>
> *Mr. C*: My name is Sato too, and our family had exactly the same problem. (He relates a long detailed story of his greedy elder brother.)
>
> *L*: We had a similar situation in our family too. (Details follow. There was enthusiastic listening on the part of all while these

accounts were being related. No religious interpretation was given.) (18)

Much of the above kind of gossip comes from the leader herself in the course of her teaching or relating of personal testimonies. As pointed out in Chapter VI, most of the instructing is done by means of the "case method," that is, through personal narratives, rather than by logical teaching of abstract concepts. But we find that many narratives told by the leader are at best only remotely related to the pedagogical point. The following cases can be cited:

Mrs. A: My son causes us so much trouble at home. (Weeping) He is so rebellious and doesn't listen to anything we say.

L: This situation reflects something in your home life and your relation with your husband. You must apologize to your husband; then things will turn out all right. An elderly woman I know raised six children, even though she had none of her own. That was a remarkable thing! She lived in a village where her family were fishermen. You know what a hard life fishermen have. (Details about fishermen's life followed.) (36)

In Session 39, Mrs. A's case of whether to take her step-son, who was seriously ill, to her home, or to send him to his real mother was under serious discussion. In the course of the discussion, the leader related two episodes of her own:

L: This problem is like one I met in Kyushu some time ago. The mother in that case had to decide whether to keep a step-son or give him back to his real mother. The child was so angry with his father that he slashed him with a knife. But that anger was nothing but the mother's bitterness showing itself through him. That reminds me of still another case where a wife was unable to have children. So she and her husband adopted a baby at the age of three. She thought the child looked just like her husband. But soon after the child died. Then they adopted another child and that one too looked very much like the husband. This child also became very sick. The mother was suspicious about the adopted children and began investigating. She discovered that both were the children of her husband and his mistress, whereupon the husband suddenly left home. (39)

In these and many similar cases the content is highly emotional and fascinating to the listeners, but apparently irrelevant either to teaching religion or to "therapy." Therefore, we would classify these conversations as gossip, dramatic human interest episodes for their own sake.

Much hoza conversation is humorous, entertaining and delightful, but irrelevant to the stated purposes of the groups. The following examples are typical.

> *Mr. A*: I've had many unusual experiences. Once I was engaged, but I didn't know how to carry on conversation with a woman, so I broke off the engagement. I've decided never to marry, since I get confused when women are around, and can't do my work. (The group was highly entertained by his talking.) (12)

> *Mrs. E*: I'd like to have you give me the answer to my problem, insignificant though it may seem. This morning I was boiling an egg in a pan which had a leak in it. The leaking water put out the gas flame, so when I lit the stove again it burst into flame and I got a burn on my neck. (She showed a red spot about an inch in diameter.)
>
> *L*: Oh, that red mark is from the flame? I thought it was a "kiss mark" from your husband last night, and I've been feeling so envious this afternoon looking at it! I wondered why you should be trying to cover it. Why don't you show it off and brag about how passionately your husband kisses you? (Group howled with laughter; Mrs. E was delightfully embarrassed.) You're so young and pretty, why don't you let your husband make a kiss mark on the other side of your neck to balance off the burn! I'm sure he would do that if you treated him properly. (32)

It is significant that only on one occasion was fear expressed by a member that if she told her problem in hoza it might become the topic of "gossip" in the bad sense. The leader emphatically replied:

> *L*: Such a thing will never happen! Hoza is not a place to expose people or gossip about people. We share things only for the sake of teaching each other. We tell these incidents only to show how the Buddha's mercy has operated in concrete cases. (6)

Instances of hoza conversations entirely lacking in religious reference have been cited. However, far more instances of conversation could be cited in which there is a superficial religious reference appended to the end of a long narrative which we would conclude was actually told as gossip rather than for pedagogical or therapeutic purposes. There are many instances where a pedagogical point is merely a "jumping off point" for launching into gossip. With regard to a very great proportion of all the conversations which we have classified as testimonies and problem-solving, there is an ambiguous line of distinction between the presentation of a problem and gossip, a testimony and gossip, or even teaching and gossip. In the following cases this ambiguous line between gossip and purposeful "case studies" is evident.

Mrs. A: I was sick for 15 years with a peculiar ailment, and no doctors could help me. I was coughing blood. Doctors treated me for TB. (She ramblingly told of the conditions of her birth, of moving to Hiroshima during the war where they underwent much suffering, and of the way in which her marriage was arranged.) Finally I humbled myself before the Buddha and went to still a different doctor. He told me that my coughing blood was not due to TB at all, but due to the fact that I menstruate only two or three times a year. (She gave much detail about her peculiar physiological condition.) This diagnosis gave me confidence to face life again, knowing that I didn't have TB. TB is due to a self-centered spirit, so I had been wondering in what way I was so selfish that I could be suffering from TB. But when I discovered that diagnosis of my physical and spiritual condition was wrong, I got a new lease on life. (5)

L: I know a case of a bride who was frantic because the groom stepped out on her just before the wedding. (Many details followed.) We wondered why such a thing should happen, and when we traced back we found that neither of them had been honoring their ancestors at all. You realize that veneration of ancestors is central to what RK stands for. I know another case of a boy who had polio. Acquaintances wondered why he should be stricken with this so they investigated his background and found that his grandfather had been a terrible person. He had once taken a fish knife to kill his wife; he often fought with his wife, so that he was arrested and put in jail. (Rambling details followed.) This is an obvious case where karma of a former generation is being manifested in a later generation. We must learn from this to follow the eightfold path of goodness so nothing like that will befall our children or grandchildren. (16)

(*Interpretation*)

It will be helpful at this point to recognize the multi-functional character of group conversation, and the distinction between conceptual and emotional content of any conversation. A distinction can be drawn between manifest and latent functions of group activity. The conceptual or intellectual content of a conversation is the manifest aspect, but this manifest function of communicating information is colored by emotional overtones which either please or displease the group. This emotional movement is the latent function of the conversation. Giving testimony of "religious experience" or teaching religious doctrine via case studies may be the manifest function of a group, while the pleasure and social warmth involved in the very act of sharing such conversation constitute the latent function. Which of these functions is the more decisive for the total impact of the group meeting may be hard to judge. In the case of hoza the latent socio-emotional function is at least as decisive for the total impact as is the manifest function of problem-solving, teaching and giving testimonies.

Another way of expressing this distinction is to recognize two aspects in any discussion—content and process. In every group experience there is a two-fold dimension, the dimension of content, that is, the subject matter talked about, and the dimension of process, that is, the atmosphere, attitudes, relationships and feelings which exist within the group. The interaction of process and content in any group meeting is the object of concern for many researchers.[19] Another relevant pair of concepts used in analyzing groups is the distinction between group task and group maintenance. Task, or goal-achievement, is accomplished through such behavior as initiating action, keeping attention focused on the goal, giving information, evaluating, etc. On the other hand, group maintenance is accomplished through such behavior as keeping interpersonal relations pleasant, arbitrating disputes among members, providing encouragement to continue supporting the group, etc. In hoza both aspects of group life—the latent, emotional, process factors as well as the manifest, content, and task-achievement factors find full expression. Hoza thus functions as both a socio-emotional agent and also as an agent of religious propagation.

The fact of the fundamental need of the Japanese for the support and solidarity of a group has already been alluded to many times. This need can be called an ethnological characteristic of the Japanese.[20]

That RK deliberately and effectively promotes this spirit of group solidarity is evidenced in such activities as the stirring festivals, the youth retreat program, and not least in hoza itself. Beyond this basic general need are the specific needs of the contemporary period and of the class of people to whom the new religions appeal. The alienation of the lower middle class, from which most of the hoza participants come, their loneliness and frustration—these find a satisfying outlet in hoza. In hoza these people have the opportunity to express their burdens and identify with other people who have similar troubles, in a genial, accepting atmosphere. Here they can make friends and gain a sense of belonging. Hoza has been called a *nakama-zukuri no ba* (a place for making friends) and *idobata kaigi* (literally, a "well-side conference") because it is a place where personal sympathy and social intimacy are fostered. This kind of "therapy" is especially needed by housewives, who need emancipation from their household drudgery as well as the pleasant socializing which hoza provides

The preceding paragraphs have indicated that regardless of the content of the conversations—whether it be religious teaching or counseling or gossip—the experience of the talking itself is a kind of therapy and salvation for lonely or deprived people. Group dynamics research corroborates this in recognizing "informal communication" as an important element in group process. Such communication is motivated by emotional states, such as joy or anger, rather than by the subject matter. It is sometimes referred to as "consummatory communication." Consummatory communication differs from instrumental communication in that the act of communication itself is the end, rather than the effect it has on the listener. What we have called "gossip" could rightly be given the more technical designation of "consummatory communication."[21]

Is hoza really "group counseling"? In the context of American concepts of counseling, perhaps not. But in the context of the strong need of the Japanese for maintaining and expressing social solidarity, RK is unquestionably effecting a remarkable socio-emotional therapy in the broadest sense through its hoza.

CHAPTER EIGHT

CONCEPTUAL CONTENT

In this chapter we will focus attention on the actual content of the speeches, conversations and discussions which constituted the substance of the hoza sessions under consideration. The material will be divided into four categories: problem-solving, instruction, testimonies and discussion of institutional maintenance.

Problem-Solving

The officially stated purpose of hoza is to apply the teachings of fundamental Buddhism to everyday life problems, to help people solve any and all the problems of their life by a proper application of Buddhist doctrine to specific situations. This process is called *musubi* in RK terminology, which literally means "tying together." The teaching is tied in with the everyday problem; i. e., the problem is solved in the light of the Buddhist Law. This activity will be described under two headings, first, the nature of the problems presented, and then the nature of the answers given.

(*Findings*)

THE NATURE OF THE PROBLEMS

Problems presented for solution are actually not as diverse as might be anticipated. They tend to fall into a few rather well-defined categories. In the following paragraphs these problems will be classified and listed with an indication of the number of cases of each problem which were discussed in the forty sessions attended.

Family

We shall further classify the cases listed as family problems and note their frequency of occurrence.

Problems in the husband-wife relationship—8 cases:

Wife complains about her husband's conduct and attitudes toward her: lazy, inconsiderate, hard to get along with, etc. 5 cases (2, 10, 12, 30, 32)

Husband complains about his wife's attitude toward him: cold, irritable, hard to get along with. 3 cases (6, 24, 29)

Problems in the parent-child relationship—9 cases:

Mother complains that her small child is difficult to handle. 1 case (10)

Mother complains that her child is rebellious and has bad behavior. 2 cases (25, 36)

Father complains that children are hard to get along with. 2 cases (24, 29)

Son complains about ill treatment from his parents. 1 case (34)

Daughter complains that her mother is hard to get along with. 3 cases (4, 10, 34)

Other family problems—3 cases:

Son complains he is not getting a fair share of the inheritance. 1 case (18)

Grandmother complains about the way her grandchild is treated by its parents. 1 case (38)

Mother has a problem regarding her step-son and his true mother. 1 case (39)

Health

The health problems are too diverse to classify according to medical categories. Instead, we shall group them according to three broad categories: disorders which are readily subject to medical diagnosis, disorders which have a high probability of being psychogenic or hypochondriacal, and those which could be considered relatively insignificant from the medical point of view. There was only one occurrence of each complaint.

Disorders subject to medical diagnosis—7 cases:

Fever (9)
Dumbness (11)
High blood pressure (23)
Appendicitis (25)
Diabetes (27)
Bladder stones (35)

Meningitis (39)

Disorders probably psychogenic or hypochondriacal—4 cases:

Stomach trouble (10)

Heart fluttering (18)

Blushing, fainting, fear of going outside (20)

Generally poor health (32)

Relatively insignificant disorders—3 cases:

Boil on knee (6)

Nosebleed (13)

Aching legs (28)

Nature of disorder not revealed—2 cases:

(27, 38)

Personal Relations Other Than Family

Cases in this category can be classified as follows:

Problem in relationship with friends. 2 cases (6, 22)

Problem in relationship with neighbors. 2 cases (2, 24)

Problem of loneliness. 1 case (24)

Institutional Maintenance

Matters of institutional maintenance also become matters for *musubi*. That is, problems encountered in doing service for RK itself become the life problems with which the members struggle.

The following cases are representative:

Difficulties in doing personal evangelism (*michibiki*). 3 cases (11, 23, 37)

Frustration over conflict between service responsibilities to RK (*oyaku*) and other responsibilities. 3 cases (14, 16, 34)

Various Misfortunes

These problems were trivial in nature, but they occurred with sufficient frequency to warrant attention as a separate category. The topics were as follows:

Purse was lost. (15)

Table leg broke, causing dishes to fall. (16)

Child fell and bumped his head. (20)

Husband got dirt in his eye. (20)

Money stolen from child at school. (20)

Face singed by gas stove flame. (32)

Other Problems

The following problems, each of which is of some importance, will be grouped together here since each occurred only once or a few times:

Problems related to occupation. (18, 26, 33)
Philosophical problem of evil (17)
Community ethical problem. (26)
Drinking problem. (27)
Problem of how to interpret a dream. (40)
Failure in college entrance examination. (3)

THE NATURE OF THE ANSWERS

Attention will now be turned to the way in which these problems were handled in the group. Perhaps the most characteristic thing about the handling of problems brought to hoza is the use of a stereotyped answer for them. Generally speaking, problems are not handled as individual, unique experiences which require an individual, unique solution. Rather, they are seen as merely a particular manifestation of a universal problem common to everyone. Therefore the solution required is a general, universally applicable one.

Thus in spite of the variety of problems presented, the solutions can be classified into relatively few categories. Furthermore, these categories do not represent different types of answers for correspondingly different types of problems. The classification is rather the identifying of the various steps or aspects of one standard solution. This standard solution consists of several parts, but in most cases the entire solution with all or most of its constituent parts is presented as the answer to any problem. The comprehensive answer will be stated in the form of an inclusive formula at the end of this section. First, cases from hoza conversations will be presented to illustrate the various aspects of this formula.

Manifestation of Karma

In RK the idea of suffering as a manifestation of karma, that is, the Buddhist teaching that the ethical consequences of one's acts determine future fate, either in one's own life, or in the experience of future generations, is a presupposition basic to the understanding of all human problems. The following are typical illustrations.

Mrs. A: My grandchild is quite sick, but is at home now. Her father says she should be in the hospital, but the doctor says she can stay home if she has no fever. Her father says the mother simply wants to have her home for her own comfort, that is, because she selfishly wants to have the child close to her. What do you think is the right thing to do?

L: Everyone, listen to this problem for it is one we should all consider. What do you think about this case? Obviously the child is sick because there is no gratitude on the part of the child toward her parents. How do I know this? Because we know the mother is selfish, and this is inevitably passed on to the child. But, Mrs. A, this unhappy situation eventually springs from you, for you are the grandmother, and the word of the Buddha is that deeds pass on through three generations. (38)

Mrs. D: My 4-year-old is dumb, but do you suppose even with this speech handicap it will be possible for him to enter the RK kindergarten?

L: We must realize that this problem is eventually related to your own treatment of your mother when you were a child. You caused your mother suffering, so now you are reaping the results of that in the suffering which your child causes you. (11)

Value of Suffering

This is an important step in the total solution. The individual is exhorted not to be bitter or despairing about karma and the suffering which has appeared as the fruit of karma, but rather to be thankful for it, recognizing that it has opened his eyes to see the need for a change of heart. Thus the disadvantageous situation can be turned into advantage for that individual's life. Phrases such as "Evil can be turned into good," and "An evil situation can be used to produce a good outcome," are heard frequently throughout hoza conversations.

(Mrs. B described her miserable home life life and says she is considering leaving her husband.)

L: Don't leave him, whatever you do! Rather, be thankful for him and for this trouble, because that will make you strong. Even in in the case of the development of cultures, it is the country which has difficult circumstances which develops faster than the one in good circumstances. That's why cold Japan has developed faster than the warm islands of the south seas. (10)

Mrs. A: My health has not been so good lately.

L: The Buddha gives us sickness so we will be led to enlightenment through it and be more thankful for our health from now on. Only those who have been sick can help another sick person. So your sickness is for the sake of helping you to help others. (32)

Self Reflected in Others

This is a central concept and is a key to answering most of the problems raised in hoza. People expose sin in one another simply by reflecting each other's character. Suffering forces a person to self-examination and investigation of the cause of his suffering. At that point his first impulse is to blame someone else as being the cause of his trouble. But RK teaches that the fault always lies in oneself. The other person's action merely mirrors or reflects the real cause, namely, a weakness in oneself.

Mrs. A: I'm very upset because the person who led me to faith has moved from Tokyo without telling me anything about it.

L: Don't blame him. There must be something in yourself which has caused this. How has your relationship with him been in the past? I hope you have learned that you shouldn't blame others for misfortune, for the fault is always in yourself. It is just as it is when you point with your finger at someone, blaming him. Notice that when you do that there are always three fingers pointing back at yourself. (20)

Mrs. B: My husband always tells me that I look sad, but he wishes I had a smiling face. But how can I look happy when he's so mean to me!

L: But you see, your husband has simply been mirroring your attitude toward him. If you don't treat him smiling and tenderly, you can't expect him to treat you with consideration either. (2)

Need for a Change of Heart

When the individual brings his problem and relates his suffering in hoza and finds the cause of his trouble to lie in his own evil past, what must he do to free himself from this suffering which karma has produced? He must have a change of heart, repent, and apologize to others and to his ancestors. Several things are especially significant here. "The first is that the vicious chain of karma, that is, the moral cause-effect law of the universe, can be broken by a change of heart. Another is that the repentance before the Buddha is indistinguishable from repentance before one's deceased ancestors. Thus repentance and veneration of ancestors are inseparably connected. Another significant point is that change of heart is also inseparably linked to the person whom one has offended. Where the problem involves broken relations with another person, part of the solution lies in going to that person and humbly apologizing for past wrongs.

(Mrs. E told her experience of having her miserable home life improved through attending hoza.)

L: If Mrs. E had not cut the causal chain of her lustful nature here in hoza through sincere repentance, her son who has just gotten married, would no doubt have the same trouble she has had. So you too, Mrs. A, must break your karma chain now through a change of heart, or your baby here will have the same trouble in his marital life when he grows up. (Mrs. A, having her child with her, had previously told her marital problems.) (30)

Mr. B: I'm worried about my younger brother. He has a fever every night, but he refuses to go to the doctor.

L: He must be a person with a very stubborn disposition.

Mr. B: Yes, I guess he is that kind of a person. He's like me. When I had appendicitis, I refused to see a doctor for a long time.

L: Then you must become humble yourself and go to your brother and apologize to him. Tell him that you realize you have been stubborn, and show him that he should not make the same mistake you made. (9)

Exhortation to Submissiveness

In most cases of problem-solving, an ethical solution which instructs the inquirer how he must behave in order to solve his problem is a part of the answer. Even this ethical solution is standardized, and can be summed up in the exhortations, "Don't be selfish, but be considerate of others and submissive to others." Humility and submissiveness are supreme virtues.

Mrs. A: I find my husband very hateful. He's a good-for-nothing! I've tried my best to be a good wife; our trouble is all his fault.

L: We all say that at first, but we learn differently after learning the Law. Every one of us wives here was bossy and irrate with our husbands at one time. But now after learning the Law, we have seen that our family strife was due to our own bossiness, and we have all become, or at least are becoming, humble and submissive persons. (30)

Mr. D: (Excitedly) Please help me; I'm having a terrible time with my parents again. Tonight when I left the house to come here, they said, "Leave home and never come back again for all we care, if you're going to spend so much time away from for the sake of RK!" I feel terribly bitter and angry toward them. I just can't make myself step down and listen to them as I know I should.

L: Don't ever talk back to your parents. Talk softly and bow to their will. (34)

Exhortation to Faithfulness in Ancestor Veneration

The last component of the standard answer is the exhortation to be devout in performing the rites of ancestor veneration. This is closely interwoven with the idea of karma, for one's personal karma is not confined to his own life as an individual, but is integrally bound up with all those who gave him his life. The comforting and appeasing of ancestors, and learning to adopt the attitude of gratefulness toward them is one of the means of breaking the chain of karma and finding release from suffering.

Mrs. A: I'm very upset because the person who led me to faith has moved from Tokyo without telling me anything about it.

L: Don't blame him. There must be something in yourself which has caused this. You must break the chain by apologizing to him first.

Mrs. A: But he's not here now, and I have no idea where he's gone.

L: If you can't find him, then apologize to your ancestors. Remember, we're not dealing with only the living. We who are alive today are only the leaves of a tree which has deep, deep roots, that is, our ancestors. (20)

Miss C: I've become afraid to go out of the house lately, so I just stay home all the time. When I do go out and someone looks at me, I blush and feel embarrassed. Once I almost fainted when I was riding the train. Tell me what's the matter with me.

L: What is your name? Did anyone in your family ever die of a neurotic condition?

Miss C: Yes, 17 years ago my mother died from a neurotic ailment.

L: You haven't been praying enough for your deceased mother. You must pray for her comfort. If you do that, you will get well yourself. (20)

A special aspect of ancestor veneration is the writing of the ancestral tablets, called *kaimyō*. As soon as one becomes a member of RK he is required to have such a tablet written for each of his deceased ancestors. On the tablet is inscribed a special posthumous name which is conceived and written by a corps of select members who execute this sacred task with great solemnity and ceremony in the *eijuden*, a sanctuary on the seventh floor of the Great Sacred Hall. Failure to have the *kaimyō* written is a blasphemous affront to the deceased, and is believed to result in sinister effects in the present life, as the following case illustrates:

Mr. A: I have one daughter and one step-son. My step-son's real mother is divorced and has remarried a man who is a member of Soka Gakkai. Now he is very sick in the hospital with spinal meninjitis.

L: Mrs. A, do you have three generations of your ancestors recorded on your ancestral tablets? (No.) Then you must get the names of all three generations written as soon as possible. (39)

In summary, then, based upon the evidence of the above cases, the standard answer to the problems presented in hoza for solution can be stated thus: Your suffering is a manifestation of the law of karma in your experience. Do not be resentful about this suffering. Rather, be thankful, for it has forced you to re-examine your life. And do not be resentful toward other people who may seem to be the cause of your trouble, for other people's behavior is simply mirroring your own. Ultimately the cause of your suffering lies in your own self. Therefore you must have a change of heart and apologize both to your ancestors and to the one you have wronged. Then you must start immediately to live right, which means you must not be selfish or proud, but thoughtful of and submissive to others. At the same time you must be faithful in venerating your ancestors, for the living cannot separate themselves

selves from their deep-rooted connections with those who have gone before.

Answers Related to Folk Beliefs

Leaders frequently make use of devices which to the Western observer can be generally described as superstitious. But in RK thought it is believed that such methods as divination, onomancy and the use of the horoscope are about 85 per cent reliable. Leaders claim that these methods are used as short-cuts in getting to know the member's character and in analyzing his problem. Cases representative of three different aspects of these folk beliefs will be cited: onomancy (*seimeigaku* or *seimei handan*), that is, the analysis of character according to one's name; use of a horoscope (*kyūsei*, *hoshi-uranai*), and the use of what we will call a psychosomatic formula.

> *L*: (To Mrs. A, who has just told her what her name is) That's a good name, but it means you are the *mokusei* (wooden) type, and such persons are selfish and get angry when someone dares to counter them.
>
> *Mrs. A*: Yes, I do tend to be stubborn.
>
> *L*: No, you're not stubborn. You're *mokusei*, and that means you're simply selfish. You also have many fine qualities of the *mokusei* type: you are bright and gentle. (30)

> *Mrs. B*: At lunch this noon my three-year-old fell off his chair and bumped his head. It swelled so badly that I had to put cold cloths on it. Do you think his head might be injured?
>
> *L*: Tell me more about your family before I can answer. What year were you born? What year was your husband born? What is the disposition of your child? Has anyone in your family ever died of an accident?
>
> *Mrs. B*: Yes, seven years ago an uncle died in an accident.
>
> *L*: (Looking through the horoscope) Oh, oh! This is a crucial year for you, Mrs. B! This accident could have very disastrous results. You must pray fervently to your ancestors all during this year, lest something terrible befall your family. (20)

By "psychosomatic formula" we refer to the system of finding cause-effect relations between physiological symptoms and moral causes. Certain type of physical ailments are believed to have direct connection with mental or moral problems. Therefore in some cases of problem-solving in hoza, a psychosomatic formula is utilized to provide the answer to individual's problems. The following cases illustrate this approach.

Mrs. B: My two children both have aches and pains in their legs. What is wrong with them?

L: The cause of this condition is lustful thinking (*shikijō*). Trouble in the legs always points to a problem of sexual lustfulness. You yourself probably have a problem with this, don't you? (28)

Mr. E: I have always had poor health. I have bad color in my skin and pains in various parts of my body, and I have bladder stones.

L: You say you have bladder stones. This is connected with a selfish spirit, you know. You have put yourself in the center of your family, wanting to be first and strongest yourself, haven't you? (35)

(***Interpretation***)

In these Findings, particularly in the solutions offered for the problems, many concepts—such as karma, the veneration of ancestors, etc.—call for some interpretation before the hoza conversations can be pieced together and become intelligible, at least for the Westerner. However, inasmuch as these subjects constitute the doctrinal content of all three of the main categories dealt with in this chapter, namely, problem-solving, instruction and testimonies, they will be considered together at the end of the present chapter. At this point only certain items relevant to the activity of problem-solving itself will be taken up.

SIGNIFICANCE OF PROBLEM-SOLVING IN HOZA

Regardless of the nature of the problems or of the answers offered them, it is necessary and valuable for common people to have such a place as hoza where they can bring their troubles. Especially people of the lower middle class experience many frustrations but have no place where they can find a listening ear.

The established religions are neither alert to this opportunity to help individuals, nor able to give what the people want and need. In this crucial situation, RK has instituted hoza as an appropriate answer to this need. Particularly in the light of the historical precedent set for hoza by the Buddhist *kō*, hoza is indeed a natural activity which finds ready response in Buddhist-tinged Japanese society. "We in the new religions are trying to satisfy the urgent needs of the citizenry and the fact that we have grown so fast proves that we have been successful in doing this", states an RK leader.[1]

A chief characteristic of the new religions is their promise to bestow concrete benefit on people if they will become believers. They promise to build the "kingdom of God" here and now by granting people what they need and want. Many of the new religions, including RK, promise happiness as the reward for joining their group and following their teachings, and happiness is interpreted in extremely concrete ways: the release from the evils of physical illness, material poverty, tension in personal relationships, etc. This kind of "gospel" has won them the name "*goriyaku shūkyō*" (benefit-granting religion, or profit-making religion), which is usually used in disparagement.

However, RK leaders recognize that crowds of people would not come to hoza just to learn the teachings of the Lotus Scripture. There must be a more urgent motivation than that. They come to have their troubles eased and their problems solved. According to RK theological interpretation, this is not a perverse motivation, for, as an RK theologian explained, Buddhism is in essence a *riyaku* (benefit-granting) theology inasmuch as it promises happiness (*shiawase*). *Shiawase* is the modern way of expressing Nirvana, which is the goal and result of the religious life. People invariably gain material and physical benefits as the result of the belief. There is no shame in being this-worldly. Rather, shame ought to lie with the old religions who are content only to bury the dead and offer prayers for them.[2]

Riyaku, or concrete benefit, is subject to a theological interpretation in RK. It is called a *hōben* (means, expedient). Although the ultimate end of religious teaching is to make people realize the meaning of their life, appropriate means (*hōben*) must be used to lead people from the point where they actually are to that ultimate end. If people can be lured into the true religion by the means of concrete benefits, then such a means is appropriate and good.

However, this materialistic approach to religious faith and to promotion of the faith is the subject of much criticism, not least by other Buddhist scholars, who say that RK does not wrestle with the basic question concerning the essence of "happiness," but is content to identify happiness with material prosperity and physical well-being. The result is a superficial religion. Original Buddhism, they point out, is not concerned with material prosperity. The Buddha himself lived an austere life of poverty, as did Saint Nichiren. RK is thus sometimes criticized for not being concerned with basic theological and philosophical problems, and for simply using theology to achieve its own ends.

NATURE OF THE PROBLEMS

Reviewing the list of problems presented for solution during hoza sessions, a few general observations can be made. First of all the matters of concern are remarkably concrete, practical and earthy, touching everyday life experience. It is very significant that out of the vast array listed there is only one instance of an abstract problem being brought up, namely, the philosophical problem of evil discussed in Session 17. Psychiatric observers note that the Japanese people live "close to their bodies," and that in order for an idea to have genuine meaning, it must be relevant to that which touches the earthy, physical part of the person. Japanese people, especially of the lower class, are attracted to a religion which has relevance to the physical. An intellectualized religion means nothing to him. He needs religion which heals his body or puts yen in his pocket, and RK is perceptive and sensitive to this way of thinking.[3]

Secondly, the matters of concern brought for solving are, generally speaking, relatively minor matters. This leads to some conclusions. One is that no item of concern is too small to merit the attention of the hoza leader and group. Participants are confident of being accepted by group regardless of how insignificant or foolish their particular problem be. But it might also be said that hoza leaders are not equipped to handle the more serious problems of human experience, and that hoza does not provide a suitable context for dealing with such problems. For instance, although there were many cases of family troubles, the problem of separation or divorce was not among them. Yet these are matters of frequent concern among contemporary Japanese. Problems concerning the meaning of life in its philosophical dimensions were never mentioned. Problems involving serious emotional or neurotic disturbance are not found in the list.[4]

It is significant that the bulk of the problems fall in the category of family problems. This would seem to indicate that problems related to family living are the most immediately pressing problems in the members' experience. This could be anticipated in view of the fact that most of the participants are housewives, and in view of the fact that the Japanese housewife is generally considered to be an oppressed person, who traditionally has lived in sacrificial servitude to her husband.[5] At the present time one of the deepest revolutionary trends in Japanese society is the revolution in the family system and family values, which causes conflict in the understanding of husband-wife roles and parent-child roles. Mita's study of the types of problems brought for counseling showed that nearly half of all the cases concerned marriage and family life.[6] Kato's study of the same subject showed that 75 out of 81 problems dealing with human relations dealt with family relationships.[7]

Although this study does not take a historical approach, but rather analyzes hoza at a certain chronological cross-section, mention should be made of the shift in interests of hoza participants, and the consequent shift in the nature of problems presented in hoza. According to a survey conducted among RK leaders, if we compare the current cross-section with the situation in hoza of the early or middle 1950's, the problems about which members are concerned have shifted from "material-phenomenological" ones to problems of human relations and problems dealing with way of life.[8] Students of the new religions are prone to conclude that they thrive among the lower classes in an atmosphere of material need and social alienation.[9] But this reasoning is no longer completely valid in Japan, which is experiencing unprecedented material affluence. Finding relief from material distress is only a very minor motivation for joining RK today, and a minor source of problems handled in hoza. Today anxiety is shifting from the material sphere to the spiritual sphere of human relations.

If the thesis that the new religions rise and flourish as a response to certain social crises be true, then in view of the radical change in Japan's social situation during the past two decades, we would expect that the content and appeal of these religions, too, must have changed or be changing. And this is exactly what is happening. RK leaders admit that the orientation of hoza must change as people's needs change in the context of changing social conditions. The success of RK itself depends on how well they are able to satisfy both those members who still seek material benefits and traditional ethical patterns, and yet at the same time develop and perfect their doctrine and outlook in order to meet the demands of younger and more highly educated people and of those in search of ethical and spiritual values.[10]

NATURE OF THE ANSWERS

Theological and Traditional Elements

According to an official RK pamphlet, hoza is described as a place where the fundamental Buddhist doctrine of the Four Noble Truths (*shitai*) is taught. The presentation of a problem by a participant is the acknowledgement of the truth of suffering, the first Noble Truth, and the probing into its background by the leader is seeking the truth of cause, the second Noble Truth. The leader then urges the member to attain happiness, or nirvana, which is the third Noble Truth, by changing his ethical way of life according to the truth of path, the fourth Noble Truth.[11] One leader expressed it this way:

> We find the root of people's suffering by searching into their karma of the former world (*shukugō*) as well as into their karma of the present world (*gengō*). This is the first time the difficult Buddhist doctrine has been applied simply and meaningfully to people's everyday life problems.[12]

The Lotus Scripture teaches the right way of life, and it is the ultimate aim of RK to teach this to everyone, but the theological principles of the ancient Scriptures must be translated in a way to meet the needs of people today. The task of the hoza leader is to apply the theological principles according to the nature of the inquirer. Principles are applied according to the intellectual and cultural level of the inquirer. If the religious teacher can grasp the individual's feeling, desires and his peculiar nature, the right answer can be given to his problem even though the leader has had little or no formal theological education. President Niwano himself sees religion not so much as a philosophy of life as a force which grips people at "gut-level," and changes their life from misery to happiness.

The Findings revealed that one standard part of the answer to personal problems is to show that no one is to blame but yourself for the problem suffered. "The fault lies with *you*," is frequently heard. This is an interesting emphasis from several points of view. It is easier to give an explanation which throws all the responsibility on one individual rather than to point out the complicated factors in society and environment which may have contributed to the problem. There is more immediate hope of change if only one subject is involved.[13] The religious institution comes to the guilty person and offers him salvation and bliss and prosperity if he believes and follows, or threatens him with ruin if he does not.[14]

This approach is also linked with the idea of karma, which traces the the cause of evil into the individual's own past. It also has affinity with economic class, in that the RK teachings appeal more to those whose pains and problems would disappear if only they changed. The small businessman or shop-keeper, in contrast to both the factory worker and those on the management level, is the one whose livelihood may be most directly influenced by his inner spiritual condition and attitudes, inasmuch as his business is directly dependent on the amount of energy he will put into it, and the kind of face he shows to his customers.

The philosophy of subjectivism and the intuitive approach of the Japanese to religion may also be a factor in producing this tendency to individualize problems and their solution. The characteristically Japanese subjective approach to religion results in a tendency to emphasize change in inner attitude only, with a corresponding neglect of changes which could reasonably be effected in the environment. "Instead of changing the environmental conditions, the religionist works for a changed attitude towards a continuing environment."[15]

The problems presented are concrete. The answers also usually contain some concrete specific suggestions. But when it comes to the heart of the problem, the answer characteristically switches to metaphysics. That is, *innen or inga kankei* (cause-effect relationship) is given as the final answer. When cause-effect relationships are interpreted concretely and rationally, proper solutions can be found, but cause-effect is interpreted in the context of karma, which includes causes lying in one's former existence, or in the deeds of one's deceased ancestors. Thus attention is distracted from the concrete circumstances of a problem and focused on a metaphysical doctrine. Although the individual might be dissatisfied with such an answer, he cannot criticize it because it is in the realm of speculative metaphysics with which he is not equipped to argue.[16]

Answers are given on the basis of traditional values more than on the basis of either theology or psychology as such. Solutions for problems are found entirely within the existing cultural order. Regardless of the content of the answers, since they are backed by the authority of President Niwano and the RK structure, the individual accepts them meekly and and gratefully. He takes whatever the leader says largely because of the authoritarian manner in which it is said. Thus it is rare to find really creative or new ideas appearing in the hoza answers. They tend rather to be a positive reaffirmation of the old ethic of traditional Japanese culture.[17]

Elements of Folk Belief

One of the most conspicuous and intriguing elements in the answers given to problems is what may collectively be called the role of folk beliefs. That is, the elements of divination and superstition, along with an emphasis on the efficacy of ancestor worship. It was mentioned above that the stated reason why onomancy and the horoscope are used is to have access to a quick and fairly sure method of knowing the individual questioner, so that an answer appropriate to that persons character can be given. As such, these constitute one type of *hōben* (means, expedient, or accommodation). The concept of *hōben* as the accommodation of method to meet people's actual ability to comprehend the truth is an acceted doctrine which is found in the Lotus Sutra. The parable of the burning house in which children are lured out of a burning house with a toy and thus saved is frequently referred to.[18] However, the magical element in this procedure is in itself a great attraction.

Relativism, syncretism and the incorporation of magical, shamanistic and superstitious elements are among the characteristics common to most of the new religions. Many make unashamed use of astrology and other types of divination as handmaidens to religion.[19] Oguchi says that "a mixture of shamanism and ancestor worship forms the basic character of the new religions."[20] President Niwano himself, in his pilgrimage of seeking for truth in his early days, sought salvation through various popular folk beliefs. Mrs. Naganuma, the co-foundress of RK, was a shamanic type of person herself. In keeping with its founders' experience, RK, especially in its early years, accommodated itself liberally to non-theological folk beliefs.[21]

There tends to be vague distinction between religion and magic in the minds of Oriental people, particularly among those not highly educated. Talcott Parsons points out that, from the functionalist point of view, magic may take the place of religion and serve as a functional equivalent to religion. Such magical belief is still surprisingly prevalent in Japan. Many Japanese even today find their religious satisfaction in a "queer combination of intellectualism and magic."[23] In the public statements made by RK, particularly those aimed at Westerners, magic is emphatically denounced.[23] However, our observation has revealed that on the actual level of hoza, leaders make no attempt to try to stop the interest in and use of magical thinking, but actually encourage it, deeming it a necessary *hōben.*

How can magic and superstition exist side by side with almost universal secondary education and widespread higher education in contemporary Japan? The penchant for holding together a multiplicity of heterogeneous, and often mutually contradictory, elements is one of the most intriguing aspects of the Japanese way of thinking.[24] The Japanese culture has never aimed to be a logically consistent system. A person who simultaneously holds various logically inconsistent "ism's" and beliefs "should be called typically Japanese, as long as he is not bothered by the inconsistency of ideas...In other words, the Japanese mind works intuitively rather than rationally," says Ariga in characterizing his people.[25]

Instruction

(*Findings*)

The second major category of material which comprises the content of hoza conversations is instruction in the doctrinal teachings of RK. Here we will make an effort to sift and classify the teaching material into a few major themes, or key ideas, which constitute the essence of RK teaching as actually presented by hoza leaders. Before turning to the doctrines themselves, a few general remarks are in order. The stated purpose of hoza is not to teach or indoctrinate, but rather to apply the teaching to people's everyday life problems. However, the fact is that a great deal of time during each hoza session is devoted to indoctrination. Typically, about the first half of a two-hour session is given over to organizational matters and instruction or to "preaching" in some form, while the second half is centered on members' questions. This proportion varies a great deal from session to session. Furthermore, the "counseling" almost invariably turns out to be an occasion for teaching. The advice given as the answer to an individual's problem is usually elaborated by the leader into an extended instructive discourse which touches the the whole range of RK doctrine. The method of teaching, which constitutes one of the keys to the effectiveness of hoza, was discussed in connection with the ability of leaders as teachers, namely, the case study method of teaching. A doctrinal point is made, and then illustrated by means of long, detailed cases which are given as proof of the truth of that doctrine. Thus it is impossible to delineate clearly between the three types of material which comprise the content of hoza, namely, the problem-solving, the teaching, and the testimonies. In most cases all three are woven into one conversation. Nevertheless, for the sake of analysis we are treating the three separately in the Findings, although the "Interpretation of Recurring Concepts" at the end of this chapter will deal with them as a whole.

THE DOCTRINE OF INTERDEPENDENCE

The doctrine of interdependence comes first because it is a key to the whole RK system for interpreting the sufferings and blessings of life and the road to self-improvement. There are different ways of expressing this concept, as indicated in the following excerpts.

> *L*: The difference between Christianity and Buddhism is that Christianity sees people as individuals, separate from one another, and created by a God who is also a separate being. Buddhism sees all things as part of the Great Whole, connected integrally by cause and effect. (8)

> All things are interrelated and interdependent. Think of your life in terms of a cross where the vertical line represents the interrelatedness of all the things existing in the world at the present moment, and the horizontal line represents the interrelatedness of all things throughout time—the past on the left side, and the future on the right side. (7)

> *L*: We live by the grace of others, for instance, by the efforts of the man who made your clothes, the one who spun the thread, the one who raised the sheep, etc. Even if you lived alone in the mountains, you would be dependent on plants for food and air for breath. (36)

The principle of interdependence has a direct application to the method of hoza organization:

> *L*: We have good rapport here in hoza, thanks to the truth that there is no independent existence. We are all basically interdependent upon each other, and our hoza circle is nothing other than the living out of this principle of interdependence. It is not even necessary to have introductions among us, for we all believe the same Law of the Buddha, which teaches us that we are all interrelated by birth. (38)

The concept of interdependence is focused in the formula, *in-en-ka-hō*, which is a dominant motif in all RK teaching. The formula can be defined thus: *in* means primary cause (cause in past time); *en* means present condition or circumstances (secondary, cause); *ka* means result, and *hō* means recompense (reward or retribution for the result). In hoza conversations the meaning of this basic concept is explained and and made operative in everyday life.

> *L*: In hoza we examine the primary cause, secondary cause, effect and recompense, good or bad, which we are actually experiencing in everyday life. Through such examination we trace the cause of our trouble and change our ways. The primary cause is like a seed which represents the causal connection between all our past up to the present moment. The secondary cause is the environment in which we live, which can be likened to the soil and wind and sun working on the seed, that is, the connection of all things working on our present situation. Effect is the fruit of the plant, the result of the interaction of primary and secondary causes. Recompense is the experience of reward or punishment which arises in connection with the effect. (9)

The *in-en-ka-hō* formula has practical value for the reshaping of everyday life.

> *L*: The practical, important thing is to be aware of this truth of cause and effect and to realize that our present troubles are caused by past mistakes, and that present mistakes will cause future trouble. In accordance with that knowledge it is our responsibility to repent of the past and resolve to do good in the future. Thus we will create good rewards for our future. To act this way is to know enlightenment. Unenlightened people don't know why they are suffering. They just say, "How awful! What shall I do!" without trying to find the cause for their trouble, so they don't know how to avoid similar trouble in the future. (8)

> *L*: We are concerned with looking to the future. We must take care now to be creating good causes which will in the future issue in good results for ourselves and for future generations. So it's the present which is important. We are piling up merits which will be justly recompensed in the future. So act rightly today! It is the knowledge of karma working in this way which makes life challenging. (29)

The significance of this approach to life's experiences is sharpened when it is compared, as it frequently is, to the Christian way.

> *Mrs. A*: You Christians teach, "Turn the other cheek," but we say, "Find out why he hit you," for that is the only way to solve the problem. (40)

THE DOCTRINE OF KARMA

Behind the *in-en-ka-hō* formula lies the basic Buddhist doctrine of karma, which recognizes the interdependence and continuity of succeeding generations, and also recognizes reincarnation of the same soul in more than one earthly existence. When these aspects of karma are brought into the discussion of "*in-en-ka-hō*," issues become blurred and unverifiable explanations are offered as reasons for a particular problem. Such explanations sometimes instill fear or distract attention from more immediate factors. A few examples will show this.

> *L*: I know of a boy who had polio. Acquaintances wondered why he should be stricken with this, so they investigated his background and found that his grandfather had been a terrible person. He had once taken a fish knife to kill his wife; he often fought with his wife, so that he was arrested and put in jail. This is an obvious case where karma of a former generation is being meted out to a later generation. We must learn from this to follow the eight-fold path of goodness so nothing like that will befall our children or grandchildren. (16)
>
> *L*: If you don't put forth your best efforts to do good works, you will surely reap punishment. The mercy of the Buddha is equal toward all, but the distinction as to whether we receive it or not is created on our part, by whether we do good or evil. Of course there is a difference in the reward of those who do good works diligently and those who don't. The fairness of the Buddha's mercy means that he recompenses each of us justly in accordance with our deeds.
>
> However, even if two people do their best all their life, there is sometimes inequality of reward. This is because of the karma working from their previous life. Previous life refers to your total past: what happened to you one minute ago, or what happened to your great grandfather. Although he has long been dead and you never

knew him at all, his soul might be living in you, and your present suffering might be because of his evil deeds. (29)

L: Your present trouble is caused by karma. After all, we all are simply the residence of some soul which has migrated perhaps many times into and out of this world. Consider your baby. Somebody's soul has simply borrowed your body to be born in this child. (30)

THE VALUE OF SUFFERING

RK teaches that suffering is a valuable part of human experience, because it is the occasion through which people are forced to reflect on and discover the moral dynamics of life. If a person repents of this evil, changes his ways and prays to his ancestors, he will be delivered from present trouble. Thus, suffering is the alarm clock which awakens the soul to its true nature and turns it toward a better life.

The frequently stated purpose of hoza is to help people find the cause of their suffering, and thus to be able to overcome it.

L: In hoza we find the cause of suffering. Usually the cause is not clear at first, and it takes some investigating. Take my case, for which I found the solution in hoza. I was cheated by a crafty salesman who came to the door offering me woolen material at a bargain price. I bought material from him, but it turned out to be some poor substitute for wool. In hoza I came to the realization that the primary cause for this misfortune was the selfish desire of my own covetous heart, and the secondary cause was the crafty salesman. The solution lay in repenting of my covetousness. (40)

Mrs. B: Unbelievers blame others for their misfortune, but we look inward and find the source of the trouble in our own heart, and then repent and nurture that heart in the right way. (23)

People are urged to recognize that suffering has a basically positive rather than negative function.

L: In former times none of us knew the truth of the universe, but now, thanks to President Niwano and his interpretation of suffering and the road to happiness, we know that suffering leads us to the right path. Therefore we should never feel resentful about suffering, but be joyful under all circumstances. (10)

L: The greater the trial, the higher we rise. Bad people show us our own ugliness, so we need them for our own growth. The essence of salvation is to be thankful for all circumstances and all people who cross our paths. (16)

ETHICAL TEACHINGS

The teaching discussed thus far lies in the realm of theological doctrine. But RK does not put primary emphasis on theology or doctrine as such. The thrust of the teaching is always aimed at concrete change of behavior. Practice of the virtues of gratitude, filial piety, unselfishness, and the like are the proof of salvation and the ultimate goal of RK's religious teaching. The prior importance of ethical behavior and actual practice as over against mere conceptual knowledge of religious doctrine is constantly emphasized.

L: Only RK is a truly practical religion, that is, it is only RK which applies religion to life. All other religions are simply intellectual doctrines to be understood in the head but not practiced in life. (40)

L: This morning President Niwano emphasized that it is not enough just to know the teaching of our religion intellectually, but that the important thing is to practice what we know. That is, we must actually do the will of the Buddha. (1)

Showing gratitude and honor to parents is the primary virtue. RK seeks to bring about a renewal and strengthening of this traditional ethical base and value system, called *oya kōkō* (filial piety).

L: You'll find that the people who cause trouble to society are the ones who do not have respect for their parents. We must be grateful to parents first of all, and then to everyone else. (36)

L: Disobedience to parents is the worst sin. We must overcome our strong-willed ego. We must listen meekly to what others tell us to do. You must appreciate the love of your mother, for nothing in the world is more sacred than that. (34)

L: In a word, RK is the teaching of filial piety, for the attitude of respect on the part of children for their parents, along with our Japanese family system, is the essence of all that is best in Japanese life. (7)

Working out from the base of the family, the RK member is exhorted to live in harmony on all levels of his social existence. The harmony which begins in the home must be carried out in the community, the nation, and the whole world. World peace is the ultimate goal, and is a motif currently being emphasized in RK public meetings. The harmonious cooperation among all religions is another area in which RK has exerted great effort in recent years, especially since the meeting of President Niwano and Pope Paul VI in 1963.

L: The idea of hoza is the spirit of harmony, i.e., mutually helping each other to live in harmony, beginning with family and neighborhood, and extending to nation and world. In all relationships we should not live for ourselves but for others. (2)

L: President Niwano has set forth two principles as a guide for our activities in RK for the coming year. They are: 1) Work for cooperation among all religions in order to establish world peace, and 2) win more members for RK. (1)

What is the path toward achieving harmony in society? It is to get rid of one's selfishness and live for others. This rule of individual ethics is constantly driven home in hoza teaching.

L: The source of evil is in our selfish heart. We must learn how to live with and for each other, and by the help of each other. No man is an island, but we are all particles in the great stream of the universe. (10)

Mr. E: We must try not to live just for our own self, but always be thinking of what is best for our neighbor. Most problems which I face as a legislator are problems of human relations, and I simply apply the RK principle of working for the good of others. (31)

Specifically, what stance should the individual take in order to live for others? The essence of the answer to this question is in the exhortation to be submissive toward others. Although this principle is applied especially to women in their relation toward their husbands, and to youth in relation to their parents, it is also advocated as a general ethical principle.

L: We must be thankful even for a mean husband, because if we learn to be submissive even to them, we have indeed perfected our character. Our spiritual task as wives is to learn to be meek before our husbands. (16)

L: Our religious discipline as wives is to learn to acquiesce to our husbands. When our husbands see that we are really more obedient and humble wives, they let us go to RK willingly. (23)

VENERATION OF ANCESTORS

RK affirms and gives fresh impetus to the traditional practice of ancestor veneration, a concept deeply rooted in Japanese religious feeling. Exhortations to be faithful in the act of ancestral veneration (*senzo kuyō*) run like a refrain through hoza discussions and teaching. The principle theological interpretation of ancestral veneration made in hoza is that this act gives recognition to one's dependence on all that has gone before as being the ground and grace of one's own existence. The appropriate attitude toward life is gratitude, and the starting place for expressing gratitude is toward one's forebearers, the source of life.

L: Mr. D, you should foster the feeling of gratitude to your ancestors. This is the basic thing in our religion. You will never understand what we are teaching here if you don't start from that point. We can't expect you to change all your Christian conceptions, but at least your must try to understand this most basic element, namely, the need for venerating your ancestors. (40)

L: Ancestral rites are for the purpose of bettering our own souls. It makes us realize our dependence on those who have gone before, and on all other persons and things of the universe. The basic principle of life is that no one lives to himself or by himself. (23)

But there is a second theme running through the emphasis on ancestral veneration, one which has even more emotional power. That is the idea of ancestral veneration as being an effectual act of comfort for or appeasement of the dead. Frequently there are emotional appeals made on the basis of the longing of a deceased parent or grandparent for the comfort of someone's prayers.

Mrs. F: My son died some years ago on the 23rd of the month. My husband had died several years prior to that on the 18th of the month. Is it all right to do the memorial service for both of them on the same day?

L: Yes, if you choose the earlier date. The earlier the better, for your son is waiting for that memorial service all the time, and it will make him happy to have it come early. You know that the memorial service is a great comfort to the deceased. (36)

(*Interpretation*)

In this section we gave an outline and illustrations of the central points of RK doctrine as it is popularized for laymen in hoza. It was observed that teachings which cluster around the concept of social and cosmological interdependence are fundamental. Teachings centering around a positive interpretation of suffering, teaching oriented toward practical, ethical admonition, and exhortations regarding the significance and necessity of ancestral veneration are all prominent in hoza instruction. These motifs deserve a degree of interpretation, and will be dealt with later. Here only some comments on the significance and nature of the element of instruction as such, and not the content of the instruction will be made.

The teaching function of hoza stands in sharp contrast to the lack of understandable, appealing teaching in the Buddhist temples of Japan today, where, generally speaking, virtually no attention is given to the responsibility to educate the laity in the content and meaning of Buddhist faith. So-called "established Buddhism" (*kisei Bukkyō*) offers the public little more than ceremonial rites, particularly at the time of funerals and memorial services for deceased ancestors.

The positive doctrinal instruction given in hoza also stands in sharp contrast to the general attitude of indifference toward particular claims to truth. Cultural anthropologists generally agree that the Japanese mind inclines toward reconciliation of opposites rather than toward polarization, and this perspective on truth produces a broad tolerance in matters of religion. The Zen authority Suzuki says that as a mother embraces all her children with unconditional love and never discriminates among them or calls some good and others bad, so man should embrace all things, not judging some good and others bad, but leaving all things as they are. It is natural and right to accept all things as they are, rather than to try to reconcile what seems to be in opposition.[26] Truth or falsehood is not the primary issue in religion. Truth and falsehood are subjective and therefore relative. The common approach to religion is expressed in the Japanese proverb: "The many paths of Mt. Fuji all lead to the summit," which implies that the various religious roads all appear to be different, but all are the same in essence.

In contrast to this general indifference toward religious truth, RK holds a clear position and proclaims a straightforward message. Its official claim is to endeavor to save all mankind through enlightenment to the Four Noble Truths, and it carries on this saving work by propagating its teachings through publications, mass meetings, personal evangelism and hoza. In a society where ethical and social structures have disintegrated and the masses are without spiritual leadership, such positive, aggressive teaching meets with ready response from many quarters.

The new religions characteristically streamline both the institutions and the dogma of the established religions, and simplicity of doctrine is one of their appealing points. RK has skillfully concentrated and simplified the opaque philosophies of Buddhism into a few lucid charts in which the entire teaching is summarized around a few slogans and symbols. Chief among these are Four Noble Truths (*shitai*), the Ten Suchnesses (*jū-nyoze*), the Eightfold Path (*hasshōdō*), the Six Perfections (*rokuharamitsu*), all of which are tenets of classical Buddhism, but which are explained in brief, clear language. Further, the most essential truths are summarized in the formula of the Three Cardinal Signs (*sanbōin*), and the way of salvation is condensed into the mono-syllabic formula of *in-en-ka-hō* (cause-conditions-result-reward). A brief creed, giving the essence of the entire thought and purpose of RK, is recited in unison by the congregation as part of the daily cultus.

Testimonies

(*Findings*)

The third major topic which describes the content of hoza discussions is testimonies, that is, the relating of personal religious experiences of how allegiance to RK has effected changes in the individual's life. The testimonies are an integral part of problem-solving. Counseling and teaching are directed toward individuals who come to hoza seeking help. But these people are also expected to return to hoza and report on what happened when they acted on the advice given them. They frequently do this, and such reporting is in the form of what we may call a testimony of religious experience. In most cases the testimonies state the same thing that was stated in the teaching, the only difference being in the grammatical mood of the sentence and the person of the pronoun. That is to say, whereas in the teaching section the material is in the form of

"You must..." and "Let us..." now the same material comes in the indicative form of "I did..."

THE NATURE OF THE RELIGIOUS EXPERIENCES

It might be supposed that this religious experience would be thought of in the traditional Buddhist terms of enlightenment (*satori*). However, this expression is seldom heard. The change in heart is rather seen simply as understanding the message of the RK teachers or hoza leaders. The awakening to truth in the tradition of RK is a more rational and practical thing than is the experience of *satori* in classical Buddhism. There are relatively few instances where basic, thorough-going awakening to the truth of the Law (*hō*) plays any important part in the testimony. Testimonies center on the more obvious phenomenon of a happy feeling, the recovery from an illness, etc.

The basic reason for religious change is usually the realization that the individual has caused his suffering by his own evil deeds and therefore should not blame others but take his suffering as an occasion for repentance. This is the realization of karma in terms of *in-en-ka-hō*, although members do not usually use these terms of theological interpretation. The following is typical.

> *L*: My daughter, at the age of 13, had a fatal heart disease. How I lamented this! But then I came to realize that this sorrow put upon me was due to the fact that I had grieved my parents when I was young. In other words, it was a case of the cause-effect rule of karma coming around full circle. I repented of my past, and immediately my daughter got well; doctors thought a miracle had happened. (7)

The elimination of resentful attitudes and the adopting of a spirit of gratitude is the fundamental change which occurs in the individual's life, simultaneous to his being saved by the realization of karma.

> *L*: I used to be resentful because I was mistreated by my mother-in-law. She treated me like a floor mop! This continued for almost twenty years of our married life until a few months ago when I had an operation for cancer and had a breast removed. Only through that experience did I learn not to be resentful, but rather to be grateful. Now I see it was not the people around me who were at fault, but my misery was my own fault, because I did not have the

spirit of gratitude. (25)

> *Mrs. C*: My son used to be in poor health, and this caused me so much trouble that I felt very bitter about the whole situation. Finally I myself fell sick. I couldn't sleep at all. I tried all kinds of treatments for a period of some six years. I had acupuncture treatment and chiropractic treatment and all kinds of treatments, but I still couldn't sleep a wink at night. Then my RK friends told me that my trouble was because of my inner attitude, my bitterness. So I confessed this, and then for the first time I could sleep again. My health used to be in such a bad way, but now I'm a changed person, both physically and spiritually. (32)

This adopting a spirit of gratitude for all things, even for adverse circumstances, appears to be the chief element in the experience of a changed life.

Along with the change in attitude comes change in behavior. RK stands for the practical application of the Buddhist Law to everyday life. Most of the testimonies tell of a change from stubbornness (*ga no tsuyoi koto*) and selfishness (*wagamama*) toward tolerance and submissiveness (*sagaru kokoro*) in personal relations. The following is typical:

> *Mrs. A*: I used to be such a stubborn person that I wouldn't give in to anyone; that had always been my nature. But at the retreat I learned the meaning of compassion for the first time. I wept one night until 2 a.m. Then I did the ancestral rites. I confessed that I had been harsh and self-centered and that I had not treated my parents properly.
>
> *L*: When I went to a retreat at Ome I had an experience like yours. I went to my area leader who was there, and she helped me to confess my past life and pray for the Buddha's help. Then I went to Mr. Y, whose mother is a Soka Gakkai member, to try to win him over to a stronger faith in RK. After some talking he made three promises: to be more loving and obedient to his parents, to exercise more patience, and to put flowers and rice on the altar in his home regularly to venerate his dead elder brother. So you see he's on the right track. (35)

As observed in the above excerpt, this change from stubbornness to submissiveness is not an abstract thing, but is linked to either or both of the following family relationships: conduct of children toward their parents, and conduct of wives toward their husbands.

Mr. C: I used to ridicule my mother, who was a very faithful member of RK. I never appreciated her or thanked her for what she did. Then last year she died. I didn't even mourn at her funeral. But recently I went to the youth retreat at the Ome Training Hall, and there I was made to see the folly of my past. I prayed for forgiveness for my sinful ways, and I wept so much. Now I feel so grateful for my mother, and even though she is now dead I am giving thanks to her. My life was changed completely by attending the retreat. (24)

Mrs. B: I feel very happy today; I want to share with you some recent events of my life. Last year I went to the Ome youth retreat and my life was completely changed. I became a true believer, and I repented of all my evil ways in the past. When I was in the hospital my husband told me that then, for the first time, I showed my true humanness. Then I realized that I had been cold and self-willed, so I apologized to him, and now I'm trying my best to be an understanding, sympathetic wife. (22)

There is an integral continuity between the ethical changes dealt with above, particularly the strengthening of filial piety, and the rites of ancestral veneration, for there is an ambiguous line of demarcation between one's relationship with the living and one's relationship with the dead. Thus the typical testimony includes in the same breath the change from indifference toward living parents to gratitude toward them, and the change from neglect of ancestral veneration to faithfulness in performing this rite of devotion.

Mr. A: Once when I returned from the races my son was very sick. The doctor pronounced it to be spinal paralysis. That very day was the anniversary date of the death of two of my ancestors. So I did the ancestral rites with fervor, but my son still remained very sick. Finally I realized that I had failed to repent of one serious fault in my family relations, namely, I had not apologized toward my father whom I had always disliked so much. So I did my act of penitence before the altar for my deceased father, under the gracious guidance of my local RK head. Then we later went together to the hospital to see my boy, and his fever had suddenly dropped. Now he's a healthy boy again. (29)

Mr. A: When I was three years old I got this severe burn on my back which left me hunch-backed. I had a resentful attitude toward this accident and toward my malformation for a long time. My mother died at the age of 48, and I grieved over her death so much, wondering why she had to die so young. Her early death made me very bitter. But recently my eyes have been opened to see that it was my own bad attitude toward the burn which caused her so much grief that she died at an early age. So now I am repenting of this past evil by doing the religious disciplines of RK, and by giving 100,000 yen as an offering to RK. This offering is for the purpose of comforting the spirit of my dead mother. (12)

There are frequent accounts of physical healing in hoza discussions. They are among the most dramatic and appealing elements of hoza conversation. However, there are actually only a very few hoza participants who give a testimony of their own experience of healing. Rather, the testimonies are usually given by the same person who repeats his narrative over and over again for the sake of listeners who have not yet heard it. Also, there are many recitals of healing which are not personal testimonies, but second-hand stories told about the healing experienced by others. Although there are exceptions, the accounts relating to physical illness and health characteristically report a changed mental attitude which enables the person to endure the ailment, rather than an actual change in physical condition. In every case it was a change in ethico-religious attitudes which influenced physical health.

Mrs. A: I had a terrible, excruciating pain in my hips recently. I thought it must be because I am getting old. But then I began being more devout in doing the ancestral rites—for I had become quite negligent—and suddenly the pain stopped.

L: Isn't that marvelous! I also have a friend who had a similar problem. She had a child who was very stubborn and wouldn't listen to its parents at all. They wondered why he should be that way. Then the mother realized that she had been that way when she was young, that is, she was very self-willed. So she repented of her past, and the pain which she had had in her hip went away. (22)

L: I had a bad case of hemerrhoids, but my condition has completely cleared up. I learned that sickness is a matter of the mind, and when I learned to think differently about myself and my health, my physical condition inproved. (27)

THE CONTEXT OF THE TESTIMONIES

A few observations need to be made regarding the giving of testimonies. One is that a testimony is thought to be a reflection from the life of one person of a universal phenomena which all people experience.

> *L*: Please speak up, everyone! It's helpful to yourself and to others to talk about your experience of enlightenment and repentance, because the only way people come to know themselves is by hearing the testimony of someone else. (22)

Thus there is no essential distinction made between one's own personal experience and the experience of others. Many testimonies are second or third hand, and do not serve the purpose of sharing personal experience. Hoza members, especially leaders, draw freely on the experience of others in relating testimonies.

Another observation is that the function of many if not most testimonies in hoza seems rather to be the recital of dramatic experience—either one's own, or someone else's experience—primarily for a didactic or persuasive purpose, rather than simply to give expression to a meaningful experience. It is obvious that nearly all of the testimonies have been repeated a number of times, some of them many, many times. The leader will frequently call on someone in the circle, asking that person to give his testimony (the content of which the leader obviously knows) for the sake of a certain person who is present for the first time that day. Most of such testimonies are narratives which relate how some evil befell the individual because he was not living right, and how happiness and other benefits resulted from a change of heart.

> *Mr. A*: My neighbor has bad stomach trouble, which shows he is disrespectful toward his parents. He was asked to have hoza in his home, but didn't want to have it, even though he is a member of RK. But the day he refused to have the hoza, he collapsed while he was at the public bath. So he decided to have the hoza meet at his home after all. After that he and also his brother both changed. Now they understand that you shouldn't feel resentful about hardships, but should see both good and bad as the will of the Buddha and give thanks for both. This is the goal of RK teaching. Let's all learn to think this way! (26)

(*Interpretation*)

A great number of the testimonies appear to be not spontaneous expressions of a personal religious experience, but rather borrowed stories of experiences which prove that RK belief results in the experience of happiness and concrete blessing, while disbelief results in suffering. It must therefore be concluded that the testimonies in hoza function largely as a means of instruction and persuasion rather than as a means of sharing inner feeling. This fact is not denied by leaders. Earlier it was pointed out that instruction is presented by means of narrative illustration rather than in propositional form. The testimonies are this narrative illustration; one person tells another about his own experiences and through this the other can analyze his own anxieties. The giving of testimonies thus functions as a persuasive means to teach and convince listeners that their life will be changed for the better if they become RK members.

The fact that the content of the testimonies parallels the content of the teaching as exactly as it does indicates a significant aspect of Japanese educational method. Typically, the Japanese teaching-learning situation is one in which the teacher repeats his material in the same form over and over again, and the pupil absorbs and memorizes this material in rote fashion, finally returning it to the teacher with a minimum of innovation or variation. This pattern is enacted in the interplay between instruction and testimonies of hoza.

Institutional Maintenance

(*Findings*)

A considerable amount of time during each session of hoza is devoted to problems of what can be termed institutional maintenance. Presenting these problems at length would mean probing into the organizational aspects of RK, which it is not our purpose to do. It will merely be observed that matters of supporting and promoting the RK organization as such do constitute a considerable portion of hoza conversations, as much as one-fourth or one-third of the morning session in many cases. The following excerpts are typical.

Mrs. D: I've had so much trouble in distributing the RK newspaper lately, and also the *Kōsei* magazine. I was supposed to give copies to X and Y and Z, but I wasn't given enough copies to go around. (Long talk about difficulties of distributing literature in the neighborhood followed.) (37)

Mrs. E: I've been expecting someone to speak up today about what we should do about following our area leader's suggestion that we should have two local meetings a month instead of one, as we've had in the past. I think we should meet twice a month so we have more time to discuss how we are progressing in our promotional work.

L: That sounds like a good idea. (This matter was discussed at length.) (37)

(*Interpretation*)

The above type of conversation suggests the possibility that hoza might not be needed to the extent to which it is were it not for the elaborate structure of the organization itself, which takes so much energy and activity to maintain. At its worst extreme, this means that people come to hoza to discuss their problems, but these problems are not concerned with life in and work for society, but are concerned with maintaining the institution itself. But from the point of view of RK as a religious institution, one of the values of hoza is that it provides an excellent occasion for fostering the organization.

(*Interpretation of Recurring Conɔepts*)

It has been indicated that the motifs which constitute the doctrinal content of all three of the main categories of this chapter—namely, the categories of problem-solving, instruction and testimonies—were to be dealt with in a separate section. We come to this point now, and offer some comment on the six items of belief which appeared over and over again throughout hoza conversations. These are: (1) the value of suffering, (2) the doctrine of interdependence, (3) the karma concept, (4) ethical teaching, particularly the "ethics of submission," (5) the exhortation to veneration of ancestors, and (6) physical healing.

THE VALUE OF SUFFERING

The stated motivation for people coming to hoza is that they are experiencing some problem or suffering from which they want to find relief. Helping people to become aware of the cause of their suffering, and to discover how to eliminate that cause and find happiness is the purpose of hoza. Leaders place heavy emphasis on the positive side of suffering, urging people always to be thankful for their sufferings, for this is the thing that opens the door for self-reflection and hence for a change of heart and a life of happiness. This emphasis, "Be thankful for sufferings!" is one of the characteristic refrains of hoza teaching and problem-solving. The affinity of this teaching with Japanese religiosity, which places an almost exclusive emphasis on subjective experience rather than on intellectual or ethical aspects, should be noted. That is, what counts is the individual's inner attitude toward his suffering rather than an objective eradication of the conditions of suffering.

One of the latent functions of this exhortation to be grateful for suffering is that it promotes a conservative philosophy of social adjustment rather than an aggressive desire for social change. Yinger posits three modes of relationship between religious change and social change: "Religious change as a result of social change; religion as a barrier to change; religion as an initiator of changes."[27] In this scheme, it would appear that RK functions strongly, but not exclusively, in the second category, namely, as a barrier to change. Yinger states that religious expression among the sects of the lower classes is inclined "to redefine the meaning of their economic status" by making poverty a virtue.[28] This may be one of the factors operative in hoza conversations. At the same time, however, strong hope for economic and social improvement for those who hold the faith is also a dominant characteristic of all the new religions, and puts RK also in the category of "religion as an initiator of change." The promise of concrete benefit was given first place in the list of characteristics of the new religions, many of which are criticized for exploiting the human longing for happiness and prosperity by promising such benefits on the sole condition of joining the organization. The promise of present material benefits rather than a future eschatological reward is a feature of the new religions of Japan which distinguishes them from many sectarian groups in America, and thus invalidates many of the analyses of the American sociologists of religion.[29]

THE DOCTRINE OF INTERDEPENDENCE

In hoza conversations there is frequent reference to the idea that one's own problem is everybody's problem, that the spiritual dynamics of a certain individual whose life problem is being considered by the group are the same as the spiritual dynamics operative universally in everyone's life. There is no such thing as a problem unique to one person only. This, in fact, is the rationale for hoza, where people are supposed to come to discover their own nature and the way of salvation by hearing other people's problems revealed and solved.

Giving a negative evaluation of this, Saki says that this is simply a way of strengthening an awareness of kinship and "togetherness" (*nakama-ishiki*), because it makes everyone see that he is no worse than anyone else; all are fallible and have "skeletons in their closets".[30] In the strong "we-conscious" society of Japan, identification with others comes easily.

However, the idea of the ontological unity and the interdependence of all things in the universe is a central theological tenet of RK. The *in-en-ka-hō* formula is a simplified version of the Buddhist *in-ga* and *innen* (cause-effect) concepts. RK theologian Obayashi states that the idea of interdependence is the basic doctrine of RK. It means that no man is an island unto himself, but that everything and everyone in the universe exists in inter-relationship, an inter-relationship throughout time so that we stand in relation to our most distant forebearers, and an inter-relationship throughout space so that all things existing at the present moment are related to all other things existing in the present.

There is mutual affinity and reinforcement between this doctrine and the primary Japanese cultural characteristic of placing ultimate value on the human collectivity. It was pointed out earlier that for Japanese, groups and group-belonging are ultimate realities. This is the thrust of Nakane's theory of "frame" as the constituting factor of Japanese society.[31] This group orientation which stresses mutual dependence and social solidarity finds a metaphysical rationale in the doctrine of *shohō muga* (non-existence of the ego) which teaches that there is no independent individual existence. The system of social obligations expressed in traditional ethics through the concepts of *on* and *giri* (favors bearing obligations) can be regarded in a mutually interacting relationship to this theological emphasis on interdependence. It is, therefore, quite plain that a strong "elective affinity", to use Weber's term, exists between social custom and religious dogma in the area under observation. It can be said that this religious teaching of interdependence gives emotional support to the fundamental values of society.[32]

The concept of ancestral veneration also illustrates this mutual reinforcement between religion and culture. In the ancestral rites the borderline of one's dependencies is seen to extend beyond the living members of the family and include the deceased ancestors. In the home there is continuous reference to the former generations to whom one is indebted for the existence of the household. The dead never cease to be members of the family. There is one eternally continuous spiritual community. "Through ancestor worship the membership of the *ie* is enhanced to such an extent that true membership is never lost; it transcends death and lasts forever."[33]

THE DOCTRINE OF KARMA

The idea of karma (*gō*), as familiar to hoza participants as it is unfamiliar to the Westerner, runs as a refrain through hoza problem-solving and teaching. Thoroughly to interpret this concept would require a treatise on the original concept as it arose in India, as it was developed in Buddhism, and as it is popularly understood today. Here will be stated simply the standard definition of karma and some interpretations by contemporary Buddhist leaders, including an RK theologian. Karma is a Sanscrit word meaning "deed" or "action." In modern use it is the doctrine that every deed, good or bad, receives due retribution.

> The supreme power which is actually operating in the world is the 'law of the deed'—an inescapable, inexorable, impersonal principle of justice and moral retribution. 'Not in the sky, not in the midst of the sea, not if we enter into the clefts of the mountains, is there known a spot where a man might be freed from an evil deed.' (Dhamma-pada)[34]

Since this reward and retribution is not always obvious as one examines actual existence, the doctrine has been combined with the doctrine of transmigration, which thus "makes it possible to explain any apparently undeserved pleasure or pain by the fact that karma causing them was performed in a previous existence." This Hindu thought found its way into Japanese Buddhism from ancient times, and is expressed frequently in hoza, where the "testimonies" are a prime example of the statement that "in all sects karma remains a powerful ethical argument, used especially in the tales invented to illustrate its effects."[35]

There are two kinds of karma, past karma (*shukugō*) and present karma (*gengō*), and in accordance with this, the idea is put to either negative or positive use. That is, looking backwards over the past we realize we are the result of the past, either of our own conscious past or of a previous existence. This tends to produce a fatalistic outlook. The positive interpretation of karma is to look forward toward the future knowing that we are creating our own karma for the future by the deeds we are doing in the present. Therefore we can break the chain of evil effects and insure happy rewards for the future by doing good deeds in the present. The basic point of karma is that moral energy and actions never disappear. Just as physical energy never disappears from the universe, so spiritual and moral energy never disappear, but will surely produce a reward or retribution (effect) appropriate to the deed (cause).

Contemporary Buddhist theologians tend to put the emphasis on the future, claiming this to be the original meaning given it by Sakyamuni Buddha, whereas the emphasis on *shukugō* (karma accumulated from past evil actions) is a mistaken, popular notion. The karma concept is not fatalism, but is simply "that one's future is determined only by one's self," as opposed to the idea that one is controlled by a power other than or above himself. One contemporary Buddhist theologian says the karma concept in Buddhism is superior to the Christian idea that everything is attributed to God's will, because "karma admits the possibility of improving human life by means of the human will or effort."[36] Although the future karma concept is taught by hoza leaders, the dramatic moments of hoza are when problems are interpreted and "solved" on the basis of past karma, that is, the discovery of some long forgotten evil deed or of some long forgotten evil ancestor. This approach tends to remove the solutions of hoza from the realm of practical workable answers into a metaphysical, intangible world.

ETHICAL TEACHINGS

In the Findings pertaining to both instruction and testimonies a strong ethical emphasis was discovered. Exhortations to practice the faith are a continual refrain. This practice mainly takes the form of being grateful, humble, submissive and peace-loving. The emphasis on obedience of children toward parents and of wives toward husbands was especially prominent. The typical sermons of President Niwano are surprisingly simple and practical: the most important thing for a good RK member to do is to help his neighbor in any way he needs it. Anyone can understand the Eight-fold Path in a few hours of study, but it takes a a lifetime to put it into practice, he says, and urges everyone to start practicing his faith immediately by doing such little things as picking up paper on the sidewalk to make his neighborhood a more pleasant place.

This ethical emphasis presents a sharp contrast to traditional Japanese thinking, which fails to see and grapple with the conflict between good and evil. The traditional view, growing out of an all-embracing naturalism and a trust in subjectivity, cuts the ground out from under the philosophy of two powers, the "flesh" and the "spirit", which are struggling for supremacy in human life, which is a world-view that lies at the center of Western thought. Sansom says that "throughout their history the Japanese seem to have retained in some measure this incapacity to discern, or this reluctance to grapple with, the problem of evil."[37] To the Japanese, human nature is naturally good and to be trusted. It does not need to struggle with "original sin." It needs only to cleanse the windows of its soul and act with appropriateness on every occasion.[38] Shinto, which colors the basic ethical attitudes of Japanese, is ethically amorphous and neutral, taking a naturalistic approach to morality. Even Nichiren Buddhism can be considered as "essentially amoral," for "the enlightenment experience involves realizing there is no real difference between good and evil."[39] Established Buddhism, taken as a whole, is virtually irrelevant to great ethical questions of the modern world, but the new religions seek to awaken their "ethically amorphous" contemporary generation to its ethical responsibilities. RK seeks to make vital and practical a religious tradition which has grown stagnant and irrelevant.

What is the content of this new ethical emphasis? As indicated in the Findings, the ethical principle proves to be not really new, but a reaffirmation of the traditional "ethic of submission"—obedience of children to parents, wife to husband, and follower to leader. Hoza leaders and RK theologians alike defend this ethic of submission, saying that taking the humble posture (*sunao na kokoro*) is the way to make true progress, for only by humbly and submissively listening to the other can one learn and thus progress. To fail to do this is to fall into the rut of self-centered stubbornness. Furthermore, this "low posture" is the only way to preserve the supreme virtue of harmony (*chōwa*)—in the home, the group and community.

Although the posture of authoritarianism on the one hand and submission on the other is in the process of change today, it is still dominant in Japanese society as a whole, as evidenced by recent studies which show that the spirit of obligation is still very much alive. A statistical study was made of the attitudes of youth toward the *bushidō* concepts studied by Ruth Benedict a decade earlier.[40] Even among contemporary youth, the sense of personal dependence was marked. When the youth were asked about their understanding of *giri* (obligations), two-thirds gave the traditional answers and one-third were unable to give adequate answers. This testing regarding *giri* "may perhaps indicate the beginning of a change in the personality structure of the Japanese," the author cautiously states.[41] Again, in the case of the husband-wife relationship, although there is lip service paid to the egalitarian principle regarding women's rights set up after World War II, both men and women still, in practice, accept the subordinate positions and inequalities which continue to exist.

The affinity between these patterns of relationships in Japanese culture and the pattern of relationships advocated as the religious ideal in hoza is obvious. That is, it would be justifiable to conclude that RK is playing the role in contemporary Japan that religion has always played in Japan, namely, the role of reinforcing the "commitment to the central value system by making that value system meaningful in an ultimate sense."[42] The Japanese value system has been characterized by primary respect for and loyalty to both family and nation. Religion in Japan has tended to accept this structure of Japanese society and its values as being in accordance with the nature of reality. The truly religious person is the person who wholeheartedly carries out his part in that society.[43]

This ethical role of hoza does tend to give stability, unity and solidarity to a society which would otherwise be on the point of social and moral disintegration. The family system, the social and national structure and the traditional religions, all of which formerly provided a stable framework in which life was meaningful, have been attacked from all sides during recent decades and are in a state of collapse or radical metamorphosis. Industrialization, democracy, and the Western notions of freedom, along with the philosophy and methodology of science, work to undercut the old foundations. Individuals are left standing alone without spiritual or social security. Hoza has much to offer these people. On the other hand, this extreme conservatism in ethical teaching does not provide the new and creative guidance so desperately needed by a nation in its infancy of democracy. "I make the assumption that a new and fundamental ethic is required for the new era in which Japan finds herself," says a prominent educator.[44] There is need for genuine spiritual renewal, but "just as Japan has never experienced a thoroughgoing religious reformation in the past, neither do the new religions promise a reformation," says McFarland. Must RK also be put in the category of the new religions which have offered a "sanctuary and a palliative, largely revisionary in character, which imparted a measure of hope to many among the frustrated masses, but offered nothing to the nation as a whole"?[45]

VENERATION OF ANCESTORS

Throughout hoza conversations, exhortations to be more faithful in the rites of ancestor veneration (*senzo kuyō*), or to hurry and get the ancestral tablets (*kaimyō*) written are heard as a constant refrain. The necessity for devout ancestor veneration is woven integrally into the conversations on various religious and ethical issues. Yet ancestor veneration is not a doctrinal teaching at all. Mention of this notion is not to be found in the Lotus Sutra, the source of RK belief. Ancestor veneration is not essentially a Buddhist rite or belief, but is "folk religion," yet a folk religion which is completely integrated into Buddhism, Shinto and Confuncian religious traditions. Bellah sees ancestor veneration as an example of the lack of differentiation, or only partial differentiation of religious and secular functions in Japanese social life.[46]

The many different meanings and functions of ancestor worship were noted in Chapter I. The most prominent meaning, which is revealed in hoza and other conversations with RK members, is the meaning of gratitude for all that has given one his life. Venerating the ancestors proves that the worshiper "is not forgetful of the ties that bind him with his ancestors, that he is conscious of his indebtedness to them and attentive to and appreciative of what they have done for him.[47] The head of the RK bureau for writing ancestral tablets (*Eijuden*) once told the writer: "Buddhists don't have to be taught about ancestor worship; we all know that this is the basis of our religious life. Ancestors are the 'other side' (*rimen*), the origin of our life; so ancestor worship is the 'other side' of our religious life."

Hotoke is the word given to both the spirits of deceased ancestors, and to the divine Buddha. This is extremely significant, and can be understood in the light of both the Buddhist doctrine of the universality of the Buddha spirit (*busshin*) and the Shinto identification of the divine (*kami*) and the human. To be grateful for all who have shared in giving one his life, especially toward parents and parents' parents is a deep-seated feeling of obligation in the Japanese. Paying the debt of gratitude toward parents is the ultimate moral responsibility of a Japanese, and veneration of ancestors gives a sacred and eternal aura to this feeling for the ultimate value of the family.

The other aspect of ancestor veneration which deserves special attention because it plays an important role in hoza is the concept of the threatening nature of the spirits of the deceased when they have not been duly honored by the rites. When the cause of an individual's suffering cannot be found in traceable conditions, it must be found in the vague metaphysical sphere of past karma, which is linked ambiguously with neglect of ancestral veneration. There is a general feeling that the ancestral spirits are miserable or malignant and need the comforting and placating which come through the faithful performance of rites on the anniversary date of the death of the deceased. There is a feeling that such performance serves simultaneously to guarantee security to the spirits of the dead and give protection to the one performing the rite.

PHYSICAL HEALING

A few comments can be made regarding the many allusions to physical healing made in hoza conversations. Many of the ailments talked about are of a psychosomatic nature. Offner calls attention to the word *byōki* (sickness) itself, which in Japanese is composed of the two characters meaning "sick" (病) and "mind" or "attitude" (気). A popular Japanese proverb states that "Sickness comes from the mind" (*byō wa ki kara*). It is natural for Japanese to think in terms of the psychological dimensions of illness. This often means that the "miracle of healing" is that "miracle" which transforms the body at the same time that the spirit is transformed by the adopting of new attitudes of hope and self-confidence. Membership in hoza provides for sympathetic concern, personal confession, congenial fellowship, purposeful activity, etc. This kind of "achievement of spiritual, mental, emotional, and volitional stabilization and amelioration is an undeniable help in bringing about a physical improvement.[48] Officially RK does not promote "faith-healing" apart from medicine. It maintains its own hospital, and the standard exhortation is both to see a doctor and to be diligent in religious exercises, for faith promotes healing.

At the same time, many questionable and bizarre interpretations of physical symptoms and magical "healings" also appeared frequently in hoza conversations. There were frequent references to various esoteric "psychosomatic formulae." An understanding of some common "folk perspectives" on healing will help interpret these peculiar ways of thinking. First is the idea of karma which holds that for every suffering there is a cause which lies either in one's own past behavior or in one's inheritance from forebearers. The second notion sees suffering as a warning from a deity or ancestor that the afflicted person is remiss in the performance of his ancestral rites. A third idea is that a person accumulates pollution or impurities that cause misfortune unless the person is purified, as in the Shinto purification rites which are performed when a pilgrimage to a shrine is made. A fourth view is that physical circumstances are a reflection of one's inner mental and spiritual attutudes. Suffering is a kind of mental projection, an idea which echoes the Buddhist teaching that the phenomenal world is unreal.[49] All of these perspectives are helpful in making sense of the way in which leaders handle problems concerning physical ailments. They underscore again the extent to which "folk ideas," in contrast to purely theological concepts, dominate the content of hoza discussions.

*

At this point the Western observer feels compelled to ask, perhaps with no little astonishment, "How is it possible that some of these concepts which comprise the content of hoza conversations can be viable for the citizens of this educated, secularized, scientifically minded nation of Japan? This anomaly cannot be explained apart from recognizing some peculiar characteristics of the Japanese way of thinking. In contrast to Western thought patterns which are characterized by a primary concern for rationality, logical analysis and reasoned conclusions, Japanese thought patterns may be described as experiential and undifferentiated. The Japanese assign priority to a living, feeling experience rather than to reasoning and logic. Kato, a native observer of the Japanese mentality, says "The Japanese attitude is phenomenological, and as such is indefinite. Phenomena are accepted as wholes, without analysis or definition."[50] Intuitiveness is a conspicuous characteristic of Japanese religion. Immediacy and direct perception take priority over deductive reasoning. Nitobe considers the faculty of perception to be a chief trait of Oriental mentality, perception meaning an immediate awareness and sensation, the immediate cognition of an object. It is the unproved foundation of proofs.[51] The enlightenment (*satori*) of Zen Buddhism exemplifies this kind of understanding, for it is a mysticism realized through the direct insight which is characterized by irrationality, intuitive understanding, and an authoritative sense of the Beyond.

During a visit to Japan, Paul Tillich asked Buddhist leaders about the necessity for bridging the vast gap between Buddhist theology and "popular piety" in Japan, to which the reply was made that "Buddhism is not a system of doctrines but is primarily an experience," with the implication that content of belief is unimportant; only a "Buddhistic experience" is important.[52] The famous Japanese Christian author, Inazo Nitobe, once defined religion in these words:

> To commune with a god, invisible to eyes of flesh, is the faith of the heart of man. Not a mental discovery of the existence of the divine but the feeling of His presence...The faith of the Japanese is not an intellectual assent...The Japanese conception of religion is clear in experience, but vague in theory. It begins in instinct, gains volume by sentiment, and grows in strength by emotion.[53]

Understood in this context, many hoza conversations which leave the Western observer perplexed become intelligible.

SECTION III

CONCLUSIONS AND COMPARISONS

THUS far this study of hoza has intended to confine itself insofar as possible to an objective presentation of Findings based on observation of hoza sessions, and of Interpretations of those Findings based on contributions from various disciplines. Although the study could be terminated at this point, we could not feel satisfied to leave the work here. The original motivation for this study of the hoza of RK sprang from a concern about the slow growth of the Christian church in Japan. It is now time to return to that concern and ask what insights have been produced by our contact with hoza which might have special significance for those who view Japanese religion and culture from a Christian perspective, and especially for those who are concerned about Christian proclamation in Japan today. Thoughtful Christian readers will already have discovered many areas for reflection and self-examination and areas of challenge. Now it is time to lift out of the study some significant issues, evaluating them and comparing them with Christian concepts and practice.

CHAPTER NINE

CONCLUSIONS, EVALUATIONS AND COMPARISONS WITH CHRISTIAN PATTERNS

The present chapter presents ten major issues which grew out of the research. The topic of each issue will be stated in a heading followed by a brief paragraph, printed in italics, which presents the conclusion regarding the RK position or practice in this matter, as discovered from the Findings. This is followed in each case by an evaluative discussion of this position. Each issue is then further discussed by comparing concepts and practices of the Christian church in Japan with those of hoza. It is the writer's intention to pin-point the problem areas of the church in a way that will, without being exhortative, indicate directions for the future.

RELIGIOUS INDIGENEITY

Both the form and content of hoza were conceived and developed by Japanese to meet the needs and interests of Japanese. Every aspect of this activity, from the physical arrangement of squatting on the floor, to the appeal to be devout in ancestor veneration, is rooted in indigenous concepts and practices.

If indigeneity is regarded as an important value for a religious movement, then hoza must be highly evaluated on this point, for both hoza and the sponsoring body, RK, are indigenous from alpha to omega. They are the "children of Japanese society and they cannot be understood apart from the characteristics of Japanese society."[1] Concrete aspects of this indigeneity will emerge in subsequent discussions.

Implicit in this positive evaluation, however, is a negative side. It is questionable whether or not it is healthy for a religion to be wholly identified with culture. It is impossible to draw a line between Japanese culture and Buddhism, or between traditional Japanese thought and RK teaching. They act in mutual reinforcement. Kraemer has said that the symbiosis of culture and religion is the very essence of the religious systems of the East.[2] But in such a case, does religion do more than simply mirror what is implicit in culture? Without a "gospel" from beyond culture, what is the source for renewal of culture? With regard to religious cooperation, despite the earnest emphasis of RK on world peace and cooperation among world religions, is it possible for a religion so rooted in one particular cultural context to be a vessel of universal understanding, or to function on the inter-cultural level?

*

The problems of the Christian church with regard to indigeneity are all too obvious. "It is probably correct to say that no charge against Christianity in this country is so old, so complicated, so painful to the missionary, and so frustratingly difficult to answer as the allegation that 'Christianity is foreign to Japan.'"[3] "For the non-Christian ordinary folk, Christianity is still thought to be a Western and white man's religion, and there has been an undercurrent of antagonism toward Christianity that has existed continuously."[4] "Christianity is still the Stranger in the land who has taken up alien residence...It is still clothed in Western garb."[5] "In sharp contrast to Confunianism and Buddhism, Christianity...has been more belligerent toward the spiritual tradition of Japan...Christianity has tended to reject not only all the rival religious systems, but also the values and meanings of the culture and historical experiences of the Japanese."[6] These poignant criticisms of Christianity, which continuously recur in printed word and public address, are enough to make the point that one of the profound weaknesses of the Christian church in Japan is its lack of indigenous qualities, and its reputation of being a foreign religion.

ACCOMMODATION TO SOCIAL STRUCTURE

Hoza is an extremely effective organ of religious propagation because, as a group movement, it is rooted in traditional patterns of collectivity orientation, group dependency, and mutually binding interpersonal relations, all of which are factors of primary importance for the maintenance of social and psychological security for Japanese.

"We-consciousness"—a commitment to the group over against individual aggressiveness—is one of the chief characteristics of Japanese culture. Hoza is a supreme example of accommodation of a religious activity to the social structure in which it exists. Given the social solidarity consciousness of the Japanese it would seem that participants find the healing they need to a greater extent through the group approach of hoza than they would through an individual approach. In hoza people find the fellowship and sense of belonging which is so vital to them.

RK is greatly concerned about accommodation to patterns of both thought and structure. It adjusts its practices readily to changing environmental needs. During its few decades of existence it has already changed its patterns several times. It thus functions as an instrument of social adjustment for its members. While this makes for popularity, it does not enhance stability or integrity. The question must be asked: What is the permanent theological principle upon which the character of the religion is based?

Regarding the group-centered orientation itself, there is danger that religiosity may be little more than group psychology, and that the fostering of individual maturity will be neglected, so that without the group to depend on, the individual will fall. The question must be raised as to whether this kind of group orientation, which lacks a fundamental sense of individual responsibility, is able to provide a basis for democracy in Japan. In fact, can it not justly be asked whether Japan's spiritual "lostness' does not lie right here—in her group dependency? For the group tends to assume ultimate value; it is idolized. Yet the group can be wrong. The possibilities of sinister socio-political movements capitalizing on such group orientation cannot be denied.

*

Christianity has come to be identified with an emphasis on the individual. This has been a needed counteractive force in this other-directed and group-directed culture. But this emphasis is an ambiguous virtue. "One feels that Protestant Christianity has become so individualized that even the family has been lost sight of as a basic unit for evangelization," yet in the Japanese social setting it is especially important to work with the family or group as the basic unit rather than with the individual.[7]

Japanese critics say that unfortunately the urban church has no primary-group character, but this is urgently needed because it gives the believer both religious security and also emotional security. If the city church does not make an effort to integrate new members into a new group solidarity, even though the individual may be interested in Christian teaching and faith, he will be distracted by the busy life of the city, fail to maintain his ties with the church, and tend to lose his faith.[8]

Too often the church, which speaks much of Christian fellowship, has left this fellowship in the realm of the God-man relationship, neglecting the man-man relationship. Japanese churches have failed to give full recognition to the strong need for horizontal relationships. They have indeed avoided the danger of absolutizing the human group, but have gone too far, and fail to see the church group as the place where spiritual life can be and ought to be nurtured.

RELEVANCE OF THE MESSAGE

Hoza, as part of a popular religious movement of and for the masses, propagates a popular message, that is, its concerns are concrete, appealing and wholly relevant to the everyday problems of common people. The message promulgated in hoza meets people on their own level of comprehension and is attractive to them because it promises happiness and many other benefits, reinforces their existing ethical values of conformity and submission, and sanctions popular folk beliefs.

RK has attempted to make Buddhism relevant to the life of every man. It has sought to make Buddhism a people's faith (*minkan shūkyō*). The ancient sutras exist in language that is not even readable to modern Japanese, but President Niwano has digested their content and proclaimed it in a form understandable even to the least educated. The aim of hoza is to help people find what *oshakasama* (Sakyamuni Buddha) is saying to them today. An effort is made to renew the people's conscience by recalling them to their ethical responsibilities: obedience to parents, submissive service of wives to husbands, humble service to others, etc.

RK believes that, although everyone wants to have a pure faith, yet that purity should not be sought at the expense of separating oneself from the world. Religion must partake of the contaminated (*doro-kusai*) world in which it exists; only thus can it truly encounter and struggle with the corruption. Furthermore, as society changes (it is said that "the contemporary Japanese way of thinking" changes every five years!), the nature of the religious appeal must also change, so the emphases of hoza are geared toward constant change. Here is the ultimate in relevance!

In the process of being relevant and struggling with the world's "dirt," the message accumulates considerable dirt upon itself. The content of some hoza discussions reveals a shocking mixture of Buddhist theology, folk religion, sheer superstitution and crassly materialistic appeals. At times truth becomes distorted into little more than a gossip session.

The ethical principles, relevant indeed to traditional ways of thinking, are extremely conservative of old modes of behavior, but hardly adequate for this new day of liberal, democratic thinking.

*

If the new religions are preoccupied with making their message popular and relevant, Christianity is preoccupied with the purity of its theology. Japanese Christianity jealously guards the traditions of classical dogma handed down from the Western forebearers. This has been both its strength and its weakness. A firm grasp of the historical faith is one of the strengths of the Japanese church as it takes its place alongside the churches of the world. At the same time this has been its weakness in that "Japanese Christianity has had no language with which it could speak directly to the Japanese laborers and masses." A noted Japanese Christian novelist says that "Christianity in Japan has been the property of a few intelligent people," and as such "floats unattached on the surface of present day Japanese society. The fact that a number of new religions are getting to the hearts of the masses may be disquieting for those Japanese Christians who deplore the decrease in the number of their believers."[9] A popular movement is bound to become dirtied with a mixture of pure and impure elements. Can the church risk becoming a popular movement? But we must also ask, Can the church risk remaining in its isolated splendor of theological purity?

TECHNIQUES OF PROPAGATION

The techniques of propagation used by hoza introduce modernized approaches into the dormant climate of established Buddhism. They are geared toward efficient operation in an urban setting, as evidenced by such things as lucid teaching, practical counseling, and zealous personal evangelism. At the same time, the methods of hoza are adapted to traditional patterns such as teaching by the case method, rote learning and counseling in a group context where dependency is fostered.

The discussion of techniques of propagation will be confined to three areas: teaching, group work and counseling. With regard to teaching, hoza's injection of practical interpretation, clear simplicity and popular appeal into the complexities of Buddhist dogma is a praiseworthy movement. The teaching aspects of hoza are open to criticism mainly on the points of over-simplification and excessive use of clichés. The teaching tends to follow a stereotyped pattern which facilitates rote learning, but does not encourage creative thinking on the part of the listeners.

Regarding the group process itself, it is remarkable that the hoza system has progressed as well as it has without technical training in the science of group dynamics and leadership. It is true that the leaders who are *seikyōshi* ("official teachers") do receive a certain amount of intensive training through experience in their own evaluated group participation, but, at least in the past, there has been no regular, systematic study of, nor even awareness of, the science of group dynamics.

As for the practice of counseling, it is obvious that the traditional Japanese approach to counseling is foreign to American concepts of counseling, the aim of which is to help individuals accept responsibility for making the significant decisions for their own life. If hoza were to be seriously studied as "group counseling," the word "counseling" would have to be used with the Japanese connotation and definition of the word, recognizing that this counseling would have a different aim and different dynamics from counseling in the Western context. This study was begun with the intent of examining a group counseling movement, but that narrow pursuit had to be abandoned as it was discovered that the impact of hoza did not originate in any significant way from the counseling function, narrowly conceived.

A chief source of the conflicting interpretations of counseling lies in the differing concepts of personality and individual responsibility, which in turn are the products of cultural and religious systems. That is to say, Western personality theory is based on the concept of respect for the individual person as being the supreme value. That fundamental respect demands that every individual be granted the freedom and responsibility to make his own choices, both in matters of religious faith and everyday decisions. This attitude toward the individual is, generally speaking, lacking in hoza as we have observed it. In its place is an approach which makes group harmony and obedience to group leadership the supreme value.

*

Where does the Christian church stand in terms of her efforts in the communication of the Gospel? As far as statistics are concerned it has to be said that evangelism in Japan during the thirty years since World War II have borne but little fruit for the churches. People give many excuses, mainly that the Gospel is alien to Japanese mentality. "But woe betide the Japanese Christian who comforts himself with such an answer. There needs to be an over-all objective and constructively critical examination of evangelism in Japan," says Kobayashi, who continues with the challenge that "the question whether or not there have been any blind spots as regards evangelism should be asked by every Japanese Christian."[10] Offner says that the new religions should encourage serious reflection on the role and methods of the Church in Japanese society today, and provide a stimulus and challenge for evangelistic advance. He admits that the Gospel itself is a stumbling block, but that much of the stumbling lies in the Church's ineffective use of method. The Church should be shamed to find that the new religions have met with success using methods similar to those of the New Testament Church, but which the Church itself has not utilized effectively.[11]

More specifically, what are the problems of the Church in the three areas under discussion? In regard to teaching method, Christian teachers on the parish level will do well to take heed to techniques effectively utilized in hoza. One is the need for the simplification of doctrinal and theological instruction, both in the sermon, the catechetical class and the Bible study. Christian pastors are notorious for their *muzukashii* (difficult to understand) sermons and studies, which tend to be lectures, with a minimum of practical application and popular appeal. The Bible is regarded by most people as a valuable book but one which is very difficult to interpret. In this respect, as in other respects, has not Christianity slipped into the unfortunate rut of the old, established religions of Japan? Like the established sects of Buddhism, Christianity has become abstruse, separated from the life of the people, and has lost the vitality and zeal which she originally had as a "new religion" in the first century, and which Japan's "new religions" have today.[12] Offner praises the simple teachings of the new religions and says: "The scholar may object that the doctrine is too simple, a gross oversimplification, but at least it is understood by the laymen, whereas the complicated reasoning of the erudite is beyond their ken." He calls the language of these religions the "*koine* of the masses."[13] The present writer concludes on the basis of his participaiton in hoza that for certain situations it can be effective to reduce religious doctrine to simple formulae and teach it in the pattern of rote learning. He admits that he himself would have had difficulty grasping the complexities of Buddhist doctrine without, for example, the catch-phrase formula, *in-en-ka-hō*.

Regarding group work as a technique of propagation, many feel the need for a Christian parallel to hoza, which does not exist at the present time. Roman Catholics have the private confessional; the Protestants have pastoral counseling, but, regrettably, there is no widespread small group movement within Christianity. Yet there is no reason why this method should not prove to have impact for Christian communication as it has for communication in other religions.

In the immediate post-war period Joseph Spae held a similar hope for the effective use of small groups in the church as he looked at the powerful impact of neighborhood associations in Japan:

> Who among us priests who saw the civil neighborhood associations at work, especially at the time of the great wave of enthusiasm, did not marvel at the concealed strength which went out from the Japanese when they banded together for the attainment of a single well-defined objective? What missionary did not hope and pray that some day the church would harness for the fulfillment of her saving mission that same irresistable force? Here was cohesion; here was a spirit of sacrifice. Here was activated the whole gamut of social virtues of which, as on a natural rock foundation, the conversion of Japan could easily be built.[14]

With these impressive words Fr. Spae made a proposal for the use of the small group pattern for the propagation of the Christian faith in Japan.

Regarding counseling, suffice it to say here that the Christian church has within its faith and theology the richest resources for conducting helpful and healing counseling based on the foundations of respect for the integrity and freedom of persons, of nurturing of socially responsible selfhood, and of the ultimate concern of love for the other. All that remains is to find a functional form—perhaps a hoza-type group—through which these resources can be channeled to the masses. Without a suitable form of expression, the Christian treasures remain hidden.

EFFECTIVE LEADERSHIP

A significant characteristic of hoza is its exclusively lay leadership. This leadership is highly authoritarian; it is part of the hierarchical structure of the religion as a whole and therefore is tinged with a divine aura and charismatic power. This type of leadership is effective in accomplishing the purposes of hoza in its given context, as evidenced by the fact that it is not only gratefully accepted, but is expected, particularly from teachers of religion.

There is no question but that lay leadership constitutes one of the the principle keys to the secret of hoza's success, as of the success of the new religions in general. Lay leadership assures that hoza will not become lost in theological abstractness but will stay close to the everyday life of the people. Whether a theologically trained priesthood could in any way strengthen the impact of the movement is highly questionable.

The authoritarian character of this leadership is, however, subject to varying evaluations. Considering the hierarchical structure which is common to Japanese social organization in general, and the strong dependency needs which characterize Japanese psychological make-up, the attractiveness of this authoritarian system to large numbers of Japanese is undeniable. Doubtlessly this approach is the most appropriate and most effective kind of leadership for this group of people at this particular time. "Many Japanese want the sense of security that comes from submitting to authority," says McFarland, who goes on to point out the negative side of this kind of leadership by indicating the potential infringement of democratic rights and processes inherent in this system.[15] The whole system seems to have leaned from the area of religious authority into the sphere of institutional authoritarianism, where authority is invested in certain persons who have a divine aura about them. This tends to make the movement one of reactionary conservatism in a day when the main stream of society is moving in a liberal, democratic direction.

In addition to this threat to democratic development is the more sinister threat of revival of potential fascistic development, which such sociologists of religion as Saki and Takagi decry.[16] Even though this does not appear to be an imminent danger, it must be recognized that the potential for such a development is there. Authoritarian leadership produces quicker results, as group dynamics research indicates, but it is a result based not on spontaneous will but on compulsion. A fundamental doubt must be raised as to whether true religious faith can be fostered in an atmosphere of compulsion. If hoza is effective in producing religious conversion and growth, the questions must be asked: What kind of religion? Growth in what values?

*

Some significant comparisons between hoza leadership and leadership in the Christian Church in Japan can be made. First it must be noted that the church has the reputation of being a clergy-centered institution. The vertical structure of God-minister-laity has been over-emphasized. The stance of obedience and reverence of parishioner towards the minister has taken precedence ever the horizontal relation of fellowship within a common body. "Theology of the laity" has been widely discussed among Japanese Christians. "They have discussed the issue, affirmed the importance of laity, and done almost nothing," says Kobayashi, who also points out that "part of this responsibility...should be borne by theologians and ministers. It is questionable whether professional Christian leaders were eager to reorganize the structure of church activities in order to give laymen more power and responsibility."[17]

There is an obvious structural difference between hoza and the Christian church on the matter of lay versus clerical leadership. When it comes to the matter of the quality of leadership, the contrast and comparison is more subtle. Signs of both the authoritarian pattern common to Japanese social organization, and signs of a uniquely democratic pattern are both present. Takenaka points out that "a strong emphasis on the personal charismatic authority of outstanding persons has been characteristic of Christianity in Japan...Churches tended to center upon the leadership of the minister, thus helping to establish an authoritarian pattern of human relations."[18] Furthermore, as one could anticipate on the basis of the general cultural pattern, the teacher-disciple relationship is the standard pattern of relationship between minister and layman in the Japanese church.

On the other hand, Japanese sociologists of religions recognize that Christianity is unique and revolutionary in its fundamental approach to people in that it is the only religion which does not appeal to the old authoritarian mind, but appeals rather to individual response. The almost exclusively individualistic appeal was noted above as a weakness of the Christian approach, but on the other hand Christians can be grateful that their church has the reputation for being a democratic institution which has advanced on the basis of individual commitment rather than coercion. Christianity is known as the home of genuine freedom of choice for the individual conscience.

But have Christian leaders not been too democratic, too *laissez faire* in their approach to Christian evangelism and education? The Japanese, conditioned by their centuries of feudal culture, expect and respond readily to authoritative leadership. The vertical structure of group organization, with its firmly fixed order of ranking, "is overwhelmingly important in fixing the social order and measuring individual social values," says Nakane.[19] Given this hierarchical way of thinking and living, would it not be possible for Christian leadership, in order to find common ground with and make an impact upon Japanese society, unashamedly to assume a hierarchical type of organization? Of course distinction must be made between hierarchical, authoritative leadership and single-handed, autocratic leadership. Unfortunately, it is the latter which tends to be characteristic of the present clergy-centered church, whereas the former system, at its best, implies a system of delegation of authority to succeeding ranks in the structure which makes for efficient communication and operation. Ultimately, the essential distinction is reduced to discovering the line between authority and authoritarianism, recognizing the need for a proper authority in the hierarchy of institutional strategy or in the communication of religious faith. Norbeck commented on a similar dilemma which he encountered in Japanese culture with these words: "Instruction in democracy backed by the force of authority seems curiously contradictory."[20] But history often moves along curiously contradictory lines.

INTERACTION BETWEEN CULTURE AND RELIGION

Hoza functions in a dual role—as a psycho-sociological movement and as a religious movement. Providing personal security and identity to the masses who are otherwise nameless and alienated constitutes the former role, which is mainly a latent one. Teaching and problem-solving based on Buddhist doctrine constitute the latter role, which is the manifest religious function of hoza.

This topic is not so much an issue as an assumption underlying the study. It is an "issue" only in the sense that the fact of this cultural-religious interaction and the dual role played by hoza need to be recognized. Failing to recognize and be aware of the multiple functions of religion can lead the religious institution into self-delusion and into paths which it might never have intended to follow.

In evaluating hoza in its dual role, it can be said that both the content and method of this activity are admirably adapted to play the dual role, or rather, they actually grow out of the dual needs of the people—their psycho-sociological needs and their ethico-religious needs. For example, it was noted how the religious exhortation to be grateful for suffering promotes a conservative philosophy of social adjustment, and makes low economic status and also physical malady not only tolerable but meaningful for those who have little chance of bettering their situation. Or again, the theological interpretation of the unity and interdependence of all things, and the affinity of that theological dogma with the value attached to group solidarity in Japanese culture may be pointed out.

What we would like to suggest here is that RK is undoubtedly not fully aware of its dependency upon these cultural patterns for the promotion of hoza. What will this mean for the future? Cultural patterns are slowly but surely changing. Will RK continue to cling to the old patterns while society moves on ahead? If so, there will doubtlessly be a decline in its popularity and growth. Or will RK change its practices and emphases in accordance with the changing cultural milieu? Judging from past performance, this may well be the case. But if that is so, will not RK lose its integrity as the proponent of "fundamental Buddhism"?

*

The realization of this principle of the interaction between cultural and religious dynamics brings both warning and encouragement to those engaged in Christian propagation—warning that unless the church finds channels of communication in this country which has greater affinity with the current social and cultural milieu, her message may continue to go unheeded except by a select few, because religious movements and cultural movements are inevitably interrelated.

At the same time recognition of this interaction brings encouragement to Christians in the form of an exhortation to patience. Just as the new religions are assured of quick success by their identification with culture, so Christianity faces inevitably slow growth because it is clear that the cultural presuppositions of Japan are non-Christian presuppositions, and hence antagonistic to the essential foreignness of the Gospel. The first century for Protestantism has passed and the church is still a "stranger in the land," for Christianity maintains an awareness that it is not primarily a cultural movement but a religious movement, rooted in divine revelation and not primarily in social needs. Thus Christianity might be called *the new* religion of Japan. Furthermore, its supra-cultural orientation permits optimism in fostering its growth as a world religion, for only a religion which is not embedded in one culture can expect a hearing outside its own cultural origins.

CLASS RESTRICTIONS

The membership of hoza is constituted predominantly by people of the lower middle class, especially those who have a generally low level of education and who are engaged in small businesses or office work. Both the theology of hoza, as evidenced by the frequent appeal to folk beliefs and to irrational elements of religiosity, and the methodology, as evidenced, for instance, by the commotion and communality of the physical environment, have strong affinity with the mode of thinking and the way of life of the lower middle class.

RK and its hoza deserve praise for their effective answering of the needs and compliance with the interests of the lower classes. These people are in urgent need of the values which religion can offer, yet unfortunately, these needs have not been met by other religions. President Niwano was a man of humble origins: he worked in a pickle shop and later delivered milk. It is to the credit of him and the movement he started that they have never been ashamed of his roots in the lower cultural strata of society. He has, in fact, capitalized on this to prove his identification and the identification of RK as a whole with this stratum.

However, the seemingly inevitable trend of movements toward a higher social strata appears already to have set in, as was noted in the discussion of current trends of the new religions. "The churches of the poor all become middle-class churches sooner or later," said H. R. Niebuhr, and in so doing they tend to "lose much of the idealism which grew out of of their necessities. There is no doubt of the truth of Max Weber's contention that godliness is conducive to economic success."[21] It would be regrettable if RK would lose its mission to the lower strata of society.

*

With Christianity the problem is quite the opposite. For various reasons related to the cultural connotations of Christianity at the time of its introduction into Japan, notable among which was its founding of many educational institutions, the influence of the church from the beginning of the Protestant century has been largely confined to a single class—middle class intellectuals. "A major factor hindering the growth of Protestantism has been that it does not spread beyond the bourgeois class in urban districts." Christianity is characterized as being of the "white collar class in urban areas."[22] Although the church has made frequent thrusts toward the rural and the laboring classes, "its feet have found it hard to go to them, and its hands have lacked the requisite skills for service. Neither the people of the villages nor the workers in the cities have been deeply reached, much less won," commented Charles Iglehart at the end of his long career in Japan. The church remains "an urban, middle class intellectuals' religion—cosmopolitan, international, enlightened, ethical and rational."[23] "*De facto*, 95 per cent of Japan's Christians (with the exception of those living in Kyushu) belong to the middle class, a situation which has always been viewed with considerable alarm, but for which no remedy could be found."[24]

The case seems to be quite clear: Christianity, while verbally proclaiming its commission to teach and preach to all people, has in fact miserably failed to do this in Japan. Why? Not because it has consciously rejected this commission or simply because it has lacked zeal, but because the form of the message and the method of communicating the message are geared toward the upper strata of the middle class. This insight came as a significant revelation to this writer, and the following personal account indicates among other things how blinded during his first decade in Japan he had been to his confinement within the upper middle class and its values:

> It is not the purpose or method of hoza which has made my contact with RK significant. What has been the eye-opening and surprising experience for me is to discover the way of thinking of the people who attend hoza. I have been amazed at how susceptible the people are to what I consider to be superstition. I have also been amazed at the degree to which ancestor veneration is accepted and practiced. Previously I thought I knew the Japanese mind, but it was only after attending RK's hoza that I realized I had known only the mind of students and professional people—the mind of those who are in our Christian churches. But now I see that they do not represent a cross-section of Japanese people. People in the church and the people whom I have come to know in hoza represent two different worlds, between which lies a wide cultural gap.[25]

The Christian church seems either to be unaware of this gap or indifferent toward the task of bridging and crossing over this gap to realize the inherent universality of its Gospel.

LEVELS OF PERSONAL NEED

The physical and affective needs of individuals, such as problems of health and marital relations, and the need for social fellowship, especially among women, are fulfilled through hoza, for it is not primarily a place of intellectual instruction, but a place of answering everyday life problems on the most concrete level. This is particularly necessary in view of the Japanese tendency to value emotional, intuitive experience above logical reasoning, and also particularly necessary for reaching the less educated strata of society.

Again, consideration of the latent and manifest functions of hoza is helpful at this point. The manifest function is to solve certain problems, to teach the Buddhist Law, and to give testimonies of religious experience, but, after these activities have been given their due recognition, it must be said that perhaps the more significant function of hoza lies in the area of latent functioning, namely, to provide a happy emotional experience for the participants. RK unhesitatingly interprets the blessings of Buddhist faith in terms of concrete benefits, the primary benefit being the experience of happiness (*shiawase*). On the basis of the achievement of this latent function, hoza must be judged eminently successful.

Joseph Spae supports the idea of happiness as a justifiable content of religious experience, pointing out that happiness is different from pleasure or well-being, being "that fulfillment and that hope which becomes ours when we obtain those 'cosmic gifts' which we crave. Its inner dynamic... acts as a transforming power."[26] The kinship between this promise of benefit and the theology of the book of Deuteronomy in the Old Testament should not be forgotten. One of the characteristic ideas of the Deuteronomic writer is that security, prosperity and possessions are the sure reward for obedience to God's Law. There is frequent repetition of the exhortation to obey the Lord in order "that it may be well with thee," "that thou mayest prolong thy days in the land," or "that the Lord may bless thee."[27]

On the other hand, the danger inherent in an emphasis on the benefits of religious faith rather than on the absolute worth of the object of faith itself seem not to be duly recognized by RK. The value of happiness and of material benefits is justified as a type of *hōben*, or means of attracting people to the true faith. But in the conversations of hoza it is painfully obvious that the meaning of religion tends to stop at the level of *hōben* in the form of experienced benefit, and seldom arrives at the ultimate realization of Truth. This stands in stark contrast to the Biblical concept expressed frequently in the Psalms, "Wait patiently for the Lord," and in that phrase which represents the antithesis of *riyaku shūkyō* ("benefit religion," a phrase often applied to the new religions), "Though he slay me, yet will I wait for him."[28]

*

The problem for the church is quite different. It is threatened by the extreme of cold intellectualism and by a lack of affective and experiential qualities. "There is no doubt that the current presentation of the Christian message is much too complicated, too theoretical and too distanced from daily concerns. Its thought patterns are too intricate; it uses too much theological jargon."[29] The church and its message have the reputation of being "primarily an affair of the mind, something rarified, disembodied, disincarnate...Not a few, therefore, are turned away by the seemingly intellectual demands of the Gospel. They come in search of bread and instead receive a stone for their starving souls."[30]

The typical Japanese minister orates learned sermons and lectures from his pulpit to a handful of "intellectuals" while the teeming crowds around the church go untouched. Hoza members occasionally made the criticism of Christianity that it lacked reality, warmth and humanness, that it is merely a conceptual, not a practiced religion.

The problems of individualism and class-consciousness have already been touched upon, and there is integral relationship between those problems and the one under discussion here. It was stated that in the church there is a strong strain of individualism and class-consciousness, that is, restriction to upper middle class intellectuals. How does this situation affect the expression of Christianity? Spae sees that these very things constitute the reason for Christianity's image of cold intellectualism. He points to parallels between upper middle class intellectuals and non-affective religion.

> If Max Weber's hypothesis on the relation between social stratification and affinity for religious doctrines is correct, then it would follow that the type of membership we find in Japan would produce Christians whose lines are characterized by a high degree of formalism and a low degree of religious affectivity. They will...project an image of sternness and suffer from lack of human warmth. They will put great stock on orthodoxy, ethical conformity and sacramental cult.[31]

There is no question about the necessity for Biblical and doctrinal teaching in Christian propagation. The distinctive content of the Christian revelation cannot be adequately communicated without a certain amount of conceptual teaching. The problem is one of balance. As Kobayashi, himself a Japanese Christian theologian and observer of the new religions, says, "Religion is basically that which is experienced by an individual, and not something that is taught or indoctrinated. Religious experience comes first, and systematization of the faith follows." He quarrels with pastors who put primary emphasis on conceptual learning and belittle the experience of faith within the the fellowship of the church. "When Japanese Christians evaluated the New Religious Movements, they made serious mistakes," he says, for "they were happy to discover the superiority of Christian theology in comparison with the systems of thought in these New Religious Movements, which were still underdeveloped." However, the intellectual understanding of religion should not be given priority over the total experience of religious reality itself.[32] Hoza has gone to the extreme of emphasizing emotional experience and affective relationships at the expense of rational interpretation, whereas Christianity has gone to the extreme of emphasizing intellectual indoctrination at the expense of affective experience and fellowship.

ESTHETICS AND ECONOMICS

At the Great Sacred Hall hoza is carried on in an atmosphere of comfort and opulence, which in itself is a great attraction to participants. Some elements of the environment appeal to traditional Japanese esthetic sense and other elements, borrowed from other cultures, appeal to the sense of modernity and eclecticism. This phenomenon is in keeping with the Japanese proclivity for embracing a multiplicity of forms. It also testifies to remarkable financial resources, which could not be available without skillful business management.

Who cannot help but be impressed by the financial genius of RK when one sees the magnificent structures and institutions that are being enjoyed by the thousands of people who daily use them! Questions might be asked, however, about the means used for accumulating these financial resources. Offner says of the new religions in general that "there is an undeniable pecuniary interest evident in the activities of many of these religions. At times it seems that healing or other benefits are dispensed for a price in a manner not greatly different than in businesses run for profit. The ethics of some...religious leaders are not above reproach."[33] But with regard to RK itself, the means of financing are unknown to the present writer except for the standard answer given to the public: "Our funds come from the voluntary offerings of our members."

As for the artistic style, it obviously appeals to the taste of the adherents. Who is to set the criterion for its "goodness" or "badness"? Whether any objective standard of esthetic values exists or not is a perennial issue among artists. What can be said is that the architectural style of the Great Sacred Hall where hoza takes place is, according to common standards, bizarre. Whether in the long run this will prove to be an asset or detriment remains to be seen.

*

The Christian Church and its esthetic style could hardly make a more startling contrast. It is exceptional to find an attractive church building in Japan, attractive either on the outside or inside. Lee's portrayal of "Workingman's Church" describes the typical church and its facilities:

> A querry to the police officer—concerning the whereabouts of "Workingman's Church" brings forth this response: "You can't miss it. You'll see a big brown building with a funny tower on top. That's the church."...On the ground floor are religious education meeting rooms...Upstairs is the sanctuary with its hard wooden pews which can accommodate 120 worshippers. Needless to say this is not the church of "the comfortable pew." Toward the rear of the sanctuary, a small coal burner emits what little heat there is for the shivering visitor.[34]

This sketch is enough to suggest that as far as physical environment is concerned the modest atmosphere of a Christian church building and the opulent atmosphere of RK's Great Sacred Hall are indeed two separate worlds.

The particular style chosen for a religious edifice would not seem to be of any great import. No one can define what constitutes the style of "modern Japanese architecture;" it is highly eclectic and international. Elements from both ancient Japan, India and America are equally auspicious in the Great Sacred Hall, yet it was our conclusion that here is a truly indigenous movement. Many people worry about the Western style of architecture common in Japanese church buildings, but, given the use of common sense, "Western" style is no worse and no less indigenous to modern Japan than is ancient Japanese style.

A further point of contrast regards the financing of religious institutions. In order for the Christian Church to break the "poverty image" and all the inconvenience and inefficiency which that implies, the concept of money as a degraded and degrading thing, all too prevalent among Japanese ministers, must be rectified. "A religion cannot demonstrate its strength and value to secular society without having enough financial backing...The lack of financial resources for religious activities can easily strangle all the activity," says a Japanese Christian, who goes on to suggest that "in this respect the Japanese churches should learn from the New Religions how to use money more effectively."[35] The current trend among churches to utilize their valuable property holdings in metropolitan areas for income-producing enterprises can be a step toward escape from the "poverty-image" and toward securing material resources sufficient to permit aggressive evangelism programs in this country, plagued by a cost of living which is one of the highest in the world.

INTEGRITY

Frequently there is boastful self-promotion of hoza by the leaders and the use of coercive methods of persuading people to join RK or to believe its teachings. Both teaching and testimonies often have the effect of pressuring people to believe. Superstitious, syncretistic and materialistic elements are used in order to gain popular support. Some religious interpretations, particularly concerning the working of karma and the necessity of ancestor veneration as these apply to the "solution" of people's problems, function as threats.

On some of these points doubts must be raised about the message and method of hoza. Methods tainted with coercion or manipulation must be questioned as being antithetical to basic respect for individual rights and freedoms. There is an unfortunate tendency in some of the new religions to undermine these priceless freedoms.[36] The strong emphasis on *riyaku*, or the material benefits which the religion claims will surely come to the true believer, must also be called into question. "The preoccupation with physical and material well-being tends to debase religion to the level of satisfying purely natural desires rather than lifting man up to a higher plane of existence." This kind of religion is easily perverted into a tool used for the purpose of attaining selfish goals.[37] Although RK has moved in the direction of a purer theology in recent years, on the level of hoza conversations there are still many elements that, at least to the Western observer, must be evaluated as a perversion of true religion. Many answers to the problems presented for solution in the *musubi* cases must be judged as psychological gimmicks and appeals to the participants' inclination toward superstition and magic rather than as true efforts to solve human problems.

To such criticisms at these, RK leaders would probably make the following responses. One response would be that a degree of coercion or materialistic attraction or a degree of interpretation based on folk belief and superstition is permissible under the rubric of *hōben*, that is, that a good end justifies even a poor means. Since affiliation with RK as the dispenser of the Truth of the Universe is the ultimate good, whatever means are necessary to draw people into that relationship are permissible. Another comment from RK leaders would be an admission that there is an unfortunate gap between the ideals and officially stated purposes of hoza and some of the actual practices found there.

*

Takagi, not a Christian adherent himself, makes a significant aside that the reason Christianity has not been successful in Japan, as success is judged by usual standards, is partly because Christians never learned to appeal to the need of the masses for unification under superior authority. Christianity has always been democratic, working from below, on the level of individual conscience and conviction.[38] The Christian church in Japan has not resorted to coercion nor compromise nor to gimmicks that might issue in quick results. The church can hold its head high and point to a record of integrity and honesty. Perhaps it is at this very point where the reputation of the church shines brightest, and in this fact lies great potential for the future.

But in the matter of effective persuasiveness, although the church's reputation for allowing free and spontaneous acceptance of its faith is granted, the church cannot afford to be proud of its record in propagation. Lee's interviews with lay leaders in local churches presents a picture not so much of the absence of coercion as the lack even of invitation on the part of Christians toward those outside.[39] The late Hendrik Kraemer, after a visit to Japan, was asked what he thought was the most urgently needed thing for the renewal of the church in Japan. His answer was one word: "Passion!"[40]

*

Passion! That is what RK members have and Christians lack. RK shows itself to be a movement of renewal, revival and reform within an old religious tradition. It is bursting with enthusiasm; its leaders are charismatic; its procedures are disciplined; its message is full of hope; its methods are experimental and experiential. In many respects, how like the Christian Church described in the New Testament!

By way of contrast, Christianity in Japan displays many of the characteristics of an old religion. Interest in theological speculation rather than in direct experience of the faith, a highly trained professional clergy—such factors as these "may easily lead to the decline of the religion unless there be a real re-awakening of the Japanese Christians to the urgent task in their own society," warns Kobayashi.[41] The impression of Christianity expressed by twelve Japanese scholars was summarized in these words:

> Christianity is foreign, strange, on the margin of everyday life, gregarious, stubborn, cold, unappealing to the Japanese *kimochi*

(feeling), dogmatic, sin-conscious and complex-ridden, authoritarian, conformist, sour, unnatural, uninteresting and, in short, absolutely in need of a radical shake-up.[42]

It is the thesis of this writer that increased understanding of the dynamics operative in the popular religious movements can help to stimulate this needed radical shake-up.

CHAPTER TEN

JAPANESE AND WESTERN RELIGIOSITY

by Susumu Akahoshi, M. D.

In this chapter I would like to discuss the foregoing Findings and Interpretations of hoza and the comparisons with Christianity from the viewpoint of developmental psychology and the psychology of religion which has been gained through my experiences in clinical psychiatry and psychotherapy. I shall divide this chapter into three sections. In the first section I shall discuss the fundamental difference in psycho-sociological mentality and religiosity between Japanese and Westerners, according to my own viewpoint of developmental psychology. In the second section I will attempt an interpretation of the Findings from hoza from the point of view of these special characteristics of Japanese psycho-sociological mentality and religiosity. Finally, in the third section I would like to state some general evaluations and insights regarding human religiosity as such, based on the comparison between Japanese and Western patterns.

A Theory of Japanese and Western Mentality

I believe that human religiosity is intimately related to the psychological development of individuals, and also that the religiosity peculiar to a certain nationality is rooted in the characteristics of the traditional psycho-sociological mentality of that culture. According to recent research in cultural anthropology, it has become more and more evident that there is a fundamental difference between the psycho-sociological mentality of Japanese and that of Westerners. In a word, it can be said that the characteristic of Japanese mentality is "collectivistic dependency" while the characteristic of Western mentality is "individualistic independency."

What is the source of this fundamental difference? It is my belief that this difference arises from the difference between the way infants are handled and raised in Japan and in the West. The tendency of the Japanese character toward collectivistic dependency and the tendency of Western character toward individualistic independency is basically formed during the first year of life, and strengthened in that pattern up to the age of six. It is a well known fact that the human infant is far more helpless at birth than other members of the animal family, and that it cannot adapt itself to the conditions of life by instinct as easily as the animals do. This necessitates a long period of dependency on parental care. From the standpoint of comparative biology, the human baby's nine months of gestation in the mother's womb is too short a time in comparison with other mammals. If human beings developed at the same rate as other mammals, the baby's first year of life ought to be lived under purely natural laws of growth within the mother's womb, but as a matter of fact the infant is forced to live that year in complicated human society under the laws of history as well as the laws of nature. Because of this biological helplessness of the human infant during its first year of life, its dependence upon the parent is extraordinarily strong and urgent, and because of this the satisfaction or lack of satisfaction of those needs has a determinative influence on the child's development.[1]

I define the experience of the satisfaction of these infancy needs, that is, the needs of the child prior to the time of ego formation, as "basic trust," and the experience of lack of satisfaction during this period as "basic mistrust." The basic trust of the infant is its trust in the gift of its mother's love, and this trust is not the act of the infant itself, but is rather the act of the mother's love. In this experience of basic trust the baby is experiencing the same feeling as it had while in the mother's womb, namely, the feeling of oneness with its mother's body. In contrast to this, in the case where the mother is absent, or where, even though she is present she is unable to show love because of her own anxieties, the infant cannot feel secure in being fed and moving its bowels, nor can it sleep well, that is, its dependency needs are not being met, and it is being made to experience basic mistrust. In this way the infant is given its first experience of social mistrust.

Thus the infant develops and grows in the midst of these experiences of basic trust and basic mistrust, but as the nervous system, the sensory system, the muscular system, etc. develop, that is, during the latter half of the first year of life, the infant realizes through the experience of basic mistrust that it has a separate existence from that of its mother. It is at that time that the ego system begins to develop. Accordingly, in the process of ego development, basic trust is overtaken by basic mistrust, and basic mistrust comes to control the ego consciousness of the child. The child, through its experiences of basic mistrust, shows two types of reaction. In the case where basic mistrust is a relatively light experience the child clings closely to the parent in an effort to satisfy its dependency need, and this I call *amae*.[2] In the case of a deeper experience of basic mistrust, the child no longer depends on the parent at all, but attempts to satisfy its dependency need by itself, and moves in the direction of self-reliant or narcissistic love of itself. Thus it is that in either of these two ways the child seeks to gain the feeling of integral unity with the mother, that is, gain the experience of basic trust. In the infant's seeking for basic trust out of its exprience of basic mistrust, the *amae*-drive, that is, the desire to be loved, and the narcissism-drive, that is, the desire to love oneself, are formed within the emerging selfhood of the infant.

Although it is true that the character of the individual mother is to a large extent responsible for the infant's various experiences of basic trust and basic mistrust, it is also true that child rearing is determined to a large extent by traditional practices held in common by a certain culture. In Japan from ancient times, as evidenced by such expressions as "*Kodakara*" (my child, my treasure) there has been the tradition of pouring much attention and affection on children. When the methods of child-raising of the Japanese and of Westerners are compared, it is generally recognized that Japanese tend to spoil their children while while Westerners tend to be more strict with children. This suggests that during the baby's first year of life, Japanese children have lighter and fewer experiences of basic mistrust, while Western infants have experiences of basic mistrust greater both in number and degree. Accordingly, we can surmise that in the process of ego formation of the Japanese child, the tendency to foster the *amae*-drive (drive toward dependency) is stronger than the tendency to foster the naricissism-drive toward autonomy, and with the Western child the case is just the opposite. It is my theory that in this way the fundamental difference between Japanese and Western mentality, namely, the traits of collectivistic dependency and individualistic independency, come into being.

So also in social life the tendency in Japanese society to permit and foster dependency is dominant, and the amae-drive is given constant impetus. Contrariwise, in Western society, the tendency to supress dependency and to foster autonomy is dominant. These fundamental differences in psycho-sociological mentality between Japanese and Westerners are recognized also in the general culture of these countries. In a word, Japanese culture can be described as the "dependency-type" and Western culture as the "autonomy-type." Furthermore, it is my view that Japanese religiosity can also be described in the same terms.

At this point we may ask the question, what is human religiosity? When persons come to a point of frustration in their cultural activities, when they feel the shallowness and meaninglessness of cultural life so that the self regresses to the stage prior to ego formation and once again longs for the basic trust relationship of infancy—at that time human religiosity makes its appearance. At that time the self seeks for the experience of basic trust in relationship to a religious object such as God. The basic nature of this experience is a complete reliance on mother-love, the feeling of oneness between mother and child. Thus the feeling of oneness between the individual and God or Truth, which we see in human religiosity, is a phenomenon of transference from infancy experience. When people reach the point of severe frustration in their daily lives, this crucial desire for integral oneness between man and some Absolute becomes a matter of what Paul Tillich calls "ultimate concern."

Thus it can be said that human religiosity is an activity of the self, and in that respect is the same as other cultural activities, but the direction of this activity is the opposite from other activities. That is, in one's ordinary behavior, the self endeavors to promote cultural activities and give richer content to the dependency and autonomy of the self, but in religiosity the self regresses to the infancy stage, and struggles to find the experience of basic trust in the midst of the shallowness, void and sinfulness of his life. Further, it is easy to see how the basic character tendencies of an individual are made manifest in his religiosity, that is, in the particular way in which he seeks for unity with the object of his faith. That is, the dependent person finds it easy to be dependent on God, and he clings to God in his feeling of *amae* and tries to cast himself into the state of oneness with God. On the other hand, the independent person tries to make himself one with God through his ethical acts of obedience to God's Law and through similar efforts of self-reliance. Generally speaking, Japanese religiosity is the former dependency-type, while Western religiosity is the latter autonomy-type. In the following section I would like to examine the Findings from RK's hoza and attempt to interpret them from this point of view.

A Psychological Interpretation of Hoza

PHYSICAL ENVIRONMENT

In regard to the physical environment in which hoza takes place, the statement was made that a gaudy, ostentatious style of building is a peculiarity of nearly all the new religions, the grandiose headquarters being a mecca and source of pride for adherents of these religions. That is true, but I think it is more important to see that this opulence and splendor serve as a satisfaction of the Japanese dependency need. There is a Japanese proverb, "When you lean, lean on a big tree" (*Tayoraba taijū no kage*). The more grandiose the meeting place is, the more secure the believers who go there feel, for they sense that they can surely rely on a place of such grand proportions. Again, the fact that the participants can feel at home, relaxed and "cozy" on the balconies of the Great Sacred Hall is playing upon the *amae* of the participants. It was stated that for these individuals, the experience of spending part of a day in the atmosphere of the Great Sacred Hall is sufficient reward in itself, apart from the content of the hoza discussions. Hoza members can find here the corporate solidarity which they lack in their everyday life. Thus their need to depend on someone is fully satisfied. We can say that the whole physical environment of RK is skillfully conceived and remarkably adapted to the Japanese dependency-type of religiosity.

ORGANIZATION

The Findings regarding constituency are extremely interesting. It was found that the ones who suffer most from the lack of corporate solidarity, that is, the lower middle class people of the large cities, and housewives, constitute the great majority of hoza participants. RK, through its hoza, offers these people a place of fellowship and a group to which they can belong, and in so doing satisfies their collectivistic dependency needs, and at the same time and through the same process achieves great success in religious propagation.

I also recognize that the Findings regarding use of various forms of subtle pressure in hoza has connection with the Japanese dependency-type of psycho-sociological mentality. It was stated that forms of coercion can be at least partially explained by the authoritarian and hierarchical structure of traditional Japanese group life, in which unquestioning obedience is a virtue. In the hoza group there is the tacit understanding that a degree of coercion may be necessary to form groups in which the members can enjoy relying on each other, and it is this which makes the use of pressure a viable means of group leadership. This psychology is revealed in the Japanese proverb, "Yield to the powerful" (*Nagai mono niwa makareru*).

LEADERSHIP

With regard to leadership, it was stated that the masses still today, as in the past, need, expect and favorably respond to authoritarian leaders. This need and expectation of authoritarian leadership is born naturally out of the dependency-type psycho-sociological mentality and religiosity. However, I do not think that we should say that the autonomy-type democratic leadership is necessarily the best leadership, placing a low evaluation on this Japanese type authoritarian leadership. As stated in the first section of this chapter, both the dependent type and the autonomous type of mentality are on the same level so far as psychological development is concerned, and both types have their strong points and weak points. I, too, am concerned about the problem of leadership and feel that we are faced with a far-reaching problem in trying to determine what does constitute appropriate and effective leadership in Japan today. I would like to discuss this further in the final section below.

SOCIO-EMOTIONAL DYNAMICS

RK advertizes hoza as a place where people can come to have their personal problems solved. In its literature, the official English translation of hoza is "group counseling." But we must understand that this kind of group counseling is purely a Japanese style of counseling, quite different from Western counseling. It is true that we cannot call hoza "group counseling" if we use that phrase in its Western technical meaning. However, that is not to say that hoza does not take a defineable form as a kind of experience-centered "Japanese group counseling." It must be understood that the assumptions, processes and goals operative in hoza are utterly antithetical to those operative in Western counseling. The dynamics of hoza are the dependency-type, whereas Western group counseling is based on the autonomy principle. The great majority of Japanese can make an effort to follow some authority and attain a degree of autonomy, but they cannot really stand alone as individuals. In the end, their efforts toward self-reliance result in making them a better "good fellow" in the group, and make them better able to live happily in the spirit of *amae*. This is what I have called "dependency-type autonomy" (*amae-gata jiritsu*).

It was correctly stated that "the spirit of hoza is the spirit of harmony (*wa no seishin*)." This spirit of harmony, or *wa*, is the fundamental spirit of the Code of Seventeen Articles which comprised Japan's first constitution, namely, that of Shotoku Taishi, and it can be said that that spirit reveals the fundamental psycho-sociological mentality of the Japanese. The spirit of harmony is that spirit which helps a person to become a "good fellow," maintaining personal virtue within the circle of dependent relationships. This spirit of harmony takes precedence over individual autonomy, and self-reliance is recognized as a virtue only insofar as it aids in the creation of social harmony. That is the kind of self-reliance which I term dependency-type autonomy. The essence of this posture comes out clearly in the following passage from Takeyoshi Kawashima, cited by Spae:

> An individual is not considered an independent entity. Rather, his interest is absorbed in the interest of the collectivity to which he belongs, and the interest of the collectivity is recognized as having primary importance, while the interest of the individual has merely a secondary importance.[3]

This frame of mind constitutes the heart of hoza.

It can be said that the goal of therapy in hoza is the attainment of this spirit of harmony. The text mentions that individual self-confidence and self-determination are not the expected nor desired goals of counseling. The core of the problem for which people are looking for salvation when they come to hoza is, in a word, "the passive dependency syndrome," the "never-fully-satisfied-desire-to-be-loved." Here lies the root of people's sorrow.[4] This dependency syndrome is revealed in pathological forms in such attitudes as sulking, self-pity, awkward self-consciousness, resentments, and similar attitudes.[5] In order to treat this syndrome—the pathological manifestation of *amae*—the individual must be made aware of the unconscious working of the dependency-drive in the depths of his heart, and must be made to see that as an adult he cannot always be leaning on others and be cared for by others, but that he must make some effort to become a mature person.

In order to do that, the client must renounce his morbid dependency, and this is what we see in the severe words of admonition which are heard as a refrain in hoza, "The fault lies with yourself." The rationale for this key phrase is that it forces the client to make a thorough examination of his pathological over-dependency. When he becomes aware that the fault lies with himself he accordingly makes an effort to cultivate the personal virtues advocated by RK. That is, he seeks to achieve the dependency-type autonomy, and by developing this posture the person becomes a "good member" of RK, and he is enabled to adjust to the dependency-type society in which they live. These are the socio-emotional dynamics of the salvation which hoza offers, seen from my point of view as a psychiatrist.

Generally speaking, the change which occurs in the personality dynamics of the clients treated by Japanese psychotherapists is exactly the same as that which occurs in hoza. That is, healing lies in returning to dependence, and maintaining a proper group-centeredness, rather than in learning to stand alone. Among the Japanese psychotherapists who have studied counseling and psychotherapy in the West, there are some who work on their own theory that their clients are healed through actualizing the autonomy of their own self in a Western individualistic manner. However, such cases are exceedingly rare, and in the great majority of cases healing occurs just as it does in hoza—through establishing dependency-type autonomy. My own view is the same as that mentioned in the text, namely, the counselor must understand and sympathize with the counselee's dependency needs, and bring him toward health by letting him depend on the counselor fully and trustingly.

Since the techniques of Western counseling and psychotherapy have been developed through adaptation to the individualistic independency mentality which is based on the self-love drive, it is unreasonable to expect that those techniques could be used in dealing with Japanese clients, who have the collectivistic dependency mentality. We can state this in a schematic form by saying that the goal of Japanese counseling and psychotherapy is, like that of hoza, the realization of group harmony through dependency-type autonomy, while the goal in the West is the realization of interpersonal fellowship by means of the self-love type of dependency, that is, fellowship is realized through a contract arrangement between independent individuals.

Thus we have arrived at some vital insights into the fundamental difference between two cultural types. It is important that we should recognize that these two types stand in integral, mutual relationship to each other, as the two sides of a coin. This understanding is essential for the advancement of counseling and psychotherapy in the future, and for the advancement of inter-cultural understanding.

CONCEPTUAL CONTENT

The psychodynamics at work in problem-solving have been described in detail above. The "manifestation of karma" is awareness of symptoms of the passive dependency syndrome which appeared as a pathological aberration. Becoming aware of the value of suffering is to become aware of the psychology of perverted dependency. When people are alerted to the psychology of perverted dependency in the context of the therapeutic human relations of the hoza group, and when ones own dependency need (*amae*) is accepted by others, members say that they discover how the "self is reflected in others." Then a "change of heart" occurs, which is the progression from morbid dependency to limited autonomy. This is the behavior described as repentance before the Buddha and apology to others. So the client gladly accepts the exhortation to submissiveness and thus becomes a contributor to the harmony of the group.

It is natural that problem-solving should be integrally related to the concept of benefit (*riyaku*) in this dependency-type religion. Happiness (*shiawase*) is promised to those who believe, and happiness is that condition which is the feeling of pleasure which comes from the satisfaction of the instinctual urges. It can be said that Nirvana, which is the ultimate happiness, is the same experience as that experience of basic trust which the infant has when it is completely satisfied with its mother's caressing and feeding. In contrast to this, the self-love drive which is at the root of Western autonomy-type religion promotes the search for self-fulfillment and the realization of personal values by following the drives of conscience and the super-ego. Accordingly, Western autonomy-type religion is strongly marked by logicality and sublimates its instinctual desires for immediate benefit and happiness to more abstract values.

Regarding the answers given in the problem-solving situations, some interesting observations can be made with regard to the participants' response to these answers. Hoza participants almost without exception express gratitude for the leader's advice and answer. However, in Miss Watanabe's interviewing of 44 hoza participants, she found that 61 per cent were "always" satisfied with the answer (*musubi*) given by the group leader, while 39 per cent answered they were "sometimes" satisfied with the solution offered.[6] These figures of 61 per cent and 39 per cent are of great interest because they represent the same proportion found within the ego psychology of the masses of contemporary Japanese between the tendency toward dependency and the tendency toward autonomy. As stated in the first section, in Japanese society from ancient times the dependency-drive has been permitted and fostered and has been definitely more dominant than the the autonomy-drive, this characteristic stemming from the experiences of infancy onward, being found in varying proportions in different individuals. The proportion of dominance of these two drives varies also from period to period, and from social class to class. The 39 per cent who said they were only sometimes satisfied with the leader's *musubi* are those whose dependency needs were not fully recognized and accepted in hoza, or those who, because of their relatively strong autonomy-drive resisted the *musubi* offered them. In contemporary Japanese society, the autonomy-drive is relatively stronger among the so-called intellectual class than among the majority of people. However, the dependency drive is basically dominant even among them, for even they have not cast off the collectivisitic dependency mentality. These are the people who are included among those who found *musubi* to be unreasonable and who were therefore only sometimes satisfied with the solution offered, thus indicating that they were not totally resisting the *musubi* based on dependency mentality.

Even the instruction in RK teaching as it is conducted in hoza reveals the psychology of dependency, as evidenced by the frequent expression of hoza leaders, "Our basic belief is that we live in dependency upon all things in the universe." The Japanese special dependency-type religiosity is verbalized in doctrinal form in this doctrine of interdependence. Indeed, this is a central and fundamental characteristic of Japanese religion from ancient times. Furthermore, such ethical imperatives as "Honor your parents," "Be unselfish," "Be humble," etc. are all for the purpose of maintaining group harmony. It is quite clear that the fundamental philosophy of the Seventeen Articles of the Shotoku Taishi Constitution, namely, "Hold harmony in honor" (*Wa wo motte, tōtoshi to nasu*) constitutes the core of RK ethical teaching, and that this teaching issues from the psychology of dependence. The exhortation to venerate ancestors is the ultimate ethical imperative expressed in the form of a religious rite. This is the final expression of the dependency-type religiosity of RK, for, as the text says, here is a recognition of one's dependency on all that has gone before as being the very ground of one's own existence.

Thus, the essence of salvation in dependency-type religion consists of a change of heart from sheer dependency (*amae*) to dependency-type autonomy (*amae-gata jiritsu*). Conversely, it can said that in Western autonomy-type religion the essence of salvation consists of a change of heart from sheer autonomy (*jiritsu*) to self-love dependency (*jiko-ai-gata izon*).

A Comparison of Japanese and Western Religiosity

In the first and second sections we came to a clear realization that RK is a dependency-type religion. It is my opinion that all Oriental religions, especially Japanese religions, are of this type, and particularly Japanese Buddhism after the Kamakura Period. On the other hand, Western religion is an autonomy-type religion, and institutional Christianity is representative of this. Within the history of Christianity this special characteristic can be recognized both on an individual and social level. Especially does Anglo-Saxon Puritanism strongly reveal this tendency toward autonomy-type religiosity. I think the degree of the spirit of autonomy in Western religion is equivalent to the degree of the spirit of dependency in Japanese religion. In this section I would like to compare Japanese religiosity as revealed in the study of hoza with Western religiosity, clarifying the differences, and also showing that these two exist as two sides of an integral whole. Finally I would like to point out the relationship of both of these types of religiosity to the Christian Gospel.

THE CHRISTIAN CHURCH IN JAPAN

The text stated that both hoza and the sponsoring body, RK, are indigenous from alpha to omega, whereas the problems of the Christian church with regard to indigeneity are all too obvious. But these problems are not only the problems of the Christian church in Japan, but are equally much problems for the church in the West too. The problems of indigeneity are especially complicated in Japan because here the dependency-type person meets an autonomy-type religion. Spae says that the principle of indigenization is identical with the principle of the Biblical idea of incarnation. If this is so, then the Western cultural package in which the theological message is wrapped must be stripped off to a greater extent than it has been in the past. In order to Christianize Japan, Christianity must be incarnated into Japanese culture.

In the light of this, how can the Christian church become established in Japan? First of all, there must be a correct recognition of the collectivistic dependency dominant in the psycho-sociological mentality and religiosity of the Japanese. This must be seen from the point of view of history, sociology, cultural anthropology and developmental psychology. Secondly, there must be an understanding of the Western autonomy-type religiosity which is based on the self-love drive, and of the basic difference between these two, as understood from the point of view of developmental psychology. Thirdly, there must be the recognition of the fact that both types of religiosity are based on drives which are motivating forces in the life of every person, and further, recognition that the self-love drive in Westerners and the dependency-drive in Japanese have become dominant simply through psycho-sociological factors and that both are related to each other as the two sides of a coin. Recognizing this, there must be the subsequent understanding that both Western religiosity and Japanese religiosity are in themselves one-sided, and that it is not a matter of one type being right and the other wrong. Fourthly, there must be a recognition of the bias of each type of religiosity and the validity of each type, and there must be an effort to integrate the two extreme tendencies into the formation of a world-wide type of religiosity.

There is an intrinsic foreignness of the Gospel in relation to any human culture. The Christian Gospel is a "stumbling block" to both the Oriental dependency-type religiosity and the Occidental autonomy-type religiosity, and even if an international type of religion devoid of particular nationalistic bias is established in the future, the Christian Gospel would continue to be a stumbling block for it also. For all human religiosity is an act of the human ego, no matter how advanced and refined it becomes.

COLLECTIVISTIC AND INDIVIDUALISTIC RELIGIOUS CONSCIOUSNESS

The fundamental character of Japanese religiosity is expressed in the term "collectivity orientation," as was discovered in the observations of hoza. I would like to point out a few problems which arise as we attempt to compare this characteristic with Western religiosity. It was stated that in Japan there is danger that religiosity may be little more than group psychology, and that the fostering of individual maturity will be neglected, so that without the group to depend on, the individual may fall. As was stated in the above section, Japanese religiosity purposes to maintain group harmony, and considers group harmony to be more vital than individual maturity. Moreover, personal maturity in Japanese religiosity is the maturity of dependency-type autonomy, and maturity is recognized as the ability to promote group harmony, not as the fulfillment of the self based on rational values, such as marks Western individualistic maturity. Such maturity is possible only within the context of a group. Indeed, without the group to depend on, the individual falls. Hence, Japanese religiosity lacks a fundamental sense of individual responsibility. The writer asked whether Japan's spiritual lostness might not lie right here—in her group dependency, for the group tends to assume ultimate value; it is idolized. But this is a way of thinking which reflects a Westerner's approach. Japan's "spiritual lostness" has not come about because a fundamental sense of individual responsibility has been lost—such a sense never existed in Japanese mentality—but because the group to depend on has been lost. Perhaps we can call this "dependency-type nihilism." We must recognize this weak point in Japanese collectivity-oriented dependency-type religiosity.

However, we also ought to recognize accurately the weak points in Western individualistic autonomy-type religiosity. In Western society, rather than the group, the individual, grounded in self-love type autonomy, is idolized, as a result of which the concept of the "man-god" appears, exemplified, for instance, by Ivan in Dostoyevsky's *The Brothers Karamozov*. Western man's spiritual lostness stems from the time Nietzche proclaimed, "God is dead." That is to say, along with the emphasis on the sense of individual responsibility came an awareness of personal authority to the point of personal deification. When the man-god is born and "God is killed," the discipline inherent in autonomy is destroyed. Consequently, in the present age Western individualistic democracy has fallen into danger. We cannot forget that the reign of terror of the Nazis and the Fascists broke out in Christian countries. The grave condition of Western man's spiritual lostness showed up again after World War II. During this time the autonomy-type religiosity reached its ultimate in producing the "death of God theology." It can be reasoned that this spiritual lostness of the West is the result of the the sense of individual responsibility which had supported the individualistic independency mentality. We can call this lostness of Western man a "self-love type nihilism."

Further, it now appears that contemporary Western youth are not content with their self-love type of existence and are instead beginning to seek for an existence in mutual dependency (*amae-gata izon*). What Riesmann spelled out in his *The Lonely Crowd* regarding American youth turning from the inner-directed type to the other-directed type points to this phenomenon. I think this phenomenon shows that there is a strengthening of the dependency drive and a weakening of the self-love drive in Western youth. Or again if we look at the confusion in sexual morality among Western youth we see one of the most specific symptoms of this phenomenon. Here is the most extreme expression of the strengthening of the dependency drive. For the dependency drive which is not harnessed into the discipline of group harmony (*wa*) leaves the instinctual urges to their primitive expression.

Thus, can it not be observed that in contemporary Western society there is a gradual, unconscious movement from individualistic independency to collectivistic dependency, even while, on the conscious level, the emphasis on individual freedom and responsibility is maintained as before? On the other hand, in Japanese society, along with the emphasis on democracy in the post-World War II period, there has been a conscious effort to move from collectivistic dependency to individualistic independency, but that effort has been almost entirely on a superficial level. For at the unconscious level we must admit there has been virtually no change. I believe that not until there occurs a change in religion itself will there be any fundamental changes in social patterns.

Hoza leadership can be described as authoritarian and charismatic. This type of leadership satisfies the Japanese collectivistic dependency need, and, as the text concludes, is probably the most appropriate and most effective kind of leadership for this group of people at this particular time. McFarland is quoted as saying that, "This makes the movement one of reactionary conservatism in a day when the main stream of society is moving in a liberal, democratic direction...In addition to this threat to democratic development is the more sinister threat of revival of imperial authority and potential fascistic development." We must fully recognize these weak points in hoza leadership. However, in Western democratic leadership, along with the strong points of individual freedom, responsibility and spontaneity which come from individualistic independency, there are also the weak points of the man-god concept and authoritarianism which can produce fascism. Thus there are strong points and weak points in both authoritarian leadership and democratic leadership, so that it is impossible to say which is best. The former is a type of leadership which developed in a psycho-sociological milieu where the dependency-drive is dominant, and demonstrates its effectiveness there, while the latter is a leadership which developed in the psycho-sociological milieu where the self-love drive is dominant, and it likewise demonstrates its effectiveness in that milieu.

Leadership in the Christian church of Japan is caught in a dilemma between these two leadership styles. As K. Dale says in an article on this subject, "We want to see the democratic side of Japanese personality developed, in line with the Christian concepts of individual freedom and responsibility, yet we must at the same time adapt our methods of propagation to the actual cultural milieu."[7] The thing we must make clear is that democratic leadership, which of course did develop within the Christian milieu of the West, is based on the individualistic independency mentality of Westerners, which in turn stems from the dominance of the self-love drive, and is not based on the Christian Gospel as such. Likewise the authoritarian leadership found in RK developed within Japanese culture, and is based on the dominance of the dependency-drive manifest in the mentality of the Japanese, and is not based on the teaching of Buddhism as such. Japanese authoritarian leadership is basically a concern for harmony, in which the strong atmosphere of compulsion which marks Western authoritarian dictatorship is absent. Only after we have insight into the nature of the dependency-drive and the self-love drive will we be able to discover a common foundation on which both can supplement each other, function cooperatively, and be integrated together. For just as instruction in democracy backed by the force of authority may be necessary for Japanese, so instruction in inter-dependent solidarity backed by the force of individual conscience may be a necessity for Westerners.

RELIGIOUS PROPAGATION AND SOCIAL CLASS

Regarding the social class of religious adherents the text indicated that hoza participants are mainly people of the lower middle class having relatively little education, while most Christian church members are middle class intellectuals. That is, the common people of Japan look to religion for the satisfaction of their collectivistic dependent religiosity, and RK fully responds to this need. On the other hand, the Christianity spread in Japan was brought here by American and European missionaries, and so it shows a tendency toward Westerners' autonomy-type religiosity. Consequently, that type of religion has found ready acceptance among the strongly autonomous type of persons, namely, a few middle class intellectuals, and it is mainly these people who have been responsible for the spread of Christianity in Japan during subsequent decades. Furthermore, there is a considerable gap between the middle class intellectuals with their relatively strong spirit of autonomy and the common people who are generally controlled by the psychology of dependency.

Thus the Japanese who were receptive to Western autonomy-type Christianity turned out to be the autonomy-type middle class intellectuals, and this is still the situation today. However, their autonomy is strictly the autonomy which grows in this dependency-type society, that is, the dependency-type autonomy, and this is essentially different from the Western self-love type autonomy of the West. I think that the reason why not a few of those intellectuals who were attracted to Christianity and became Christians because of its surface identification with "autonomy" in later years rejected or denounced the faith was because of this fundamental difference. Of course they were not consciously aware of this difference between dependency-type autonomy and self-love type autonomy, but they nevertheless felt it in some form, whereupon they either took the road of return to their old dependency-type religion, or the road of settling for the imitation of superficial features of Western culture, devoid of religious content, while continuing their daily-life activities in the mood of their old dependency-type mentality.

Then how are we to understand the many Japanese who have persevered sincerely in the Christian faith? We must realize that the Christians of Japan have believed the Gospel of Christ while bearing the heavy burden of being a people with a tradition of dependency-type religiosity. They have, in spite of that, accepted the Westernized autonomy-type religiosity of Christianity. I believe that because of this special burden and challenge, Japanese Christians as a whole have been given a special historical vocation by God.

Since the autonomy of Japanese intellectuals is an autonomy securely predicated on existence within the dependency-type society, it is fundamentally different from the individualistic autonomy of the West. Their autonomy is the type of autonomy which can easily fall back on and rely on the dependency-type society—unconsciously of course—whenever it is threatened. Conceptually speaking, it is autonomous, but in actuality it easily reverts to dependency on the group. Hence Japanese Christianity is keen and sternly disciplined when evaluated conceptually, but is easy-going in actual life, and is prone to fall into the pattern of "conceptual autonomy—actual dependency."

The failure of the church to reach the lower strata of Japanese society lies in the form of its message and the method of communicating it, both of which up till now have been geared toward the upper strata of the middle class. Not the essence of the Gospel itself, but the interpretation of it and the means of propagating it must undergo radical revision. In order for this actually to occur, first of all there must be an adequate understanding and acceptance of the dependency psychology of the masses. Next there must be insight into the fact that the psychology of dependency lies at the bottom of the seeming autonomy of Japanese intellectual Christians; that is, theirs is the dependency-type autonomy. Thirdly, there must be an understanding that Western Christianity reveals the tendency toward the Westerners' self-love autonomy-type religiosity. In order for there to be a change in the church's growth pattern in Japan, I deem it necessary for these three understandings to become operational.

Conclusion

From my viewpoint and using my methodology I have interpreted the Findings produced from the analytical study of hoza, clarifying the character of Japanese religiosity, and evaluating it while comparing it with the religiosity of Westerners. The religiosity of Japanese people is dependency-type religiosity (*amae-gata shūkyōshin*) based on collectivistic dependency which originates in the dependency-drive (*amae no shōdō*). In contrast to this, the religiosity of Western people is the autonomy-type religiosity (*jiritsu-gata shūkyōshin*) based on individualistic independency which in turn originates in the self-love drive (*jiko-ai no shōdō*). In terms of developmental psychology, both types appear at the same level of development and each has its strong points and weak points to the same degree. We must correctly acknowledge the strong points in both Japanese religiosity and in Western religiosity. Likewise, we must rightly discern the weak points in each. And further, both types must seek cooperation by reinforcing each other's strengths and by rectifying their weaknesses, making an effort to produce a religiosity common to all the peoples of the world.

However, it must never be forgotten that no matter how refined and globally ecumenical human religiosity might become, faith based on human religiosity is only faith as an act of the human ego. In his *Introduction to the Epistle to the Romans*, Martin Luther says that faith is not that belief or thought which man thinks is faith, but is that act of God in our midst which is given to us as the gift of God's love in Christ. This view recognizes faith as an act of God. That is, when man experiences the love of God revealed through the death and resurrection of Christ, the longings of man's religiosity are fully satisfied and faith as an act of God, which far surpasses any act of the human ego, is given to him. The death of Christ on the cross, while it completely satisfies both Japanese religious feelings and Western religious feelings, at the same time transcends them and in so doing denies them. And furthermore, the resurrection of Christ means the dissolution of the transference relationship to the Christ born out of human longing. Meeting the resurrected Christ abolishes the Christ-image which existed as a phenomenon of transference in human religiosity, and actualizes a personal fellowship between the real Christ and men.

EPILOGUE

We set out in this study to discover the factors which are responsible for the impact of RK's hoza as a means of religious propagation and education. We classified these factors into five categories and discussed them on the basis of Findings from actual participation in and observation of hoza sessions, together with Interpretations drawn from various studies in Japanese religion, society and culture. If there is any merit in this book, we feel it lies in the case study method which has been used. At the present time there is a great deal of curiosity about Japanese religion and culture, but there is still a dearth of actual case studies and a lack of investigation via first hand observation of the current Japanese scene. We hope that our efforts will serve as a stimulus for further field studies of what is actually happening in Japanese religious and social institutions today. Understanding, appreciation and evaluation—all so essential for living in today's shrunken world—must first of all be based on accurate knowledge.

In the course of the study many implications for a better understanding of Japanese religion, Japanese character, and Japanese social patterns have come to light. At the same time, many insights helpful for analyzing the Christian movement in Japan have been drawn out, as have insights for a better understanding of what constitutes effective counseling in Japanese society.

Although we have arrived at a better understanding of hoza and have been impressed with the many benefits it bestows on participants, in the end we are left with more questions than we had at the outset. Is the hoza activity faithfully propagating genuine Buddhism to its participants? Is its manifest function of answering people's problems in the light of the Lotus Sutra actually being carried out, or are its latent functions working in contrary motion to the stated purposes? The study has made is quite plain that mutual dependency centering around authoritarian leadership is the pattern of interpersonal relationships fostered in hoza. It has also been shown that the ethic of submission—submission of children to parents, of women to men, of workers to managers—is forcefully taught in hoza. Or again it has become obvious that various elements deriving from astrology, folk religion and the practice of ancestor veneration are not only permitted but are aggressively promoted.

Viewed from the standpoints of a Western Christian counselor and of a Japanese Christian psychiatrist, such elements as the above are hardly positive factors in contributing to the growth of Japanese thought and behavior patterns in such a way as to make them compatible with the contemporary international culture, which is based on concepts of liberation and rational freedom. Rather, these elements are preserving and strengthening ancient patterns of thought and behavior. But international communication, higher education, the introduction of Christianity, and other similar forces are all acting as catalysts of change in this old order. Must it not be said that these are the really new forces at work in Japan, while the so-called "new religions" are actually the conservative, reactionary forces in society?

Yet we recognize that our friends in RK might turn the questions back at us and point to our Western prejudice which attempts to evaluate the personal, ethical and religious patterns of the various cultures of the world by its own standards. They would ask, "Is the Eastern way of mutual dependency a less viable way of personal relations than the Western way of autonomous independence? Is the Eastern pattern of authoritarian leadership a less viable way of social organization than the Western democratic ideal? Or again, are the mysteries of the universe, including the mystery of existence beyond death, to be swept away in deference to the rational dogmas of the West?"

We feel that through this study we have come a long way not only toward understanding strengths and weaknesses in traditional Japanese mentality and religious practice, but also toward understanding strengths and weaknesses in traditional methods of Christian education and propagation—the task which we confronted at the outset. We attempted in Chapter IX to point out the contrasts between the methods of hoza and the methods of the Christian church. We found much to appreciate in RK's hoza, and also much to question. Likewise we found much to criticize in the strategy of the church, but also much to be grateful for.

So where do we go from here? We leave this as the next step, the ongoing challenge which confronts both the writer and the readers. But just this final thought: the main concern of this work has been with means and method, not with theological essence, and there is nothing absolute or sacred about methodology or strategy. The Christian Gospel, as a transcendent revelation of the Way shown in Jesus

Christ, cuts through and judges the strategies of the church just as it judges the strategies of Buddhism. Man is saved neither by his religiosity nor by his methodology, but by the transforming power of God. With regard to methods, a posture of openness and flexibility, an eye to scrutinize and criticize, and an ear to listen and learn—these are surely becoming to Christian workers who seek to teach this Way with efficiency and effectiveness.

APPENDIX

The writer actually participated in forty sessions of hoza, most of which were held on the balconies of the Great Sacred Hall, the main temple of Rissho Koseikai. Verbatim reports of these sessions are available but have not been included in this publication because of their excessive length. In lieu of these reports, the date, place and designation of each hoza meeting attended are listed below, along with an assigned number. The word of designation indicates the section of Tokyo or its suburbs where the participants in that group live. The numbers which appear at the end of each citation from a hoza session used in the text refer to these session numbers.

SESSION NUMBER	*DATE*	*PLACE*	*DESIGNATION OF GROUP*
1	Dec. 5, 1965	Great Sacred Hall	Nakano
2	May 9, 1966	,,	Mitaka
3	May 15, 1966	,,	,,
4	May 23, 1966 (a.m.)	,,	,,
5	May 23, 1966 (p.m.)	,,	,,
6	June 7, 1966	,,	,,
7	June 14, 1966	,,	,,
8	June 21, 1966	,,	,,
9	Oct. 14, 1966	,,	,,
10	Oct. 19, 1966	,,	Nerima
11	Oct. 20, 1966	,,	Nakano
12	Oct. 24, 1966	,,	,,
13	Nov. 1, 1966	,,	Mitaka
14	Nov. 20, 1966	Youth Training Hall	Youth Group
15	April 13, 1967	Great Sacred Hall	Mitaka
16	April 14, 1967	,,	Koto
17	April 19, 1967	,,	Mitaka
18	April 21, 1967	,,	,,
19	April 23, 1967	G.S.H. Conference Room	Nakano Men's Group
20	April 24, 1967 (a.m.)	Great Sacred Hall	Nakano

21	April 24, 1967 (p.m.)	,,	Setagaya
22	April 25, 1967	,,	Mitaka
23	April 30, 1967 (a.m.)	,,	,,
24	April 30, 1967 (p.m.)	,,	Shinjuku
25	May 1, 1967	,,	Mitaka
26	May 2, 1967	,,	Edo
27	May 5, 1967 (a.m.)	,,	Nakano
28	May 5, 1967 (p.m.)	,,	,,
29	May 6, 1967	,,	Edo
30	May 8, 1967	,,	Sumida
31	May 11, 1967	Private home	Saginomiya
32	May 16, 1967	Great Sacred Hall	Koto
33	May 17, 1967	,,	Mitaka
34	May 18, 1967	Private home	Shinjuku Youth Group
35	May 19, 1967	Great Sacred Hall	Koto
36	May 22, 1967	,,	Mitaka
37	May 23, 1967	,,	Koto
38	May 25, 1967	,,	Mitaka
39	May 29, 1967	,,	,,
40	May 31, 1967	,,	,,

(Note: The reason why the Mitaka group was attended most frequently is that the writer lives in Mitaka, and people are ordinarily expected to attend the group of their own locality.)

NOTES

CHAPTER I. HISTORICAL RELIGIOUS TRADITIONS

1. *Shūkyō Nenkan* (Yearbook of Religions), pp. 70–77 ff.
2. D. C. Holtom, *The National Faith of Japan*, p. 6.
3. *Ibid.*, pp. 53—76.
4. For example, there is currently a movement to place Yasukuni Shrine in Tokyo, where the war dead of Japan are memorialized, under federal financial support—a movement being strongly opposed by Christian and other groups.
5. H. N. McFarland, *The Rush Hour of the Gods*, p. 26.
6. K. Sekioka, "*Soteriology in Shinto*," p. 60.
7. See R. Hammer, *Japan's Religious Ferment*, pp. 44—64.
8. J. W. Hall and R. K. Beardsley, *Twelve Doors to Japan*, p. 323.
9. Hammer, p. 30.
10. See Hammer, pp. 74 f.
11. McFarland, p. 34.
12. I. Hori, *Folk Religion in Japan*, p. 18.
13. *Ibid.*, pp. 30—34.
14. *Ibid.*, p. 200.
15. *Ibid.*, pp. 217—251.
16. Y. Sasaki, "Psychiatric Study of the Shaman in Japan,' in *Proceedings of the Conference on Mental Health in Asia and the Pacific*, pp. 5—23.
17. H. Takagi, *Nihon no Shinkō Shūkyō* (The New Religions of Japan), pp. 2—6; Hori, *Folk Religion*, pp. 65—71.
18. See E. Konno, *Gendai no Meishin* (Superstitions in Contemporary Japan).
19. Takagi, *Nihon no Shūkyō*, p. 9.
20. R. P. Dore, *City Life in Japan*, p. 314.
21. H. Ooms, "The Religion of the Household," pp. 313 ff.
22. Y. Tamura, *Living Buddhism in Japan*, p. 46.
23. Ooms, pp. 250, 288.
24. Dore, *City in Life Japan*, p. 328.
25. Ooms, pp. 304 f.
26. *Ibid.*, pp. 281 f.
27. Dore, *City Life in Japan*, pp. 317—325.

CHAPTER II. CONTEMPORARY POPULAR RELIGIOUS MOVEMENTS

1. See H. B. Earhart, *The New Religions of Japan: a Bibliography.*
2. Hammer, p. 139.
3. S. Kobayashi, "The Japanese Churches and the New Religious Movements," p. 51.
4. McFarland, p. 8.
5. H. Thomsen, *The New Religions of Japan*, p. 17.
6. McFarland, p. 5.
7. *Shukyō Nenkan, pp.* 94 ff.
8. H. R. Niebuhr, *The Social Sources of Denominationalism*, p. 27.
9. J. M. Yinger, *Sociology Looks at Religion*, p. 40.
10. Takagi, *Nihon no Shinkō Shukyō*, p. 89.
11. I. Hori, *Nihon no Shukyō no Shakaiteki Yakuwari* (The Sociological Function of Japanese Religions), pp. 40, 46.
12. *Ibid.*, pp. 55 ff; see R. N. Bellah, *Tokugawa Religion.*
13. M. Anesaki, *History of Japanese Religion*, pp. 314 ff.
14. McFarland, pp. 60—63.
15. *Ibid.*, p. 67.
16. Takagi, *Shinkō Shūkyō* (The New Religions), pp. 212 ff.
17. A. Toynbee, "The Role of Japan in World History," p. 19.
18. Takagi, *Nihon no Shinko Shūkyō*, p. 44.
19. Quoted from an unpublished translation of the *Shakubuku Kyoten* of Soka Gakkai by McFarland, p. 220.
20. T. Jaeckel, "Psychological and Social Approaches to Japan's New Religions," p. 11.
21. McFarland, p. 74.
22. Thomsen, p. 28.
23. S. Kobayashi, "Religious Syncretism in Japan," pp. 48, 57.
24. T. Sugai, "The Soteriology of New Religions," p. 45.
25. McFarland, p. 227.
26. P. Tillich, *Christianity and the Encounter of the World Religions*, p. 73.
27. McFarland, pp. 227—229.
28. *Ibid.*, p. 233.
29. Takagi, *Nihon no Shinkō Shukyō*, pp. 15—17.
30. McFarland, p. 236.

CHAPTER III. RISSHO KOSEIKAI

1. The ideographs and their literal meaning are as follows: 立(*ritsu*)—to establish or to depend on, 正 (*shō*)—righteousness, i.e., the Universal Law, 佼 (*kō*)-fellowship, 成 (*sei*)—achievement or perfection of individual Buddhahood and of society, and 会 (*kai*)-association.
2. See *Risshō Kōseikai*, pp. 5—19.
3. *Ibid.*, p. 18.
4. *Ibid.*, p. 31.
5. *Ibid.*, p. 126.
6. J. Kamomiya, "Rissho Koseikai," p. 33.
7. McFarland, p. 191.
8. The following material is taken from *Risshō Kōseikai*, pp. 43—65, and from a translation of a sermon of President Niwano quoted by J. Spae in "Popular Buddhist Ethics: Rissho Koseikai," pp. 7—15.
9. Chap. XIV of the Lotus Sutra in S. Murano, "An Outline of the Lotus Sutra;" see also McFarland, pp. 179—180.
10. Kamomiya, p. 35.
11. *Ibid.*
12. *Risshō Kōseikai*, p. 51.
13. *Ibid.*, pp. 43—65.
14. *Ibid.*, pp. 135

CHAPTER IV. PHYSICAL ENVIRONMENT

1. These edifices are often of staggering magnificence and opulence. Notable are the buildings of Tenrikyo, which comprise virtually a whole city in themselves, and of Soka Gakkai at the base of Mt. Fuji, where the main worship hall is claimed to be larger than St. Peter's Cathedral in Rome.
2. McFarland, pp. 84—87.
3. H. Nakamura, *The Ways of Thinking of Eastern People*, p. 589.
4. N. Hasegawa, *The Japanese Character*, pp. 36, 50.
5. *Ibid.*, p. 51.
6. Hall and Beardsley, p. 292.
7. See Hori, *Nihon no Shūkyō no Shakaiteki Yakuwari*, pp. 95—109, and Y. Matsumoto, "Contemporary Japan: The Individual and the Group," p. 7.
8. Dore, *City Life in Japan*, p. 12.
9. McFarland, p. 83.
10. The identification of *kami* (deity) with the realm of nature, including man, is a basic concept of Shinto which deeply colors Japanese thinking in general. Any man of power or unusual capacity may be recognized as *kami*. Anything

in nature which inspires a mysterious feeling of awe and reverence can be *kami*. See I. Nitobe, *Bushido, the Soul of Japan*, p. 26. This is why observers sometimes speak of the deeply religious feeling of the Japanese, and at other times speak of their basically materialistic orientation. It all depends on how one defines "god," and consequently, "religion."

11. See McFarland, p. 60.

CHAPTER V. ORGANIZATION

1. See E. Watanabe, "Rissho Koseikai: A Sociological Observation," p. 221.
2. Bellah says that this type of society is characteristic of ancient monarchies. A universal religion was one thing which tended to break down this type of society, but Japan has resisted the break-down of this system of collectivity, in spite of modernizing in other ways.
3. Bellah, "Japan's Cultural Identity," p. 594.
4. Bellah, "Traditional Values and the Modernization of Japan," pp. 211 ff.
5. Nakamura, *The Ways of Thinking of Eastern People*, p. 313.
6. E. Vogel, "Migration to the City," in Dore, *Aspects of Social Change in Modern Japan*, p. 108.
7. The *kumi* is a voluntary association of households in which all members have equal status. Often a *kumi* is formed to serve a particular function, such as rural *kumi* for labor exchange or joint ownership of farm machinery, or a *kumi* for funerals, which is useful in taking care of the great expense and effort involved in a funeral.
8. The *buraku* is a common concept in Japanese social organization referring to the local neighborhood within a village or rural community, and also connotes the strong fellowship which exists within that group. All through Japanese life one is reminded that he exists and acts as part of a *buraku*—from children cleaning their schoolrooms according to *buraku* groups, to people participating in the *o-bon* street dances according to *buraku* grouping. *Buraku*-centered attachments become a habit of mind. See B. S. Silberman, *Japanese Character and Culture*, p. 36.
9. The origin of *kō* was in meetings for lectures on the Buddhist sutras given to local groups. There are references to *kō* in literature as early as 1275. During the Heian Peruod *kō* became formally organized as a meeting for religious instruction. *Kō* continued to develop up through the Edo Period, during which period they took on an economic character and became societies for mutual aid. In rural areas the *kō* also functioned for community recreation and spiritual nurture. See *Nihonshi Jiten* (Dictionary of Japanese History), p. 163.

10. R. K. Beardsley, J. W. Hall and R. E. Ward, *Village Japan*, pp. 248—251.
11. J. Embree, *Suye Mura: A Japanese Village*, p. 137. Embree says that a group of neighbors would form a club, each member lending a fixed amount of money to one who needed it, and would be repaid by this debtor, with interest, according to a time schedule. At the time of his study, "There was more money tied up in *kō* than in banks, village credit associations and postal savings put together."
12. Gerth and Mills, *From Max Weber: Essays in Sociology*, p. 63.
13. R. Benedict, *The Chrysanthemum and the Sword*, p. 116.
14. Japanese personal relationships characteristically take on the quality of the parent-child relation in the form of this so-called *oyabun-kobun* (parent role and child role) relation. The *oyabun* is a boss while the *kobun* is the underling and subordinate. The terms are used loosely for a wide range of situations: among gangsters, in political machines, in labor unions, in the academic world, etc. In every case, even that of the teacher and pupil, in which case it is more likely to be called the *sensei-deshi* (teacher-pupil) relationship, there is a "hierarchical system of patronage from above and loyalty from below," and the pairs preserve life-long associations colored by strong mutual affection. See Hall and Beardsley, pp. 83—84, and C. Nakane, *Japanese Society*, pp. 45 ff.
15. Nakane, p. 22.
16. *Ibid.*, p. 100.
17. In describing *kō*, Beardsley says that it is "the primary organization that takes care of problems outside the scope of the single household," and one way in which it does this is to function as a simple method of spreading news or instructions through the community. News travels along a set route of communication—the *iizutae-kōrō*—from the responsible person all through the group. See Beardsley, Hall and Ward, pp. 248—251.
18. See Chap. III for a fuller explanation of the RK organizational structure.
19. Nakane, p. 64.
20. Silberman, p. 43.
21. L. Hopkins, "The Authoritarian Group," in C. G. Kemp, ed., *Perspectives on Group Process*, pp. 56 f.
22. Matsumoto, p. 30. Ruth Benedict points to *chū*—loyalty to Emperor—as the highest law of the land, and indicates that this was responsible for the unbelievably sudden change in Japanese allegiance before and after surrender in 1945. The Pacific War was not a popular democratic war. It was a war for the Emperor, fought by the citizens in loyalty and fidelity to him. An irrational conformity to the word of highest authority made possible the amazing phenomenon of a nation hating America one day and loving her the

next. See Benedict, pp. 131 ff.

23. E. Norbeck, "Associations and Democracy in Japan", in Dore, *Aspects of Social Change*, p. 195.
24. Nakane, p. 100.
25. Watanabe, "Rissho Koseikai," pp. 85—87.
26. K. Wada, *Shinkō Shūkyō-dan no Kenkyū* (A Study of the New Religions), p. 110.
27. Watanabe, "Rissho Koseikai," p. 90
28. *Ibid.*, 89.
29. M. Mita, "Patterns of Alienation in Contemporary Japan," p. 164.
30. A. Saki, *Shinkō Shūkyō* (The New Religions), pp. 186 ff.
31. McFarland, p. 233.
32. A significant finding on the current attitude of women toward their husbands and homes comes from an investigation conducted among the wives of 287 workers of the Ishikawajima Shipbuilding Company. Respondents were asked to reveal their value orientations by marking one of four statements of philosophy of life. The two which received far the highest marks were the following: 168 out of 287 selected as their statement of philosophy:

    I do my humble best to take care of myself and manage the household efficiently and cheerfully, not caring whether we ever become famous or rich. I always consider the welfare and happiness of my children and home rather than concern myself about matters of the larger society.

    63 of the 287 selected the following statement:

    Because my husband supports the family through his work, it is my duty as a wife to take good care of him (*taisetsu ni suru*) and, even if it means sacrifice for me, to watch over the children and household so they will be of no worry or trouble to him.

    The other two statements put the husband's advancement in the world as primary value (17 affirmations) and put self-advancement as the primary value (only two affirmations). *Shufu no Seikatsu Kōzō* (The Housewife's Pattern of Life), pp. 127—188.
33. Matsumoto, pp. 26 f.
34. Vogel, "Migration to the City," in Dore, *Aspects of Social Change*, p. 102.
35. *Ibid.*
36. S. Mishima, *The Broader Way: A Woman's Life in the New Japan*, p. 173.
37. T. Brameld, "Ethics of Leadership," in National Training Laboratories, *Leadership in Action*, pp. 62—67.
38. F. French and B. Raven, "The Bases of Social Power," in D. Cartwright and A. Zander, eds., *Group Dynamics: Research and Theory*, pp. 607—622.

CHAPTER VI. LEADERSHIP

1. See Gerth and Mills, pp. 245—250, 262. Weber says: "Genuine charismatic domination knows of no abstract legal codes and statutes. Its 'objective' law emanates concretely from the highly personal experience of heavenly grace and from the god-like strength of the hero. Charismatic domination means a rejection of all ties to any external order in favor of the exclusive glorification of the genuine mentality of the prophet and hero."
2. *The Random House Dictionary of the English Language*, Unabridged Edition.
3. Gerth and Mills, pp. 245—249.
4. McFarland, p. 72.
5. See Holtom, p. 24.
6. Anesaki, p. 21.
7. For example, see Chaps. XI and XVIII of the Sutra in Murano, "An Outline of the Lotus Sutra," pp. 43, 58.
8. Gerth and Mills, p. 262. Weber says: "Precisely this quality of charisma as an extraordinary, supernatural, divine power transforms it, after its routinization, into a suitable source for the legitimate acquisition of sovereign power by the successors of the charismatic hero."
9. French and Raven, "The Bases of Social Power," in Cartwright and Zander, pp. 607—622.
10. Ariga speaks of the love of forms as being a dominant characteristic of the Japanese. "The most creative aspect of the Japanese mind may perhaps be found in its esthetic activities. It is fond of discovering forms everywhere. Whether in matters of etiquette, art, education or religion, the original form established by the founder of a particular sect or school of thought is held in high esteem. Furthermore, it is the solemn duty of a teacher to pass on the original form with precision and authenticity. See T. Ariga, "The Meeting of East and West on the Japanese Scene," p. 7.
11. R. Bellah, *Tokugawa Religion*, p. 213.
12. See H. Kato, *Japanese Popular Culture*, p. 140.
13. Hopkins, "The Authoritarian Group," in Kemp, p. 56.
14. R. White and R. Lippitt, "Leader Behavior and Member Reaction in Three 'Social Climates'," in Cartwright and Zander, pp. 527—553.
15. P. Hare, *Handbook of Small Group Research*, p. 226.
16. Kemp, p. 226.
17. Takagi, *Nihon no Shinkō Shūkyō*, pp. 15—17, 49.
18. Matsumoto, p. 30.
19. Nakane, p. 62.
20. See McFarland, pp. 84—87.

CHAPTER VII. SOCIO-EMOTIONAL DYNAMICS

1. Kemp, p. 144.
2. N. Hobbs, "Group Centered Counseling," in Kemp, p. 156.
3. Kato, p. 72.
4. *Ibid.*, pp. 73 f.
5. S. Southard, *Family Counseling in South-East Asia*, chap. 2.
6. *Ibid.*
7. W. Caudill and T. Doi, "Interrelations of Psychiatry, Culture and Emotion in Japan," in I. Galdston, *Man's Image in Medicine and Anthropology*, pp. 382 ff.
8. T. Doi, *The Anatomy of Dependence*, p. 7.
9. Interview with Dr. H. Kondo psychotherapist, Yagumo, Tokyo.
10. Quoted by Verba, p. 11.
11. E. Thomas and C. Fink, "Effects of Group Size," in P. Hare, E. F. Borgatta, and R. F. Bales, *Small Groups: Studies in Social Interaction*, p. 533.
12. *Ibid.*, pp. 532 f.
13. Cartwright and Zander, pp. 69 f.
14. Kemp, p. 108.
15. Southard, chap. 6.
16. Dore, *City Life in Japan*, p. 12.
17. Y. Sasaki and Others, "The Social-Psychiatric Study of Religious Movements in Japan," pp. 50 ff.
18. *A New English Dictionary*, J. A. H. Murray, ed.
19. See L. Goldman, "Group Guidance: Content and Process," in Kemp, pp. 41 ff.
20. See Hall and Beardsley, p. 360. Beardsley writes of this characteristic:

    > Social life throughout Japan is noted for the solidarity of group associations. To be a Japanese is to be involved in close, complex, and enduring relationships with one's family, one's neighbors and other specific associates.

    He asks, why this extraordinary sense of group solidarity? Any explanation of this phenomenon must take into account Japan's historical and geographical position. "Few areas of comparable population anywhere in the world have had such culturally homogeneous people who were so long isolated from other peoples." From the beginning of history these islands were the home of essentially a single people speaking one language having a common body of traditions and values. "In isolation, the Japanese missed what most people have experienced, a constant rubbing of elbows with outsiders." These elements are commonly referred to as *shima-guni konjō*, which means "the spiritual character of an island country."
21. Festinger, "Informal Social Communication," in Cartwright and Zander, pp. 286—299.

CHAPTER VIII. CONCEPTUAL CONTENT

1. Interview with the Secretary to President Niwano.
2. Interview with representatives of the RK Seminary.
3. Interview with Dr. M. Tatara, psychotherapist.
4. Yoshida discusses this as one of the problematic aspects of hoza. See Y. Yoshida, *Rissho Koseikai: Egao no Himitsu wo Saguru* (Rissho Koseikai: In Search of the Secret of the Smiling Face), pp. 163 f.
5. See R. Lee, *Stranger in the Land*, p. 125. Lee describes the lot of the suburban Japanese housewife by painting the picture of the typical husband's average day: He has a hectic day at his office, works until five or six, then drops in with a few of his companions to several bars, cabarets or other places of amusement. Having thus taken the long way home, he arrives home very late but invariably finds his long-suffering, patient wife waiting for him with hot tea. He goes to bed and sleeps late although his wife gets up early to take care of the children and cook the rice, etc., for breakfast. On Sundays and holidays the husband will probably go golfing, returning in the evening with some candy or cookies as a present for his wife and children, making up for his long absence. "The point is," says Lee, "that the cultural pattern which views the wife as an insignificant creature, as a chattel, as one who obediently serves her lord and master—has not completely died out."
6. See Mita, p. 139. Mita analyzed the types of problems by classifying them into the following categories. The number following the complaint indicates the number of problems, out of a total of 508:

   Love, 31
   Marriage, 81
   Conjugal disharmony, 80
   Family, 71
   Livelihood, 89
   Youth, 45
   Miscellaneous, 111
7. Kato, pp. 69 ff.
8. Watanabe, "Rissho Koseikai," p. 148.
9. See, for example, Jaeckel's analysis in "Psychological and Social Approaches to Japan's New Religions," p. 9.
10. See Yoshida, pp. 166 f.
11. See Chapter III for a fuller explanation of these concepts.
12. Cited in Wada, p. 191.
13. See Kato, p. 75. Kato found the same tendency in newspaper counseling columns, where every problem is narrowed down to a very personal problem. When troubles are presented by the client, the consultant usually gives the

advice, "Be patient," and assures him that everything will be all right if he just tries to be nice to everyone. The social dimension of the problem is overlooked.

14. See Wada, p. 192.
15. Hammer, p. 28.
16. Saki, p. 160.
17. *Ibid.*, p. 202.
18. Murano, p. 29.
19. Kobayashi, "The Japanese Churches," p. 28.
20. I. Oguchi, *Nihon Shūkyō no Shakaiteki Seikaku* (The Sociological Character of Japanese Religions), p. 80.
21. McFarland, p. 191. The author says, "RK's early success owed much to its accommodation of a largely undifferentiated popular piety, which includes but was not really governed by specifically Buddhistic considerations." RK leaders themselves admit this and refer to the period from 1949 to 1957 as the "period of accommodation."
22. Kobayashi, "The Japanese Churches," p. 31.
23. See, for example, Kamomiya.
24. See Hasegawa, who says, "It is safe to say that almost no other people in the world has shown such a readiness to welcome incursions by other peoples and other faiths...It is the tendency to assimilate...which truly characterizes the national personality." p. 8. However, Hasegawa goes on to say that side by side with this susceptibility to foreign influence has also been an obstinate clinging to traditional Japanese things. Both of these tendencies exist simultaneously in the culture, and in every individual as well. p. 70.
25. Ariga, p. 6; see also McFarland, who says that Western thought patterns tend to see reality in dualistic terms of such opposites as truth-falsehood, good-evil, divine-human, etc. These are assumed to be absolute opposites, and hence irreconcilable. But in Japan there is a different orientation to reality, "one in which apparent opposites are seen as complements or factors of each other. The discovery of the real does not result from the elimination of contradictions; it comes instead from the awareness of the unity of opposites." p. 23. Nakamura say the Japanese "are by nature inclined to rapprochement without thrashing out an issue." Nakamura, "Some Features of the Japanese Way of Thinking," p. 300.
26. Y. Kitamori, "A Theology of Dialog," p. 9.
27. Yinger, *Religion, Society and the Individual*, p. 266.
28. *Ibid.*, p. 205.
29. See, for example, *ibid.*, pp. 471 ff.
30. Saki, p. 5.

31. See Nakane, chap. 1.
32. See J. M. Yinger, *Religion, Society and the Individual*, p. 65.
33. Ooms, p. 287.
34. R. Hume, *The World's Living Religions*, pp. 69 f.
35. "Karma," in *Encyclopedia Britannica*, 1960 ed.
36. See Tamura, pp. 11—14.
37. Cited by Benedict, p. 190. Benedict points out a useful insight regarding the rough and gentle polarity in contradistinction to the good and evil polarity: "They (the Japanese) believe that man has two souls, but these are not his good impulses fighting with his bad. They are the 'gentle' soul and the 'rough' soul. There are occasions in every man's—and every nation's—life when he should be 'gentle' and when he should be 'rough.'...They are both necessary and good on different occasions." Benedict, pp. 189 f.
38. Although such a doctrine seems to Westerners to lead to a philosophy of self-indulgence and license, the Japanese sense of obligation to fellow men enters as a salutary factor at this point. Eating, sleeping, intoxication, sexual indulgence, etc., are considered part of the "circle of human feelings" to be accepted as good on the appropriate occasions, but to be stoically curbed when they interfere with social obligations. The Japanese sees the circle of human feelings and the circle of social obligations as both good in themselves, but requiring careful balancing. See Nakamura, *The Ways of Thinking of Eastern People*, p. 553.
39. T. N. Callaway, *Japanese Buddhism and Christianity*, p. 169.
40. *Bushidō*, "the way of the samurai," demands the courage to fulfill the obligations of inter-personal relations regardless of cost. It demands self-discipline and sacrifice of personal feelings, health, and life itself in the discharge of one's obligations to superiors or to one's own honor. Benedict, p. 116.
41. J. Stoetzel, Without the Chrysanthemum and the Sword, pp. 195 ff.
42. Bellah, *Tokugawa Religion*, p. 194.
43. Yinger, *Religion, Society and the Individual*, p. 301.
44. A. Osada, "Problems Involved in Providing Ethical Education," p. 67 f.
45. McFarland, p. 227.
46. Bellah, *Tokugawa Religion*, p. 55.
47. Ooms, pp. 301 f.
48. C. Offner and H. van Stralen, *Modern Japanese Religions*, p. 257.
49. McFarland, p. 80.
50. Kato, p. 140.
51. Nitobe, pp. 30 ff.
52. R. Wood, "Tillich Encounters Japan."
53. Quoted in Spae, "Japanese Religiosity as Experience," p. 29.

CHAPTER IX. CONCLUSIONS, EVALUATIONS AND COMPARISONS WITH CHRISTIAN PATTERNS

1. Kobayashi, "The Japanese Churches," p. 50.
2. See H. Kraemer, *The Christian Message in a Non-Christian World,* p. 102.
3. J. Spae, *Christianity Encounters Japan*, p. 177.
4. M. Takenaka, *Reconciliation and Renewal in Japan*, p. 90.
5. Lee, p. 156.
6. J. Kitagawa, *Religion in Japanese History*, p. 337.
7. Lee, p. 182.
8. Y. Okada and K. Morioka, "Christianity and Postwar Japanese Society," in *Japan Christian Yearbook* 1966, pp. 29—31.
9. R. Shiina, cited by Kitagawa, p. 306.
10. Kobayashi, "The Japanese Churches," p. 44.
11. C. Offner, "Resurgence of non-Christian Religions," in *Japan Christian Yearbook* 1966, p. 42.
12. See Kobayashi, "The Japanese Churches," p. 47.
13. Offner and van Stralen, p. 268.
14. J. Spae, *Neighborhood Associations—A Catholic Way for Japan*, p. 33.
15. McFarland, pp. 85 f.
16. See Saki, p. 185.
17. Kobayashi, "The Japanese Churches," p. 55.
18. Takenaka, p. 90.
19. Nakane, pp. 26 f.
20. See Dore, *Aspects of Social Change*, p. 194.
21. H. R. Niebuhr, pp. 54 f.
22. A. Ebisawa, *Gendai Nihon Shūkyō no Shiteki Kenkyū* (A Socio-Historical Study of Modern Japanese Religions), p. 110.
23. C. W. Iglehart, *A Century of Protestant Christianity in Japan*, p. 346.
24. R. Hara and P. Pfister, "Ecumenism and the Future of Christianity in Japan," in *Japan Christian Yearbook* 1968, p. 191.
25. K. J. Dale, "*Senkyōshi ga Mita Nihon to Nihonjin*" (Japan and the Japanese Through the Eyes of a Missionary), pp. 29 ff.
26. J. Spae, *Japanese Religiosity*, p. 36.
27. For example, see Deuteronomy 4 : 40, 5 : 16, 6 : 3, 14 : 29, etc.
28. See Job 13 : 15, Psalm 37 : 7.
29. J. Spae, "The Image of the Church, an Ecumenical Responsibility," in *Japan Christian Yearbook* 1968, p. 192.
30. Lee, pp. 161—163.
31. Spae, "The Image of the Church, an Ecumenical Responsibility," p. 190.
32. Kobayashi, "The Japanese Churches," pp. 46 f.

33. Offner and van Stralen, p. 274.
34. Lee, p. 73.
35. Kobayashi, "The Japanese Churches," p. 59.
36. See Saki, p. 236.
37. Offner and van Stralen, p. 273.
38. Takagi, *Nihon no Shinkō Shukyō*, pp. 23 f.
39. Lee, p. 126.
40. H. Shinmi, "Insights, Wisdom and Challenge," in *Japan Christian Yearbook* 1966, p. 67.
41. Kobayashi, "The Japanese Churches," p. 59.
42. Spae, *Christianity Encounters Japan*, p. 158.

CHAPTER X. JAPANESE AND WESTERN RELIGIOSITY

1. This theory is expounded by A. Portmann in his *Zoologie und das neue Bild vom Menschen.*
2. *Amae* and its verb form *amaeru* are impossible to translate accurately into English. The general meaning of *amae* is "the desire to be loved". Doi's book, *The Anatomy of Dependence*, is a study of this concept and its significance in Japanese culture.
3. Spae, *Japanese Religiosity*, p. 165.
4. Caudill and Doi, "Interrelations of Psychiatry, Culture and Emotion," in Galdston, pp. 382 ff.
5. Doi, p. 29.
6. Watanabe, "Rissho Koseikai," p. 130.
7. Dale, "Authority in Rissho Koseikai," p. 466.

BIBLIOGRAPHY

Books

Anesaki, Masaharu, *History of Japanese Religion.* Tokyo, Tuttle Publishing Co., 1963.

Beardsley, R. K., ed., *Studies in Japanese Culture: I.* Center for Japanese Studies, Occasional Papers No. IX. Ann Arbor, University of Michigan Press, 1965.

———, and Hall, J. W., *Japanese Culture, its Development and Characteristics.* Chicago, University of Chicago Press, 1962.

———, and Ward, R. E., *Village Japan.* Chicago, University of Chicago Press, 1959.

Bellah, Robert N., *Tokugawa Religion.* Glencoe, The Free Press, 1957.

Benedict, Ruth, *The Chrysanthemum and the Sword.* Boston, Houghton Mifflin Co., 1946.

Brannen, Noah S., *Sōka Gakkai, Japan's Militant Buddhists.* Richmond, John Knox Press, 1968.

Callaway, Tucker N., *Japanese Buddhism and Christianity.* Tokyo, Shinkyo Shuppansha, 1957.

Cartwright, D., and Zander, A. eds., *Group Dynamics: Research and Theory,* 2nd ed. Evanston, Row, Peterson and Co., 1960.

Doi, Takeo, *The Anatomy of Dependence.* Tokyo, Kodansha International, 1973.

Dore, R. P., ed., *Aspects of Social Change in Modern Japan.* Princeton, Princeton University Press, 1967.

———, *City Life in Japan.* London, Routledge and Paul, 1958.

Earhart, Byron, *The New Religions of Japan: A Bibliography of Western Language Materials.* Tokyo, Sophia University, 1970.

Ebisawa, Arimichi, *Gendai Nihon Shukyō no Shiteki Kenkyu* (A Socio-Historical Study of Modern Japanese Religions). Tokyo, Natsume Press, 1952.

Embree, J. F., *The Japanese.* Washington, Smithsonian Institute, 1958.

———, *Suye Mura: A Japanese Village.* Chicago, University of Chicago Press, 1939.

Galdston, Iago, ed., *Man's Image in Medicine and Anthropology.* New York, International Universities Press, Inc., 1963.

Gerth, H. H., and Mills, C. W., trans. and eds., *From Max Weber: Essays in Sociology.* New York, Oxford University Press, 1958.

Hammer, Raymond, *Japan's Religious Ferment.* London, S.C.M. Press, 1961.

Hare, Paul, *Handbook of Small Group Research.* Glencoe, Free Press, 1962.

———, Borgatta, E. F., and Bales, R. F., *Small Groups: Studies in Social Interaction.* New York, Alfred Knopf, 1965.

Hall, J. W., and Beardsley, R. K., *Twelve Doors to Japan.* New York, McGraw Hill, 1965.

Hasegawa, Nyozekan, *The Japanese Character.* Trans. by John Bester. Tokyo, Kodansha International, 1965.

Holtom, D. C., *The National Faith of Japan.* New York, Paragon Book Reprint Co., 1965.

Hori, Ichiro, *Folk Religion in Japan.* Chicago, University of Chicago Press, 1968.

———, *Nihon no Shukyō no Shakaiteki Yakuwari* (The Sociological Function of Japanese Religions). Tokyo, Miraisha, 1962.

Hume, Robert E., *The World's Living Religions.* New York, Charles Scribner's Sons, 1947.

Iglehart, Charles W., *A Century of Protestant Christianity in Japan.* Tokyo, Charles Tuttle Co., 1959.

Japan Christian Yearbook, The, 1966 and 1968. Tokyo, Kyobun Kan.

Kato, Hidetoshi, *Japanese Popular Culture.* Tokyo, Tuttle Publishing Co., 1959.

Kemp, C. G., ed., *Perspectives on Group Process.* New York, Houghton Mifflin, 1964.

Kitagawa, Jo, *Religion in Japanese History.* New York, Columbia University Press, 1966.

Konno, Ensuke, *Gendai no Meishin* (Superstitions in Contemporary Japan). Tokyo, Shakai Shiso Kenkyukai Shuppan-bu, 1961.

Kraemer, Hendrik, *The Christian Message in a Non-Christian World.* New York, International Missionary Council, 1946.

Lee, Robert, *Stranger in the Land: A Study of the Church in Japan.* New York, Friendship Press, 1967.

McFarland, H. Neill, *The Rush Hour of the Gods: A Study of New Religious Movements in Japan.* New York, The Macmillan Co., 1967.

Mishima, Sumie, *The Broader Way: A Woman's Life in the New Japan.* London, Victor Gollancz, 1953.

Nakane, Chie, *Japanese Society*. Middlesex, England, Penguin Books, 1970.

National Training Laboratories, *Leadership in Action*. Washington, National Education Association, 1961.

Niebuhr, H. Richard, *The Social Sources of Denominationalism*. Cleveland, World Publishing Co., 1957.

Nitobe, Inazo, *Bushido, the Soul of Japan*. New York, G. P. Putnam's Sons, 1905.

Nottingham, E. K., *Religion and Society*. New York, Random House, 1954.

Offner, Clark, and van Stralen, Henry, *Modern Japanese Religions*. New York, Twayne Publishers, Inc., 1963.

Oguchi, Iichi, *Nihon Shukyō no Shakaiteki Seikaku* (The Sociological Character of Japanese Religions). Tokyo, Tokyo University Press, 1953.

Portmann, Adolf, *Zoologie und das neue Bild vom Menschen—Biologische Fragmente zu einer Lehre vom Menschen*. Schweiz, Benno Schwabe, 1944.

Proceedings of the Conference on Mental Health in Asia and the Pacific. Honolulu East-West Center, 1966.

Rissho Koseikai. Tokyo, Kosei Publishing Co., 1966.

Saki, Akio, *Shinkō Shūkyō* (The New Religions). Tokyo, Aoki Shoten, 1960.

Schneider, Delwyn B., *Konkokyo: A Japanese Religion*. Tokyo, International Institute for the Study of Religions, 1962.

Shufu no Seikatsu Kōzō–Toshi to Nōson no Seikatsu Report (The Housewife's Pattern of Life—A Report on Urban and Rural Life). Tokyo Kokumin Seikatsu Kenkyu-jo, 1965.

Shūkyō Nenkan (Yearbook of Religions). Tokyo, Mombusho, Bunka–cho, 1974.

Silberman, B. S., ed., *Japanese Character and Culture*. Tuscon, University of Arizona, 1962.

Southard, Samuel, *Family Counseling in South-East Asia*. Unpublished manuscript, 1969.

Spae, Joseph, *Christianity Encounters Japan*. Tokyo, Oriens Institute for Religious Research, 1968.

———, *Neighborhood Associations—A Catholic Way for Japan*. Himeji, Committee of the Apostolate, 1956.

———, *Japanese Religiosity*. Tokyo, Oriens Institute for Religious Research, 1971.

Stoetzel, Jean, *Without the Chrysanthemum and the Sword*. New York, Columbia University Press, 1955.

Nakamura, Hajime, *The Ways of Thinking of Eastern People.* Tokyo, UNESCO, 1960.

Takagi, Hiro, *Nihon no Shinkō Shūkyō* (The New Religions of Japan). Tokyo, Iwanami Shoten, 1959.

——, *Shinkō Shūkyō* (The New Religions). Tokyo, Kodansha, 1958.

Takenaka, Masao, *Reconciliation and Renewal in Japan.* New York, Friendship Press, 1957.

Tamura, Yoshiro, *Living Buddhism in Japan.* Tokyo, International Institute of the Study of Religions, 1960.

Thomsen, Harry, *The New Religions of Japan.* Tokyo, Tuttle Publishing Co., 1963.

Tillich, Paul, *Christianity and the Encounter of the World Religions.* New York, Columbia University Press, 1913.

Verba, Sidney, *Small Groups and Political Behavior.* Princeton, Princeton University Press, 1961.

Wach, Joachim, *The Comparative Study of Religions.* New York, Columbia University Press, 1958.

Wada, Katsutoshi, *Shinkō Shūkyō-dan no kenkyu*: *Risshō Kōsei-kai no Jirei* (A Study of the New Religions: the Case of Rissho Koseikai). Unpublished Master's dissertation, Dept. of Sociology, Tokyo University of Education.

Watanabe, Baiyu, *Gendai Nihon no Shūkyō* (Modern Japanese Religions). Tokyo, Daito Shuppansha, 1950.

Yinger, J. Milton, *Religion, Society and the Individual.* New York, The Macmillan Co., 1957.

——, *Sociology Looks at Religion.* New York, The Macmillan Co., 1961.

Yoshida, Yutaka, *Risshō Kōseikai*: *Egao no Himitsu wo Saguru* (Rissho Koseikai: In Search of the Secret of the Smiling Face). Tokyo, Hyakusen Shobo, 1971.

Articles

Abbreviations of journals referred to in the following list of articles:

CRJ—*Contemporary Religions in Japan* (predecessor of *Japanese Journal of Religious Studies*)

JMB—*Japan Missionary Bulletin*

JR—*Japanese Religions*

JSPIJ—*Journal of Social and Political Ideas in Japan*

MN—*Monumenta Nipponica*

Ariga, T., "The Meeting of East and West on the Japanese Scene." *JR*, I (1960).
Bellah, Robert, "Japan's Cultural Identity." *The Journal of Asian Studies*, XXIV (August, 1965).
———, "Traditional Values and the Modernization of Japan." CRJ, III (1962).
Dale, Kenneth J., "Authority in Rissho Koseikai." *JMB*, XXIII (September, 1969).
———, "*Senkyōshi ga Mita Nihon to Nihonjin.*" (Japan and the Japanese through the Eyes of a Missionary) *Gekkan Kirisuto* (Christian Monthly) (September, 1968).
Doi, Masatoshi, "Religion and the Social Structure of Japan." *JR*, V (December, 1967).
Dumermuth, Fritz, "Religion in Sociological Perspective." *CRJ*, IX (March-June, 1968).
Holtom, D. C., "The Meaning of Kami: III." *MN*, IV (1941).
Jaeckel, Theodore, "Psychological and Social Approaches to Japan's New Religions." *JR*, II (1960).
Kamomiya, Jokai, "Rissho Koseikai." *CRJ*, II (March, 1961).
Kitamori, Y., "A Theology of Dialog." *JR*, III (1963).
Kobayashi, Sakae, "The Japanese Churches and the New Religious Movements." *Studies in the Christian Religion, XXXIII* (March, 1965).
———, "Religious Syncretism in Japan." *Kwansei Gakuin University Annual Studies*, VII (1959).
Matsumoto, Y., "Contemporary Japan: The Individual and the Group." *Transactions of the American Philosophical Society*, L, Part I (1960).
Miyazaki, Akira, "Risshō Kōseikai-ron" (Introducing Rissho Koseikai). *Deai* (Dialog), I (May, 1966).
Murano, Senchu, "An Outline of the Lotus Sutra." *CRJ*, VIII (March, 1967).
Mita, Munesuke, "Patterns of Alienation in Contemporary Japan." *JSPIJ*, I (1963).
Nakamura, Hajime, "Some Features of the Japanese Way of Thinking." *MN*, XIV (1958—59).
Ooms, Herman, "The Religion of the Household: A Case Study of Ancestor Worship in Japan." *CRJ*, VIII (September-December, 1967).
Osada, A., "Problems Involved in Providing Ethical Education." *JSPIJ*, I (1965).

Sasaki, Y. and others, "The Social-Psychiatric Study of Religious Movements in Japan." *Seishin Igaku* (Psychiatry), VIII, 11 (1966).

Schiffer, Wilhelm, "Necromancers in the Tohoku," *CRJ*, VIII (June, 1967).

Sekioka, Kazushige, "Soteriology in Shinto." *JR*, VI (January, 1970).

Spae, Joseph, "Japanese Religiosity as Experience." *JR*, V (July, 1968).

———, "Popular Buddhist Ethics: Rissho Koseikai." *JMB*, XX (1966).

Sugai, Taika, "The Soteriology of New Religions." *JR*, VI (January, 1970).

Toynbee, Arnold, "The Role of Japan in World History." *Japan Quarterly*, IV (1957).

Watanabe, Eimi, "Rissho Koseikai: A Sociological Observation of its Members." *CRJ*, IX (March-June, 1968).

Wood, Robert, "Tillich Encounters Japan." *JR*, II (May, 1961).

ASIA AND OCEANIA TITLES

Published by
The William Carey Library
533 Hermosa Street
South Pasadena, California 91030
U.S.A.

Aspects of Pacific Ethnohistory **by Alan Tippett $3.95**

The Baha'i Faith: Its History and Teachings **by William Miller $8.95**

A Century of Growth: The Kachin Baptist Church of Burma **by Herman Tegenfeldt $9.95**

Christ Confronts India **by B.V. Subbamma $4.95**

Church Growth in Japan **by Tetsunao Yamamori $4.95**

A New Day in Madras **by Amirtharaj Nelson $7.95**

People Movements in the Punjab **by Margaret and Frederick Stock $8.95**

Taiwan: Mainline Versus Independent Church Growth **by Allen Swanson $3.95**